DANDY OF
JOHNS HOPKINS

Walter Edward Dandy, 1886–1946

DANDY OF
JOHNS HOPKINS

WILLIAM LLOYD FOX, Ph.D.

Professor Emeritus of History
Montgomery College
Rockville, Maryland
Doctoral Research Advisor
The American University
Washington, D.C.

With the sponsorship of the
Congress of Neurological Surgeons

WILLIAMS & WILKINS
Baltimore/London

Editor: Carol-Lynn Brown
Copy Editors: Andrea Clemente, Stephen Siegforth
Design: JoAnne Janowiak
Production: Carol Eckhart

Made in the United States of America

Library of Congress Cataloging in Publication Data

Fox, William Lloyd.
  Dandy of Johns Hopkins.

  "With the sponsorship of the Congress of Neurological Surgeons."
  Bibliography: p.
  Includes index.
  1. Dandy, Walter Edward, 1886–1946. 2. Neurosurgeons—United States—Biography. 3. Johns Hopkins University—Faculty—Biography. I. Title. [DNLM: 1. Dandy, Walter Edward, 1886–1946. 2. Physicians—Biography. WZ 100 D178F]
  RD592.9.D36F69 1984   617'.48'00924 [B]   83-27379
  ISBN 0-683-04903-8

Composed and printed at the
Waverly Press, Inc.

To Lynn

Foreword

Walter Dandy was a neurosurgeon who embodied many of the ideals and spirit of the Congress of Neurological Surgeons.

His innovative brilliance in research and neurosurgical technique continue to serve as a model for all neurosurgeons. His unresting inquisitive mind and his courage in facing technically difficult surgical problems set him apart from many of his colleagues and made him one of the great figures in the evolution of modern neurosurgery.

The Congress of Neurological Surgeons is happy to have the opportunity to assist in the publication of this biography. We are most grateful to Dr. William L. Fox for the enormous amount of work required to author such a biography, to Mrs. Dandy, Dr. Walter E. Dandy, Jr., Dr. Hugo V. Rizzoli, and to the Archives of the Johns Hopkins Medical Institutions. Special thanks are due to Constance B. Hoeft who expertly prepared the manuscript for publication.

It is our hope that this biography will inspire members of the Congress of Neurological Surgeons for years to come, and that it will be of more general interest to those interested in medical history, underscoring Walter Dandy's position as a pioneer in neuroscience and clinical neurosurgery.

Edward R. Laws, Jr.
Peter W. Carmel
Congress of Neurological Surgeons
September, 1983

Preface

The origins of this biography date from a telephone conversation I had during the winter of 1964 with the late Morris C. Leikind, an enthusiastic scholar of the history of medicine, who then lived in Washington, D.C. During the course of our exchange Leikind spoke of the need for a biography of Walter E. Dandy. At the time I knew very little about Dandy, but my friend's reference to him and my interest in medical biography prompted me to learn more about Johns Hopkins' renowned neurosurgeon. In the weeks that followed, I learned enough about the man to realize that there was a gap in American medical history that a full-length biography warranted filling and that I wanted to do it. With the subsequent approval and kind support of Mrs. Walter E. Dandy and her son, Walter E. Dandy, Jr., M.D., I began this biographical undertaking. Two other publishing projects, however, were to intervene, thereby causing a delay in its completion.

In undertaking this portrait of Dandy my aim was directed at two audiences: medical people, especially neurologists and neurosurgeons, and nonmedical men and women who enjoy reading about someone of great accomplishment. For the benefit of the latter group I have occasionally given a parenthetical explanation of a technical word or term, to which I trust the professionals will not object.

It is a truism in the writing of history and biography that a work is never the result of a solo effort. Inevitably the contributions and suggestions of others go into its preparation. Without the help of many people this biography would not have been possible. (In the acknowledgements that follow, space will not permit, I regret, listing geographical identifications or institutional affiliations.)

I wish to express my special thanks and warm appreciation to Mrs. Dandy for her many kindnesses and to the Dandy children, Walter E., Jr., Mrs. Mary Ellen Marmaduke, Mrs. Kathleen Louise Gladstone, and Mrs. Margaret Gontrum; to Hugo V. Rizzoli, M.D., my technical advisor; the late Frederick L. Reichert, M.D., Warfield M. Firor, M.D., Charles E. Troland, M.D., the late Frank J. Otenasek, M.D., John W. Chambers, M.D., the late Winterton C. Curtis, Ph.D., Edward R. Laws, Jr., M.D., and the Congress of Neurological Surgeons. Dr. Laws' enthusiastic support and the ready approval of the Congress of Neurological Surgeons made possible the publication of this biography.

I also would like to thank the following people for their readiness to lend a hand: A. Earl Walker, M.D., the late Madeline Stanton, the late R. S. Battersby, M.D., W. James Garner, M.D., Robert L. Glass, M.D., Jean J. Madden, Richard S. Brownlee, Ph.D., the late Mrs. H. O. Foraker, Mrs. Edith F. Hill, Elmer Ellis, Ph.D., Mrs. Helen Dorsey, William Dwight Curtis, D.D.S., Dean Francis English, Peter D. Olch, M. D., Alexander T. Bunts, M.D., Rear Admiral Alfred H. Richards, U.S.N. (ret.), Jo and Ralph Grimes, the late Mary Brooke Hutton, R.N., Mrs. Janet B. Koudelka, the late Louis L. Austin and family, Grace L. Smith, R.N., Elizabeth Thomson, Raymond E. Lenhard, M.D., the late Harvey B. Stone, M.D., Clark Ammos, Daniel Pachino, the late R. Eustace Semmes, M.D., the late William F. Reinhoff, Jr., M.D., Lindsay Rogers, William Dock, M.D., Edwin B. Grauer, Barnes Woodhall, M.D., Tom Mahoney, Alice Grauer D'Angelo (Mrs. Lou), the late James P. Leake, M.D., Lola M. Kilmon (Mrs. Charles E.), Thomas L. Taylor, Bertha Fisher Ray (Mrs. Wilbur), Sister Mary Raymond, Warde B. Allan, M.D., Arthur B. King, M.D., Myron E. Goldblatt, M.D., Thomas B. Turner, M.D., Mrs. Miriam C. Benson, Edward Brecher, Richard J. Otenasek, Jr., M.D., the late C. William Schneidereith, Sr., Edwin N. Broyles, M.D., A. McGehee Harvey, M.D., Mrs. Joy S. Richmond, Mark M. Ravitch, M.D., the late Frank R. Ford, M.D., Curt P. Richter, Ph.D., Dennis Gaffney, Carol Dresner, John S. Tytus, M.D., the late Owen H. Wangensteen, M.D., Antonio Gonzalez-Revilla, M.D., Peter S. Moon, Irving J. Sherman, M.D., H. B. Maroney, Mrs. Alma Vaughan, Mather Pfeiffenberger, M.D., L. G. Shreve, Jamie T. Poteet, Hugh E. Stephenson, Jr., M.D., William R. Blalock, Paul C. Bucy, M.D., Ralph N. Greene, Jr., M.D., William J. Graham, Frank Padberg, M.D., Russell H. Morgan, M.D., Donlin M. Long, M.D., and Zigmond M. Lebensohn, M.D.

I am most grateful to the staff of Williams & Wilkins for their superior help and guidance, especially to Carol-Lynn Brown, Editor, and to the kindness of the following publishers: Little, Brown, and Company, Williams & Wilkins, Charles C Thomas, W. B. Saunders, Alfred A. Knopf, Harper & Row, Hoeber Medical Division, Prentice-Hall, Johns Hopkins University Press, Collier Books, Blackwell Scientific Publications, Vantage Press, W. F. Prior Company, Hafner Publishing Company, Paul C. Bucy & Associates, Charles Scribner's Sons, Munksgaard, and Princeton University Press for their permission to use quoted material.

Biography, to both reader and author, should be an instructive, insightful experience. I have learned much from a man I have come to know but never met.

William Lloyd Fox
Silver Spring, Maryland

Contents

CHAPTER 1

Neurological Surgery before Walter E. Dandy: A Brief Introduction

Three hundred years ago the English physician Thomas Sydenham wisely observed: "As no man can say who it was that first invented the use of clothes and houses against the inclemency of the weather, so also can no investigator point out the origin of Medicine—mysterious as the source of the Nile. There has never been a time when it was not" (1). The beginnings of neurological surgery, in which Walter Dandy became a master, are likewise obscure. Trephination (trepanation) of the skull by which a piece of the bone is removed may date back to 10,000 B.C. It is generally believed that this was the earliest surgical operation. "Why prehistoric man made holes in the cranium can only be conjectured," wrote Desmond C. O'Connor and A. Earl Walker in *A History of Neurological Surgery* (2). In some instances, no doubt, trephination as a therapeutic step was undertaken following a head injury; yet most of the trephined skulls of prehistoric man have not revealed pathological lesions. "The idea has been prevalent that the holes were made to allow demons, spirits or supernatural elements to escape from the head. Such sprites might well have been considered by primitive people as responsible for convulsions, idiocy, insanity, or headache" (2). It may also have been true that trephination was in some instances a ritualistic rite of sacrifice. In addition, prehistoric man apparently trephined skulls of the dead in order, as Walker suggests, "to obtain amulets or to allow suspension of the cadaver for embalming or other purposes" (2). Following trephination on the living, new bone, easily detectable by a later scientific eye, would develop around the hole; hence the ability of modern scientists to distinguish between trephination practiced on the living and the dead.

This earliest surgical procedure, strange to say, seemed to have been unknown to or avoided by the Mesopotamians and Egyptians. Nevertheless, the Egyptians, as reflected in the Edwin Smith papyrus, knew of the convolutions of the brain, the cerebrospinal fluid, as well as the meninges (membranes that envelope the brain and spinal cord: the dura mater, pia mater, and arachnoid). They also "... recognized that injuries and dislocations of the spine associated with cord damage caused paralysis of the arms and legs and also bowel and bladder incontinence as well as erections with seminal emissions. Such injuries were given a hopeless prognosis (3). Although the Egyptians knew much about the nervous system, both its anatomy and physiology, they apparently did not resort to surgery for the treatment of injuries to the head and spine.

In the time of Hippocrates (ca. 460–355 B.C.) the Greeks' knowledge of the nervous system, though rationally based, was understandably superficial. "Hippocrates trephined for skull fractures, epilepsy, blindness and headache" (4). While the Greeks and the Romans developed trephination into a fine art, they could not undertake intracranial surgery because they lacked effective anesthesia and asepsis. These deficiencies continued for centuries; not until the 19th century were they overcome.

During the thousand years of the Middle Ages surgery, including its neurological branch, was at a standstill, in contrast with the appearance of hospitals and the rise of universities embracing medical faculty and students. Contrary to a commonly held misconception about the medieval church's prohibition against the clergy engaging in surgery—the misconception having stemmed in part by generalizing from the edict of 1163, "Ecclesia abhorret a sanguine" (The church abhors the shedding of blood), some clergy were permitted to practice the art (5). Nevertheless, "the general practice of surgery, including most of the major operations, was, in the end, relegated to barbers, bath-keepers, sowgelders and wayfaring mountebanks..." (6).

From the beginning of the Renaissance till the latter half of the 19th century no significant developments in neurological surgery occurred. It was a period, however, when important gaps in the knowledge of anatomy, physiology, and pathology were overcome by the publication of such writings as Andreas Vesalius' epoch work in human anatomy, *De Humani Corporis Fabrica Libri Septem*

(1543), which Sir William Osler called the greatest medical book ever written; William Harvey's classic description of cardiac function and circulation of the blood, *Exercitatio Anatomica de Motu Cordis et Sanguinis in Animalibus* (1628); Domenico Cotugno's discovery of the cerebrospinal fluid (1774); and Marie Francois Xavier Bichat's study of tissues and "...the important concept that disease of a tissue is essentially the same, in whatever organ it may be located" (7), as reflected in such work as *Traité des Membranes* (1800), *Sur la Vie et la Mort* (1800), and *Anatomie Generale* (1801). In addition, Bichat's *Traité d'Anatomie Déscriptive* in five volumes (1801–1803) provided "a structural basis for the understanding of neurological syndromes" (8). Another invaluable addition to the storehouse of knowledge applicable to neurology and neurological surgery was Giovanni Battista Morgagni's great work in pathological anatomy, *De Sedibus et Causis Morborum per Anatomen Indagatis* (1761), in which he noted that hemiplegia (paralysis of one side of the body) occurred on the opposite side of the cerebral lesion.

A little more than a half century following the appearance of Bichat's *Descriptive Anatomy*, Rudolf Ludwig Karl Virchow published his landmark work, *Die Cellular-pathologie in ihrer Begrundung auf physiologische Gewebelehre* (1858), in which he argued that "if one admits that normal life comes from the normal functioning of the body cells, it is evident that changes in form and therefore in function should give rise to disease" (9). In his inclination to attribute all disease to cellular change Virchow went too far. Nonetheless, his imprint on pathology is still felt today.

From Vesalius to Virchow—300 years—the foundation stones on which modern neurological surgery was to be built were laid as shown in the works previously mentioned. Three years after the publication of Virchow's *Cellular Pathology*, Paul Broca gave "the first precise proof of cerebral localization" before the Anthropological Society of Paris by showing the brain of a man who for more than 20 years had been unable to speak. Broca demonstrated that "there was softening of the third left frontal convolution" (10).

In 1870 Gustav Theodor Fritsch and Eduard Hitzig published their important findings on electrical stimulation of the motor areas of a dog's brain (11). They showed that "...within the brain, a separate mechanism ... must go into action during the animal's voluntary use of the leg, a motor mechanism in which the activating energy is electrical" (12). In turn, David Ferrier carried Fritsch and Hitzig's work forward by charting the motor and sensory areas of the brain. Such information was of fundamental importance to those who pioneered in neurosurgery.

"Surgery of the brain," began Walter Dandy in his definitive treatment of the subject, "is the outgrowth of three discoveries of the nineteenth century, namely anesthesia, asepsis and cerebral localization. Without asepsis or antisepsis, surgery of the brain would never be possible. With asepsis and without cerebral localization, it could be of but little value. With both asepsis and cerebral localization and without anesthesia, it would be possible but greatly limited" (13). Between 1846 when William T. G. Morton introduced anesthesia and 1867 when Joseph Lister demonstrated antiseptic surgery, no advancement in brain surgery was made. "And," added Dandy, "seventeen additional years were required before the three combined discoveries were sufficiently secure and adequately correlated to permit this field of surgery to be fairly launched" (14).

Using Lister's antisepsis Sir Rickman Godlee, on November 25, 1884, partially removed a brain tumor from a patient of Dr. Hughes Bennett who had localized the lesion. The tumor was a subcortical glioma and so could not be totally extirpated. "This was not the first brain tumor removal; it was not even the first time antiseptic methods had been used in cerebral surgery, nor was it the first time the results of the experiments of Fritsch and Hitzig had been applied to a case to be operated upon, but it was the first time that under all these conditions a tumor had been found and successfully though only partially removed" (15). Unfortunately the patient died from meningitis a month later.

Before Godlee's operation in 1884, Sir William Macewen, whom Dandy considered the "father of modern neurological surgery," had performed under antiseptic conditions several craniotomies. In 1876 he diagnosed an abscess of the frontal lobe in which there was contralateral hemiplegia. Macewen recommended surgery, but the patient's parents were opposed. At necropsy Macewen located the abscess where he had expected it to be. For Dandy this "... was the real beginning of neurological surgery." Twelve years later Macewen published his remarkable report of 21 operations with 18 recoveries, which "... probably more than all else opened the eyes of the world to the possibility of safely operating upon the brain" (16).

Meanwhile, Victor Horsley (later to be Sir Victor), whom Gilbert Horrax referred to in his *Neurosurgery: An Historical Sketch* as "the father of neurological surgery," was appointed surgeon to the National Hospital for the Paralyzed and Epileptic, Queen Square, London, in 1886. With a sound background in neurophysiology as well as surgery, Horsley that year did 10 cranial operations. Ironically, although he was the neurosurgeon in the National Hospital— the first to be so appointed in the specialty—"he operated only by invitation. He had no beds of his own, he had no surgical service, no laboratories" (17). Horsley insisted that "diagnosis of disease of the central nervous system means an intimate acquaintance with its physiology and pathology, and this we may hope to see widely generalized in spite of iniquitous opposition to scientific experiment and foolish ignorance, which, so to speak, boasts that it 'does not believe in localization' " (18).

Two years after Horsley joined the staff of the National Hospital in London, William Williams ("W. W.") Keen of Philadelphia, called by Dandy "America's pioneer neurological surgeon," reported on "Three Successful Cases of Cerebral Surgery." In one case Keen removed a large intracranial fibroma (a tumor composed mainly of fibrous or completely developed connective tissue); in another case he excised damaged brain tissue; and in the third, he excised the cerebral center for the left hand (19). The patient from whom the tumor was completely removed was well 30 years later. Dandy thought that this was "...the first case of all brain tumors to be permanently cured" (20).

Another leading neurosurgeon of the period was Fedor Krause of Berlin who in 1895 removed the gasserian ganglion (a collection of nerve cells on the larger root of the 5th cranial nerve), the source of the exceedingly painful trigeminal neuralgia or *tic douloureux*. That same year Macewen published his monumental work on *Pyogenic Infective Diseases of the Brain and Spinal Cord* (21).

These developments in neurological surgery as well as those which followed could not have taken place without the necessary technical advancements such as the invention of the ophthalmoscope by Herman Ludwig von Helmholtz in 1850, which made possible the direct examination of an important area of the nervous system. In 1893 formaldehyde or formalin as a fixative, which was important to microscopic analysis, was introduced. Two years later Wilhelm Conrad Roentgen discovered the x-ray, which was followed the next year by Scipione Riva Rocci's development of the sphygmomanometer (an instrument for measuring blood pressure). In turn, August Bier in 1898 successfully demonstrated true spinal anesthesia. By 1900 neurological surgery was ready to advance as a specialty. What was needed, aside from further technical advancements, was the determination of a select few who were willing to concentrate their talents and energy in mastering the very demanding skills of this field.

One of the important figures in its early development was Harvey Cushing who arrived at The Johns Hopkins Hospital and Medical School in the fall of 1896 as William Stewart Halsted's assistant resident in surgery. Cushing subsequently worked out an arrangement with Halsted whereby he handled the neurological cases. By 1904 when he delivered a paper before the Cleveland Academy of Medicine on "The Special Field of Neurological Surgery" (22), his enthusiasm for the specialty was well established. The increasing interest in and knowledge of neurosurgery was reflected 4 years later in the publication of Cushing's monograph, "Surgery of the Head," in Keen's *Surgery: Its Principles and Practice* (23) and Edward Archibald's chapter, "Surgical Affections and Wounds of the Head," in Bryant and Buck's *American Practice of Surgery* (24).

If Victor Horsley, William Macewen, and others previously mentioned comprised the pioneer school of neurosurgeons, then, according to Wilder Penfield, "Cushing, [Sir Geoffrey] Jefferson, Dandy and others are technically separated from them in the modern school of neurosurgery. It was the transformation of surgical technique led by William Halsted that separated the two schools" (25).

In 1910 when Walter Dandy graduated from medical school, neurosurgery was still a young specialty that offered a challenge to one of brilliant mind who had the courage and the skill to meet it. Dandy would answer the call.

END NOTES

1. Strauss MB: *Familiar Medical Quotations.* Boston, Little, Brown, 1968, p 213.
2. O'Connor DC, Walker AE: *A History of Neurological Surgery.* Baltimore, Williams & Wilkins, 1951, ch 1, p 6.
3. Horrax G: *Neurosurgery: An Historical Sketch.* Springfield, Ill, Charles C Thomas, 1952, pp 15–16.
4. O'Connor DC, Walker AE: *A History of Neurological Surgery.* Baltimore, Williams & Wilkins, 1951, ch 1, p 11.
5. Amundsen DW: Medieval canon law and surgical practice by clergy. *Bull Hist Med* 52:22–44, 1978.
6. Garrison FH: *An Introduction to the History of Medicine,* ed 3. Philadelphia, WB Saunders, 1924, p 134.
7. Castiglioni A: *A History of Medicine,* ed 2, revised and enlarged. New York, Knopf, 1958, p 673.
8. O'Connor DC, Walker AE: *A History of Neurological Surgery.* Baltimore, Williams & Wilkins, 1951, p 20.

9. Castiglioni A: *A History of Medicine*, ed 2. New York, Knopf, 1958, p 696.
10. Ballance CA: *A Glimpse into the History of the Surgery of the Brain.* The Thomas Vicary Lecture delivered before the Royal College of Surgeons of England on Dec. 8, 1921. London, Macmillan & Co, 1921, p 86.
11. Fritsch G, Hitzig E: Uber die elektrische Erregbarkeit des Grosshirns. *Arch Anat Physiol Wissenschaftl Mediz* 37:300–332, 1870. For a careful review of the subject, see Young RM: *Mind, Brain and Adaptation in the Nineteenth Century.* Oxford, Clarendon Press, 1970, ch 8, pp 234–248.
12. Penfield W: *No Man Alone: A Neurosurgeon's Life.* Boston, Little, Brown, 1977, p 168.
13. Dandy WE: *The Brain.* New York, Harper & Row, Hoeber Medical Division, 1969, pp 6–7. This was originally published as Surgery of the Brain, in Lewis D: *Practice of Surgery.* WF Prior, 1932, vol 12, p 682.
14. Dandy WE: *The Brain.* New York, Harper & Row, Hoeber Medical Division, 1969, p 7.
15. Dandy WE: *The Brain.* New York, Harper & Row, Hoeber Medical Division, 1969, p 12.
16. Walter E. Dandy (hereinafter cited as W.E.D.) to Dr. A. K. Bowman, Ayr, Scotland, letter, June 11, 1936. Dandy Papers, Alan Mason Chesney Medical Archieves of The Johns Hopkins Medical Institutions.

    Macewen was invited to be the first head of the department of surgery at Johns Hopkins but declined because, according to Dandy whose informant was Dr. William Stewart Halsted, he could not have controlled "the nursing situation which he considered so important for the surgeon's work." Instead, Halsted received the appointment.
17. Penfield W: *No Man Alone: A Neurosurgeon's Life.* Boston, Little, Brown, 1977, p 50.
18. Horsley V: Remarks on ten consecutive cases of operations upon the brain and cranial cavity to illustrate the details and safety of the method employed. *Br Med J* 1:863–866, 1887.
19. Keen WW: Three successful cases of cerebral surgery. *Am J Med Sci* 96:329–357, 452–465, 1888.
20. Dandy WE: *The Brain.* New York, Harper & Row, Hoeber Medical Division, 1969, p 14.
21. Macewen W: *Pyogenic Infective Diseases of the Brain and Spinal Cord: Meningitis, Abscess of the Brain, Infective Sinus Thrombosis.* Glasgow, J. Maclehose & Sons, 1893, vol 24, 354 pp.
22. Cushing H: The special field of neurological surgery. *Cleve Med J* 4:1–25, 1905.
23. Keen WW (ed): *Surgery: Its Principles and Practice.* Philadelphia, WB Saunders, 1980, vol 3, pp 17–276.
24. Bryant JD, Buck AH (eds): *American Practice of Surgery: A Complete System of the Science and Art of Surgery, by Representative Surgeons of the United States and Canada.* New York, William Wood, 1908, vol 5, pp 3–378.
25. Penfield W: *No Man Alone: A Neurosurgeon's Life.* Boston, Little, Brown, 1977, p 89.

CHAPTER 2

Early Years

No decade in the half century between Appomatox and the assassination of the Austrian Archduke Franz Ferdinand and his wife, which began a train of events leading to the First World War, reflected more clearly the vibrant character of American life and the accompanying social changes than did the 1880s. The population increased by some 25%; and immigration underwent a shift from the "old" to the "new," from an alteration in numbers coming from northern and western Europe to those coming from the southern and eastern regions of the Continent. The formation of large corporate combinations such as the Standard Oil Trust was paralleled by the growth of labor unions and the organization of the American Federation of Labor (1886). Congress early in 1883 passed the Pendleton Act which established a federal civil service, based on a (limited) system of merit through competitive written examinations. That same year the Supreme Court's rule in the Civil Rights Cases practically ended the federal government's attempt to protect Negroes against discrimination by private white persons. A year later the country witnessed what perhaps was the dirtiest presidential campaign (Blaine vs Cleveland). Meanwhile, the Chicago architect William LeBaron Jenney was putting up the Home Insurance Building, America's first skyscraper, and the Baltimore printer Ottmar Mergenthaler was perfecting the linotype machine which was to revolutionize printing composition. While these developments were in progress, William Stewart Halsted, a young New York surgeon, demonstrated nerve block anesthesia by the injection of cocaine. Toward the end of the decade The Johns Hopkins Hospital in Baltimore, in which Halsted was to become surgeon-in-chief and Walter Dandy's mentor, opened its doors, a milestone in American medical history. Meanwhile, in the spring of 1886 the bloody Haymarket Affair occurred in Chicago, resulting in the deaths of 7 policeman and injury to 67 others. It was also in the spring of that year that Walter Dandy was born.

Among the thousands of immigrants who arrived on these shores while all of these developments were taking place were John Dandy of Barrow-in-Furness, Lancashire, England, and Rachel Kilpatrick from Armagh in northern Ireland. Dandy, having been a railroad man in England, became an engineer on the Missouri-Kansas-Texas Railroad and later the engineer for that line's celebrated passenger train, the Katy Flyer. On May 23, 1885, Rachel and he were married in St. Louis, Missouri. They then began housekeeping in Sedalia, Missouri, a railroad town, once the eastern terminus for the long cattle drives from Texas. A little less than a year later— April 6, 1886—their only child, Walter Edward Dandy, was born in the little house at 1323 East 5th Street.

Though they were to spend the rest of their lives in the United States except for a sojourn of 3 years in England before the First World War, they did not become naturalized citizens until 1919, some 33 years after Walter's birth. Like many other immigrants of the day, the so-called "birds of passage," the Dandys may have entertained the desire to return to the old country following retirement.

In the meantime, aside from their labors and the love they gave to rearing their son, they were active members of the Plymouth Brethren, a fundamentalist sect which ". . . had risen in England and Ireland during the 1820s as a protest against any union between church and state and stereotyped forms of worship" (1). Though Dandy rejected the doctrine of the Plymouth Brethren upon reaching manhood, he never let his feelings interfere with his devotion to his mother and father. In addition, he was never able to accept his father's political beliefs, as John Dandy was a Socialist who regularly voted the Socialist Labor Party ticket. John's daughter-in-law has referred to him as "an independent thinker," (2) a quality which it would seem he passed on to his son.

Life in Sedalia for Dandy centered about his family, friends, and school. A bright, active boy, he was one of the best students in his class at Summit School. Recognizing his ability, one of his teachers, Laura T. McGowan, arranged to have him skip a whole grade (3). Out on the school's cinder playground he joined in the games of ball and pom-pom-pull-away which occasionally resulted in skinned hands and knees. Though small for his age and "the target for the boys who were larger," Walter could handle his own in a fight.

With "the Simpson boy who sucked his thumb until it almost withered away," he had "two big fights" before his schoolmate stopped bullying him (4). And at the old 5th Street marble ring Dandy regulary won, annually winning ". . . all the marbles each boy in the neighborhood possessed" (5). He thus acquired a jar of lovely flints, an accomplishment which boyhood friends never forgot (6). Among other diversions were skating on Fishers Lake in the winter and a cool dip in the old swimming hole in the summer. "It's remarkable," wrote Dandy years later, "what little insignificant occasions flit through one's mind when passing the scenes of boyhood days" (7). He remembered how a friend and he ". . . drew a wagon all the way across town to Stevenson's ice plant to bring back ice more cheaply—5¢—and make some salty old ice cream at his [friend's] house . . ." (7). For passive amusement Dandy and his friends would occasionally watch a 10¢-show from the balcony of the old Woods Opera House. When he was old enough to deliver newspapers, Walter would walk with a companion, Harry T. Lewis, to the railroad station, which was about a mile and a half from their homes, to pick up the St. Louis morning papers. Then in the evening they would deliver two more routes of the *Sedalia Democrat*. On one occasion during his boyhood days Dandy had a frightening experience with a gun. Before crawling through a fence, he had put the gun down; it then went off accidentally near his ear. After this unsettling incident, he never had much use for guns or hunting (8).

In the spring of his senior year in high school (1903) Dandy's ability as a student—he was just 17 years old—was reflected by his serving as the valedictorian of his class. Only the title of his commencement oration, "Education," remains. At the time of his graduation he was of medium height, about 5 ft 8 inches (perhaps somewhat short by present American standards), and of slight build. The most striking feature of the young man was his deep, penetrating blue eyes.

Recalling years later his boyhood days in Sedalia after a few return visits, he expressed what others have likewise experienced upon visiting the scenes of their youth: ". . . The houses seemed so much smaller and the streets so much narrower and the block so much shorter than the measurements of my memory" (9).

The fall following his graduation from high school Dandy entered the freshman class at the University of Missouri at Columbia where within a short time he "stood out among students" (10). Sharing a dormitory room first with Ike Ikenberry, a fellow Sedalian, he later roomed in Benton Hall (Room 38) with Stanley Battersby whose family in Sedalia, like Dandy's, were British railroad people and members of the Plymouth Brethren. During his senior year Dandy shared no. 38 with Franklin P. Johnson, another friend.

Though he was not poor, Dandy was, according to his boyhood friend and college roommate, Stanley ("Bat") Battersby, frugal. Thus he had no interest in joining a Greek-letter fraternity, which aside from the expense included in those days more than a few four-flushers, the kind of people who were anathema to him. "Social activities were a waste of time" (11). Dandy did become, however, a member of the YMCA and the University Boarding Club, one of the men's clubs, ". . . which had given so many boys a start" but which in later years, he lamented, were eliminated (12).

"A hard student, a hard player and a hard sleeper (almost as in a coma)" is the way Battersby has described Dandy's student days at Missouri. "My hardest job as a roommate was to get him up for breakfast. The whole floor knew of my trials, so one morning a group came in and we [moved] him and his bed into an adjoining room. The joke went a little stale in that it never phased [sic] him. After some time someone threw a bucket of water on him and ran. Dandy woke and was terrified when he could not find his clothes and was bewildered when he realized that he was in his own bed but in a strange room" (13).

Throughout his life Dandy took sports seriously and played to win. On a nearby vacant lot he and the boys in his dormitory would play baseball at odd hours. Although he was a good fielder, he initially could not hit. One day an engineering student noticed how Dandy held the bat. A right-handed hitter, he "held the bat with his right hand below the left, a grip that is called cross-handed. With a correction of the grip he became a fair hitter and was greatly pleased with his performance" (13). In later years Dandy lost track of his friend Hart, the engineering student, but was always grateful to him: ". . . I wish I could run across Hart sometime. I am still thankful for his baseball advice" (13).

While he was at the University Dandy also learned something about boxing from one of the students in his dormitory who owned a set of boxing gloves and who would regale his listeners with fight stories and his experiences as a sparring partner with a well-known lightweight. Dandy thought it would be a good opportunity to learn something about boxing, and the fighter was willing to give him instruction. "After a month or six weeks Dandy accused the fighter of letting him have the better of thing[s] and sternly demanded that [the] fighter really fight. Well, it happened after a minute or so; the fighter landed a comparatively soft blow on Dandy's chin. Dandy was chagrined, put off the gloves and quit for good and did [not] relish any reference to his boxing lesson" (13).

It was also at Missouri that Dandy was introduced to golf, a sport which he came to love and to play until the end of his life. His introduction to the game was quite inauspicious, however. One day his friends, including Battersby, persuaded him to join them on the University's "near cow pasture golf course." As Dandy had no clubs, his friends arranged to borrow a set. When it was his turn to tee off, he "with a mighty wallop hit the dirt just behind the ball. The ball trickled off the tee and the head of the driver went 50 or 75 ft down the fairway. Dandy walked away in disgust, refusing to pick up the extra clubs, knowing that he would have to buy a new driver and that hurt his frugal spirit" (13).

Dandy's frugality while in college was revealed on another occasion, an evening ice-skating party for which his friend "Bat" had arranged for him to bring "a charming little nurse." Upon meeting the girl Dandy learned that she had no skates. "In those days," according to Battersby, "$1.50 or $2.00 bought a fair pair of skates. They were detachable (You did not have to buy shoes, etc. like the modern outfit[s].) As we were to walk to the pond and had to go through the business section we needled Dandy into buying his date a pair of skates. We had a lovely time and when we returned to the hospital Dandy's date said 'thanks' for a lovely evening and a nice pair of skates. Dandy was boiling but had to accept. (He fully expected to take the skates home.) So skates and golf were nasty words to Dandy for his remaining time at M.U." (13). As these incidents have revealed, Dandy without intent or expectation could be funny on occasion. His intensity of thought and behavior in school as well as in later life probably contributed to such droll incidents as we have noted.

While Dandy occasionally had time to indulge his love of sports or to play a game of whist, most of his time was devoted to studying and working. In order to help defray his college expenses he worked, among other jobs, as a barn painter during his summer vacations. One summer he was employed as a conductor by the Sedalia Traction Company which operated a trolley line from the town to an amusement park. The following summer he worked as a motorman, a position which he had wanted as he had a lifelong interest in trains, possibly due to his father's occupation (14). In a letter to his parents some years later Dandy made a passing reference to nursing "old man Larry," who lived at 10th and Ohio Streets in Sedalia (15). This experience in practical nursing may have occurred during a vacation while he was a student at Missouri.

When Dandy began his freshman year in September 1903, he was committed, so it appeared, to the premedical program. Besides freshman English, his schedule included elementary Greek, second-year German, inorganic chemistry, physics, and gymnasium. He did well in his courses except for slipping in both English and physics from an A in the first semester to a B in each for the second, the only instance during his 4 years at Missouri that his academic work declined slightly. His second-year schedule was just as demanding as the first: Greek—Anabasis, Latin—Livy, qualitative analysis, general zoology, organic chemistry, and gymnasium, all of which included both the first and second semesters. Again Dandy did well except for a C in the first semester of qualitative analysis. The only other C he received in college was in bacteriology, which he took in his senior year.

Beginning with his junior year Dandy was enrolled in the University's School of Medicine, which since 1899 had provided a 4-year program leading to the M.D. degree (16). His third year was clearly his best, as he received in his courses no grade less than A: descriptive anatomy and osteology (1 semester), histology, anatomy of vertebrates, French I, and embryology (1 semester). In his senior year (second year of preclinical medicine), except for bacteriology as mentioned earlier, Dandy did superior work in such courses as dissection, topical anatomy, experimental physiology, pathology, cytology, and advanced anatomy (17).

It is a truism that inspiring teachers quite often bring out the best in able students. Professor C. M. Jackson, who taught Dandy anatomy, was such a teacher, as was also Professor C. W. Greene in physiology. Some years later in asking Jackson for his photograph Dandy acknowledged: "I am sure it is needless to tell you the great debt I feel to your guiding influence and stimulation. The spirit of research, which I hope will always be uppermost in my work, was, of course, directly and solely due to your influence" (18). Dandy's tribute stemmed in part from his service as a student assistant to Dr. Jackson in the anatomy laboratory during his junior and senior years.

With the record he had compiled it is not surprising that Dandy was one of the "First Five" elected from the class of 1907 to Phi Beta Kappa, into which he was received on December 5, 1906 (19). And 4 months later he was elected to Sigma Xi, the national scientific honorary society (20). In addition to these honors Dandy was tapped for membership in QEBH, a university honorary society limited to ten men. An indication that he had other than academic talents was his election as president of the Pettis County Club, composed of students from that county.

Meanwhile, Dandy became a candidate for a Rhodes Scholarship, having taken the examination in January 1907. He did sufficiently well so as to be excused from responsions, the first examination at Oxford University which a candidate for a B.A. degree must pass (21). As a consequence he made the initial selection. For its final selection the screening committee, however, chose someone else, inasmuch as a University of Missouri student had received the previous appointment for that region. "Dandy took [it] in stride," Battersby recalled, "and I never heard him express any disappointment" (22). In the meantime, Dandy had written to Sir William Osler, Regius Professor of Medicine at Oxford, who had left Johns Hopkins 2 years before, about the prospects of studying medicine at Oxford. In his usual, thoughtful manner Osler replied:

Dear Sir:
    To take the Oxford degree you will first have to take the Oxford B.A., which would be scarcely worthwhile to spend all that extra time. It would be very much better to finish at the Johns Hopkins Hospital and then come abroad for postgraduate work (23).

Perhaps of even greater importance for Dandy than becoming a Rhodes Scholar was the question of transferring to another medical school, one of greater stature and with a stronger program, especially in the clinical years, than Missouri then offered. Professors Winterton C. Curtis and George Lefevre in zoology, who had received their Ph.D.s from Hopkins, and Dr. W. J. Calvert, who had graduated from the Johns Hopkins Medical School and was then teaching in the Missouri School of Medicine, were eager for him to go to Hopkins and wrote letters of recommendation on his behalf. Moreover, Dandy's father approached Charles E. Yeater, a prominent citizen of Sedalia and a former vice governor of the Philippines, about the desirability of his son transferring to Johns Hopkins. Like the professors just mentioned Yeater, whose picture Dandy later had in his study, recommended the transfer. At about the same time that he took the Rhodes Scholarship examination,

Dandy wrote to the registrar of Johns Hopkins as follows (24):

Dear Sir:
    I have for sometime been thinking of stud[y]ing medicine at your university but as yet am undecided for the following reason. I will graduate from Missouri University this year and also have finished the first year & 6 hours of the sophomore [course] of medicine. Now could I get credit at your school for my medical work done here and enter up a full Sophomore at John[s] Hopkins without taking the examination[?]
    My work has been very satisfactory in both Academic and Medical Departments so far, the grades of which you are perfectly welcome to if desired; I am satisfied I could do the work satisfactorily with the foundation of freshman medicine here, which I think is almost as good as any in the Country.
    Hoping to hear from you soon in regard to this matter I remain,

Yours respectfully,
W. E. Dandy

38 Benton Hall
Missouri University

About a month before he graduated from Missouri, Dandy wrote to the dean of The Johns Hopkins Medical School, Dr. William H. Howell, indicating that he wished to continue his medical education at "John[s] Hopkins or Harvard preferably John[s] Hopkins" but providing that he could enter with advanced standing. He also wondered if he could get credit without having to take examinations (25). Dean Howell promptly replied that the medical faculty might raise some objection to Dandy's application inasmuch as he had taken 2 years (actually 1½ years) of medical work and applied it to his bachelor's degree, and the faculty wanted students to have 4 years of college work before entering medical school. Howell also indicated that Dandy would have to pass examinations in such fields as anatomy, histology, physiology, and pathology (26). Later, after reviewing his application Howell informed Dandy that he would ". . . have to take an examination in histology and physiological chemistry and a provisional examination in anatomy covering the parts that you have dissected" (27). Dandy was thus admitted to The Johns Hopkins Medical School with advanced standing as a second-year student, having meanwhile received the A.B. degree at commencement exercises on June 5 with an accumulation of 138 semester hours of credit, 18 more than was necessary for graduation. He ranked second in a class of over 100. Though Dandy did not stay to receive the M.D. degree, he nevertheless was considered "a member of the Medical Class of 1909, Q.E.D.," according to his old physiology professor 25 years later (28).
    Letters of recommendation, in addition to his superior academic record, helped to make it possible for Dandy to enter Hopkins with

advanced standing. In his letter C. M. Jackson spoke of him as "an unusually good student" while Charles W. Greene in his correspondence made the interesting observation: ". . . While I do not regard him as an extraordinarily brilliant student, still I think he is the type of man who will succeed at Hopkins, and I have all confidence in him in that regard" (29). Of all his Missouri professors, Dandy always thought George Lefevre was the one primarily responsible for his going to Hopkins: "I am sure had it not been for him I should never have come to Hopkins and, of course, my opportunity could never have been so great in any other place" (30).

With his graduation from Missouri and his admission to Johns Hopkins Dandy began his medical career of nearly 40 years in Baltimore. Beneath his picture in the 1907 *Savitar*, the University of Missouri's yearbook, was, in an attempt to be alliteratively humorous, the quip "Little, but loud," which his friend and classmate, Stanley Battersby, interpreted to mean: He "had little to say but when said it was really right" (31). As his professional career would reveal, Dandy was a good listener, a clear thinker, and a relentless investigator who only spoke or wrote when he was sure that he was right.

During the summer following his graduation he made a trip to California—no doubt using the family railroad pass—where he visited San Francisco and Palo Alto. We know of this trip only by a letter he wrote to his father 32 years later in which he spoke of the heavy fog in leaving San Francisco Bay on his way to Hawaii (1939) and remembering "so well in 1907 how I took the train to Palo Alto 30 miles away to escape the fog and cold & there it was an entirely different climate" (32). The trip, no doubt, was an elixir to Dandy who throughout his life enjoyed traveling, particularly by train.

The following September found him ready to embark on another adventure, the completion of his medical education at Johns Hopkins, which Robert P. Sharkey has aptly described as "the pioneer university in this country" for ". . . it set the pace and established the standards for a host of institutions which followed" (33). As one who was to become a trailblazer in surgery, attendance at such a pioneer institution was somehow quite appropriate.

END NOTES

1. Olmstead CE: *History of Religion in the United States*, Englewood Cliffs, NJ, Prentice-Hall, 1960, p 426.

2. Mrs. Walter E. Dandy, Baltimore, interview with the author, June 3, 1975.
3. Writing to Dandy thirty years later, Laura McGowan declared: "Your successes have always been a source of great pride and pleasure to me for they have justified my hopes and assured my predictions of a brilliant future for you." Laura T. McGowan to W.E.D., letter, Oct 5, 1934, Dandy MSS.
   Another of Dandy's grade school teachers was Mrs. Mary Evelyn Offield whose son became the well known actor Jack Oakie.
4. W.E.D. to Herschel V. Ford, Houston, letter, Jan 12, 1934, Dandy MSS.
5. Herschel V. Ford, Houston, to W.E.D., letter, Dec 28, 1933, Dandy MSS.
6. R. S. Battersby, Columbia, MO, to W.E.D., letter, Aug 10, 1925, Dandy MSS.
7. W.E.D., El Paso, TX, on a train, to Mr. and Mrs. John Dandy, Baltimore, letter, June 21, 1928, Dandy MSS.
8. Mrs. Walter E. Dandy, Baltimore, interview with the author, June 3, 1975.
9. W.E.D. to Herschel V. Ford, Houston, letter, Jan 12, 1934, Dandy MSS.
10. Dr. Winterton C. Curtis, Columbia, MO, interview with the author, Aug 25, 1965.
11. R. S. Battersby, M.D., Columbia, MO, to the author, letter, Sept 27, 1965.
12. W.E.D. to R. S. Battersby, Columbia, MO, letter, Aug 19, 1925, Dandy MSS.
13. R. S. Battersby, Columbia, MO, to the author, letter, Sept 27, 1965.
14. Mrs. Walter E. Dandy, Baltimore, interview by telephone with the author, May 28, 1977. Frank J. Otenasek, M.D., "Ruminations about Walter E. Dandy," unpublished ms. delivered at the annual meeting of the Florida Association of Neurosurgeons, Hollywood-By-The-Sea, FL, May 19, 1963.
15. W.E.D., Baltimore, to Mr. and Mrs. John Dandy, London, July 25, 1914, Dandy MSS.
16. *The Advisory Council of the University of Missouri* (booklet), Dec 9–10, 1932, pp 21–22. In 1910 the University discontinued the last two years of the medical program because of a lack of funds for providing adequate hospital facilities for teaching the clinical courses.
17. Academic Record of Walter Edward Dandy, University of Missouri, Columbia.
18. W.E.D. to C. M. Jackson, Minneapolis, Nov 23, 1926, Dandy MSS.
19. *Savitar* (University of Missouri yearbook), 1907, Walter E. Dandy alumnus file, no 927730, University of Missouri.
20. Some years later The Johns Hopkins Chapter of Sigma Xi, unaware of his earlier election to membership, invited him to join.
21. University of Oxford, Delegacy of Local Examinations.
22. R. S. Battersby, Columbia, MO, to the author, letter, Sept 27, 1965, Dandy MSS.
23. Sir William Osler, Regius Professor of Medicine, University of Oxford, to W.E.D., Columbia, MO, letter, June 25, 1907, Dandy MSS.
24. W.E.D., Columbia, MO, to Registrar, The Johns Hopkins University, Baltimore, letter, Jan 26, 1907, File of Walter Edward Dandy (M.D., 1910) deceased, School of Medicine, JHU. No reply to this letter has been found.
25. W.E.D., Columbia, MO, to Dean of Medical Department, Johns Hopkins University, Baltimore, letter, May 5, 1907, File of Walter Edward Dandy (M.D., 1910) deceased, School of Medicine, JHU.
26. William H. Howell, Dean, Medical Dept, Johns Hopkins University, to W.E.D., Columbia, MO, letter, May 10, 1907, Dandy MSS.
27. William H. Howell, Chebeague Island, ME, to W.E.D., Sedalia, MO, letter, June 16, 1907, Dandy MSS.
28. C. W. Greene, Columbia, MO, to W.E.D., letter, Nov 17, 1934, Dandy MSS.
29. C. M. Jackson, Junior Dean of the Medical Department of the University of Missouri, Columbia, to Dr. William H. Howell, Dean of the Medical Department, Johns Hopkins University, letter, June 4, 1907; Charles W. Greene, Dept. of Physiology and Pharmacology, University of Missouri, Columbia, to Dr. William H. Howell, Johns Hopkins University, letter, June 13, 1907, File of Walter Edward Dandy (M.D., 1910) deceased, School of Medicine, JHU.
30. W.E.D. to W. C. Curtis, Columbia, MO, letter, Nov 23, 1926, Dandy MSS.

31. R. S. Battersby, Columbia, MO, to the author, letter, Sept 27, 1965.
32. W.E.D., Honolulu, T.H., to John Dandy, Baltimore, letter, Sept 13, 1939, Dandy MSS.
33. Sharkey RP: *Johns Hopkins: Centennial Portrait of a University.* Baltimore, Johns Hopkins University Press, 1975, p 1.

CHAPTER 3

Student Days at Hopkins

When Dandy went to Baltimore in the fall of 1907 as a 2nd-year medical student, The Johns Hopkins University was a little more than 30 years old; and The Johns Hopkins Hospital was entering its 19th year of operation. The Johns Hopkins Medical School (1), 4 years younger than the Hospital, was beginning its 15th. The Hospital, the University, and its medical school already enjoyed international eminence by the time Dandy arrived. "To Hopkins, more than to any other one institution, the country was indebted after 1890 for a veritable revolution in the nature and status of the medical sciences—with all that this implied for human welfare. This was a development of major importance in the social and cultural life of the nation, and the meaning of the Hopkins epic is missed if these wider relationships and consequences are ignored" (2).

For Dandy and his fellow medical students, including two class-mates from Missouri, Thomas Grover Orr and Raphael Eustace Semmes, Jr. (3), the annual tuition was $200.00, the figure set at the School's opening and which remained unchanged during Dandy's 3 years there. Having found a room at 141 Jackson Place, the young man from Sedalia quickly immersed himself in his studies. He liked the University and got along well with the students (4). Yet he remained uninvolved with social organizations. "A young man from a small town in Missouri was not the type to appeal to the medical fraternities or the Pithotomy (5), the oldest of the Hopkins medical student organizations having been established in 1897. "They were Ivy League only," notes Dr. Warfield M. Firor; and Dandy both in background and social orientation was clearly not "Ivy League" (6).

By the end of his first trimester he had succeeded in winning the respect of Professor Franklin P. Mall for his ability and interest in research in anatomy. Mall whose ". . . colleagues almost without exception believed that he was the leader of them all" (7) was so pleased with Dandy's efforts that he recommended him for membership in the American Association of Anatomists (8), indeed an honor for one who was only a 2nd-year medical student and especially as it was arranged by one of the leading anatomists of the day.

After an intensive first year at Hopkins, Dandy had an opportunity during the summer of 1908 to do something which, though of a scientific nature, was different from his academic work. His former zoology professors at Missouri, George Lefevre and Winterton C. Curtis, had undertaken research on the reproduction and artificial propagation of fresh-water mussels for the U.S. Bureau of Fisheries. As they noted in their subsequent report:

> The threatened extinction in the upper Mississippi River and its more important tributaries of those species of the Unionidae whose shells have been taken in enormous numbers in recent years, both for the manufacture of pearl buttons and for the pearls which they occasionally contain, had led the United States Bureau of Fisheries to undertake an extensive investigation of the possibility of artificially propagating the commercial species and of devising practicable means of restocking depleted waters which present favorable conditions for the maintenance (9).

To help in their investigations, Lefevre and Curtis invited several of their old students to join them, including Dandy and his former room- and classmate, Franklin Paradise Johnson. The members of the field study investigation lived during June, July, and August 1908 on the Bureau of Fisheries' small sternwheeler, the *Curlew*, at La Crosse, Wisconsin, where the Bureau had a substation, a small building containing tanks and running water which the expedition was allowed to use. Each member of the expedition had his own screened stateroom on the *Curlew* which transported the investigators as necessary from Lake Pepin to Davenport, Iowa, on the river, although most of their work was done near La Crosse. Aided by Dandy and the other student assistants, Lefevre and Curtis sought to determine ". . . the breeding seasons of the commercial species of mussels as far as possible at that time of the year and an examination of the depleted mussel beds in the upper Mississippi River . . ." (10). While a considerable quantity of data was collected, Lefevre and Curtis thought that there was much yet to be learned about such subjects as the food of mussels, their enemies and diseases, and the causes of pearl formations (11).

At the close of the summer's work a humorous incident involving Dandy occurred, which Curtis with a light touch has recalled:

A few days before the season's work was at an end I was away from the party and joined them at a hotel in Davenport, Iowa, where Lefevre had the four boys for a few days before they left for home. There seemed to be an air of restraint over the company and I learned of an episode the previous evening.

In an attempt to give the boys something better to do than wandering about the town that night Lefevre had suggested a poker game, playing for beans. [Howard] Welch and [W. E.] Muns had some knowledge of the game. Since Dandy had never played they nursed him along. Johnson was an expert. Lefevre knew the game well enough. I heard the story later that Johnson paid a part of his expenses through the J.H.U. Med. School from his winnings at poker. Apparently it had not been explained to Dandy, and when Johnson raised out the group on a bluff, Dandy became furious, accused Johnson of cheating and ungentlemanly conduct. Almost they came to blows when Lefevre ruled that no one should contradict anyone else during the few days they would be together. "If anyone says anything which you do not agree with, you are to say, 'I agree with you completely and consider you a perfect gentleman' " (12).

Thus ended an interesting as well as rewarding summer for Dandy who had learned something about fresh-water mussels as well as the game of poker.

Upon his return to Baltimore in the fall, he began his clinical studies which included not only attendance of clinics and dispensary exercises in medicine and surgery but completion of the required work in obstetrics, gynecology, and nervous diseases. For elective courses during the year Dandy chose anatomy and operative surgery, his subsequent grades in them being 10 and 8.2, respectively. (The grading system in the Medical School began with 10 as the highest grade.) In view of his later career his grade in operative surgery is somewhat surprising if not amusing.

Later that year he announced to his mother and father that he was no longer going to work for superior grades. His father's response revealed how well he knew his son:

. . . I think it would be impossible for you to do it. It is against your nature, and you can't very well reverse yourself for ever since you were a little boy you always wanted to beat in games. You remember how you used to cry if I beat you in little games at home and while I think it would be wrong for you to hurt yourself by over study to accomplish supremacy, I think any man is not much who has not some of this ambition about him . . . (13).

It was not in Dandy's nature to stop striving for superiority. In his senior year he was upset by a grade he had received in one of his courses. His father reminded him of an instance when he was a small boy: ". . . One of the teachers had not graded you as you thought she should and you was [sic] vexed and afterwards you was defiant [sic] [and] said with rage in your little face I can beat her" (14). During his last year in medical school Dandy did well in the obligatory courses (medicine, surgery, and ophthalmology) as he did also in the elective courses, including surgical pathology in which he received a grade of 10 (15).

His life as a medical student was made easier during the last 2 years by sharing a room with Ben Kline, also a student at Hopkins, in the home of Mr. and Mrs. Millard Fillmore Grauer who lived at 1029 North Broadway, only four blocks from The Johns Hopkins Hospital. The Grauers and their three sons made "Walt" feel at home. In time, they became very fond of him and he, of them (16). Ten years after graduation from medical school Dandy recalled with appreciation all that Mrs. Grauer had done for him in a letter which, lacking the correct address, she never received: "I often think of you and how good you were to me when I was a mere student. I shall never forget you . . ." (17).

As he seldom if ever went home for the holidays, letters from the family meant much to him. His mother's letters, other than dealing with family concerns, were gossipy; and his father's correspondence, besides reporting on financial matters, often included railroad news, which he thoroughly enjoyed receiving. (". . . As I came home yesterday on No. 3 from Junct. A. A. Allen's car was attached on his way to Texas" (18).) In one of her letters to Walter in the spring of 1910, Mrs. Dandy referred to her husband's avid interest in socialism, an enthusiasm which the son never shared: "We got the paper you sent about the Socialist mayor [of Milwaukee, Emil Seidel]. Pa was helping to clean house, but he couldn't do much after that paper came till he read it. That is a great mayor sure enough. I am rather inclined to be socialist. We could not have anything much worse than the present state of affairs, but politics is out of my line" (19). Clearly the Dandys' correspondence reflected the deep devotion that father, mother, and son had for one another and their candor in discussing whatever was of immediate concern, whether it was a gynecological problem affecting Mrs. Dandy or Mr. Dandy's selling of their houses in Sedalia (20).

By the end of his junior year Dandy stood among the top ten in his class. His ability in anatomy and surgery had drawn the attention of Harvey Cushing, who had come to Hopkins in the fall of 1896 as William Stewart Halsted's assistant resident in surgery and who by this time was ". . . widely known to the general public for his attainments as a 'brain' surgeon" (21). Cushing, meanwhile, had been instrumental in the establishment of the Hunterian Laboratory of Experimental Medicine at the Medical School. Soon the Laboratory gained recognition for its experimental work in surgery and pathology, using mainly dogs for the research. For one with Dandy's abilities and interests the Hunterian would be an exciting place in which to work. He apparently sought and obtained Cushing's consent to do research in the Laboratory during his senior year (22). Thus began Dandy's association with Cushing which was to continue until Cushing's departure from Hopkins 3 years later in 1912 (23). Following his graduation from Hopkins, Dandy became the sixth in line of Cushing's Hunterian appointees (1910–1911). "Cushing was a dramatically good teacher" (24), and Dandy was eager to get on his service.

In the meantime, while still a student, Dandy's ability in anatomy was demonstrated when he was asked to reconstruct and describe one of the youngest human embryos in Franklin P. Mall's collection, which is known in the literature as the "Dandy embryo." This work lead to his first article, "A Human Embryo with Seven Pairs of Somites Measuring about 2 mm in Length," published in *The American Journal of Anatomy* 5 months before his graduation (25). In the introduction Dandy briefly explained how "embryo 391" was added to Mall's collection:

> This very rare specimen came into Professor Mall's possession through the kindness of Dr. R. W. Pearce, of Albany, New York, with the following history from the physician who handed the specimen to him. "The woman had passed her period about two weeks when she performed an abortion with a stick about 8 inches long, which she whittled out for the purpose. This she passed into the uterus and 24 hours later this specimen was aborted. Her purpose in calling me was to see if her object had been attained. I have kept the specimen two years in a bottle of weak formaldehyde" (26).

Later Mall upon receipt of the specimen took the necessary, preparatory steps for its anatomical study, including cutting it ". . . into serial sections 10 microns in thickness" (26). It was from these sections that Dandy reconstructed the embryo using a scale of 200 magnifications.

Besides his interest in anatomy, Dandy had a talent for drawing which taken together induced him, at the time of his graduation, to consider momentarily becoming an anatomist—a professor of anatomy in a medical school. But the interest he had in surgery, especially the neurological field, and Cushing's influence proved more compelling (27).

The spring of 1910 was indeed a happy time for both Dandy and his mother and father. For him it marked his graduation from medical school ". . . in the fourth [highest] quarter of his class but not at the top" (28). For them it was the observance of their 25th wedding anniversary and Walter's remembrance of the occasion. In a letter written at the end of May, Rachel Dandy expressed their feelings of what their son had meant to them:

> Just received your letter this morning. We were very agreeably surprised on the 25th anniversary of our marriage to receive your congratulations which touched us deeply & brought tears to our eyes. We both had to weep, wept to think my life did not compare with that standard of perfection. May we have more desire than ever to count those gifts & to press onward, upward, homeward to a higher & holier life. It has been a great privilege & pleasure to do what little we could for you. Your progress in life has made us very happy & has more than repaid us for anything we have done.

> Well, your present has just arrived. While I was writing it came. On opening [I] was surprised to see such a brilliant display of silverware, nicest I ever saw[,] simply gorgeous. Nearly took our breath (29).

At Dandy's urging his mother and father, meanwhile, had been considering the desirability of moving to Baltimore following Mr. Dandy's retirement from the railroad. The young doctor, after all, was going to be in Baltimore for at least another year, as Cushing had appointed him Assistant in Surgery in the Hunterian Laboratory. But despite John and Rachel Dandy's talking about moving East, they were hesitant to pull up stakes. "In R.R. slang I think we need," Walter's father admitted, "a pusher to help us over the hill" (30). Ultimately they decided to join Walter in Baltimore where, except for a hiatus of 3 years in Britain, they were to spend the rest of their lives.

Shortly after graduation Dandy appeared before one of the state boards of medical examiners and was found "proficient and qualified to practice Medicine and Surgery in the State of Maryland as Physician and Surgeon" (31). He was now ready to practice the healing art, though initially in the role of a researcher.

END NOTES

1. In 1924 the name of the school was changed to The Johns Hopkins School of Medicine.
2. Shryock RH: *The Unique Influence of The Johns Hopkins University on American Medicine.* Copenhagen, Ejnar Munksgaard, 1953, p 69.
3. Semmes became another great pioneer in American neurosurgery.
4. Mrs. John Dandy, Sedalia, MO, to W.E.D., letter, Oct 30, 1907, Dandy MSS.
5. Mrs. Walter E. Dandy, Baltimore, interview with the author, Jan 17, 1976.
6. W. M. Firor, M.D., Baltimore, to the author, letter, Dec 30, 1975.

7. Harvey AM: *Adventures in Medical Research: A Century of Discovery at Johns Hopkins.* Baltimore, Johns Hopkins University Press, 1974–1976, p 97.

8. C. M. Jackson, Columbia, MO, to W.E.D., letter, Jan 6, 1908, Dandy MSS.

9. Lefevre G, Curtis WC: Studies on the reproduction and artifical propagation of freshwater mussels. *Bulletin of the Bureau of Fisheries,* XXX, Document no. 756. Washington, DC, Government Printing Office, 1912, p 109.

10. Lefevre G, Curtis WC: Studies on the reproduction and artificial propagation of freshwater mussels. *Bulletin of the Bureau of Fisheries,* XXX, Document no. 756. Government Printing Office, Washington, DC, 1912, p 187.

11. Lefevre G, Curtis WC: Studies on the reproduction and artificial propagation of freshwater mussels. *Bulletin of the Bureau of Fisheries,* XXX, Document no. 756. Government Printing Office, Washington, DC, 1912, p 193.

12. Winterton C. Curtis, Columbia, MO, to the author, "Memos re Walter Dandy," Aug 26, 1965.

13. John Dandy, Sedalia, MO, to W.E.D., letter, March 16, 1909, Dandy MSS.

14. John Dandy, Sedalia, MO, to W.E.D., letter, Dec 20, 1909, Dandy MSS.

15. Official Record, File of Walter Edward Dandy (M.D., 1910) deceased, School of Medicine, JHU.

16. Mrs. Rebecca Grauer, Chicago, IL, to W.E.D., Baltimore, postal card, Aug 21, 1926; W.E.D. to Mrs. Rebecca Grauer, Chicago, letter (returned), Aug 25, 1920; Mrs. Milton H. Grauer, Glencoe, IL, to Mrs. Walter E. Dandy, Baltimore, letter, April 20, 1946, Dandy MSS. Alice Grauer D'Angelo (Mrs. Lou D'Angelo), New York, to the author, letter, Oct 16, 1967.

17. W.E.D. to Mrs. Rebecca Grauer, Chicago, letter, Aug 25, 1920, Dandy MSS.

18. John Dandy, Sedalia, MO, to W.E.D., letter, Dec 7, 1908, Dandy MSS.

19. Rachel Dandy, Sedalia, MO, to W.E.D., letter, April 24, 1910, Dandy MSS.

20. Rachel Dandy, Sedalia, MO, to W.E.D., letter, March 8, 1909; John Dandy, Sedalia, MO, to W.E.D., letter, April 19, 1909, Dandy MSS.

21. Fulton JF: *Harvey Cushing: A Biography.* Springfield, IL, Charles C Thomas, 1946, p 256. This is Cushing's official biography. See also Thomson EH: *Harvey Cushing: Surgeon, Author, Artist.* New York, Collier Books, 1961.

22. "It must have taxed the limit of your nerve to follow him [Cushing]," wrote John Dandy to his son, "in order to get to work with him." John Dandy, Sedalia, MO, to W.E.D., letter, June 7, 1909, Dandy MSS.

23. "That Dr. Cushing is certainly a great man," noted Rachel Dandy in a letter to Walter. "While reading about him & his wonderful operations I felt myself wishing wouldn't I like to hear of my boy doing those wonderful operations. I believe someday someone will say just such grand things about you, as you have said about Dr. Cushing." Rachel Dandy, Sedalia, MO, to W.E.D., letter, May 8, 1909, Dandy MSS.

24. Harvey B. Stone, M.D., Baltimore, interview with the author, May 25, 1967.

25. Dandy WE: A human embryo with seven pairs of somites measuring about 2 mm in length. *Am J Anat* 10:85–108, 1910.

26. Dandy WE: A human embryo with seven pairs of somites measuring about 2 mm in length. *Am J Anat* 10:85, 1910.

27. Mrs. Walter E. Dandy, Baltimore, interview with the author, June 3, 1975. John Dandy, Sedalia, MO, to W.E.D., letter, June 6, 1910, Dandy MSS.

28. Alan M. Chesney, M.D., Dean, Johns Hopkins School of Medicine to Dr. Eldridge Campbell, Albany, NY, letter, Sept. 13, 1950, File of Walter Edward Dandy (M.D., 1910) deceased, School of Medicine, JHU.

29. Rachel Dandy, Sedalia, MO, to W.E.D., letter, May 30, 1910, Dandy MSS.

30. John Dandy, Sedalia, MO, to W.E.D., letter, June 6, 1910, Dandy MSS.

31. License by The Board of Medical Examiners of the State of Maryland, July 28, 1910, Dandy MSS.

CHAPTER 4

The Young Doctor

"I think you and Dr. Cushing would make a great team" (1), wrote John Dandy to his son in the spring of 1910, a little more than a month before graduation. It was an innocent hope, one which could never be fulfilled, as clashing tempers and searing words would reveal. The young doctor's vacation in Sedalia following graduation was cut short because Dr. Cushing wanted him to begin work that summer as Assistant in Surgery in the Hunterian Laboratory, which somewhat annoyed Rachel Dandy; for she felt that her son needed ". . . to loaf awhile to recuperate after the trying ordeal of those exams. You are young & can't stand it like Dr. Cushing[,] a man of mature years" (2).

By the middle of the following November, the Dandys had finally decided to move to Baltimore, Walter having meanwhile written that he could rent a house for them. Shortly the Dandys moved east, but they lived in Baltimore less than a year, for they sailed early in October 1911 for England and Ireland, where they were to remain for the next 3 years until the outbreak of the First World War encouraged their return to the United States. Before taking rooms in London, the Dandys visited County Armagh in northern Ireland, where Rachel had spent her childhood with her Presbyterian family, and Barrow-in-Furness in the west of England on the coast of the Irish Sea, John's boyhood home. While in the English town, they enjoyed, among other things, watching the tide come in one morning ". . . across [sic] old Barrow at the docks. When we got there she had got in & was about ready to recede. A few days before that we went & it was clear out, no water at all. Next time full up to the wall. The tide is a strange & beautiful thing to see" (3).

The Dandys were not sure whether they should settle in Barrow or return to America. Whenever they thought of Walter being in the United States where their money was also invested, they leaned towards returning to Baltimore. They wanted Walter to help them decide (4). Some weeks after the war in Europe had begun, Dandy urged his parents to return: ". . . You don't seem to be bothering much about the war, but I think you had better come back now while the coming is good. It is about the right time of year now and I think you had better start back right away. Take the *Lusitania* or *Mauretania* [;] they are as safe as American boats, but I wouldn't wait any longer" (5). The Dandys were not long in returning to Baltimore, where they were to spend the rest of their lives. By the time they reached the city, Dandy had bought and furnished a house on Arunah Avenue in the northwest section. The property included a yard large enough for his father to cultivate year after year a productive vegetable garden.

Meanwhile, Dandy was busy in the Hunterian Laboratory during the months following graduation with research on the canine and feline pituitary bodies, a subject which greatly interested Cushing. This research led to the publication of an article early in 1911 with Emil Goetsch, who had immediately preceded Dandy as Cushing's Hunterian Appointee, on "The Blood Supply of the Pituitary Body" (6). It was Dandy's first publication following his graduation from medical school. Two years later he published under his own authorship a second article stemming from continued research on the hypophysis entitled "The Nerve Supply to the Pituitary Body" (7). It is worth noting that "the beautiful drawings in these papers were made by Dandy himself, under the coaching of Max Broedel" (8), Hopkins' renowned medical illustrator. These papers were but the first of more than one hundred and fifty articles which were to come from Dandy's pen.

After spending a year in the Hunterian Laboratory and having also received a Master of Arts degree (1911) for postgraduate work, Dandy entered the regular surgical service of The Johns Hopkins Hospital as one of Cushing's assistant residents along with Howard C. Naffziger. It was to be a trying year for the young doctor from Missouri as he had already experienced Cushing's quick temper and caustic tongue.

The first in a series of unpleasant encounters between the two men occurred in the Hunterian Laboratory (9). Dandy had conducted a series of experiments on the production of glycosuria (an abnormal amount of glucose in the urine) in animals by the stimulation of the sympathetics. He told Cushing that in stimulating the central end of the sympathetics he had obtained "tremendous glycosuria." Elated with these results, Cushing, Dandy later recalled, ran out to tell Emil Goetsch. Then Dandy added that when he stimulated the central end of the cut sympathetics he got the same results. Cushing, as Dandy related in a letter in 1945 to John F. Fulton, Cushing's official biographer, replied irritatingly, "Dandy, nobody could think of such a thing as that but you . . ." (10). Cushing afterward added that he was going to St. Louis (Washington University) and that there would be no place on his staff for the current Hunterian appointee but that Goetsch and possibly Conrad Jacobson were going. "I told him," remembered Dandy, "I was only trying to check the results" (10).

Instead of going to either Washington University or Yale, from which he had also received an offer, Cushing in 1910 accepted the professorship of surgery at Harvard and the post of surgeon-in-chief at the Peter Bent Brigham Hospital, which opened in January 1913. Cushing, however, did not move to Boston till the fall of 1912.

After the incident concerning the production of glycosuria in rabbits, relations between Dandy and Cushing seemed to be tranquil. Dandy may very well have heeded the advice his mother sent him from England:

> Very glad you are having such good work even though it is with a hard master, never mind. Some day you will be your *own* master & can do just as you please, but in the meantime you must submit to the powers above you. Try & bear patiently with him for your own good. Don't let anything come between you & Cushing that would spoil your future. His wonderful operations must be very trying on his quick irritable temper. So you must overlook his temper. It is the great strain of his work that makes him so irritable. Probably you would be the same if in his position (11).

This counsel of Rachel Dandy's reflected a degree of innocent foresight about her son that was remarkably intuitive, for her comments about Cushing's temper and what triggered it were said of Dandy in later years.

In the meantime Dandy believed that his mentor had probably forgotten the matter related to the production of glycosuria in rabbits. "However," as Dandy later wrote, "at the end of the (academic) year when he was going to Boston he came to the Hunterian where I was working and wanted to see my results on experiments with hydrocephalus. I showed them to him and he put them in his box of materials from the Hunterian. I took them out and told him they were going to stay there as they were mine and he had nothing to do with them. He flared up but quickly calmed down and said he guessed they did not amount to anything anyhow" (12). This was another episode in the series which comprised the Cushing-Dandy quarrel or controversy, one of the most bitter in the annals of American medicine.

In reminiscing about this conflict more than 30 years later Howard C. Naffziger who, with Dandy, was on Cushing's service in The Johns Hopkins Hospital in 1911 and 1912, recalled:

> As far as the unpleasant relationship with Dandy, about all I can say is that it certainly existed. The reasons for it must have antedated the time of my association because it was quite evident to me from the beginning. All of us felt that Dandy was very badly treated. I think that the trouble must have had its origin during the time that Dandy was in the Hunterian. I know that Dandy worked very hard on the service and that he gave all that was in him. I have always felt that Cushing's treatment had a good deal to do with stimulating Dandy to make a good showing in neurological surgery (13).

The climax to this phase of the quarrel came when Cushing informed Dandy shortly before his departure that he was not taking him to Boston. Dandy was deeply disappointed ". . . not because Doctor Cushing had changed his mind, but because," according to Samuel J. Crowe, who knew Dandy well, "this change of mind had deprived him of his position on Halsted's staff," and to make matters worse, Halsted was gone for the summer (14). It is no wonder that at this moment Dandy ". . . thought his career ruined" (15). There was no position in Boston, and there was no longer a position at The Hopkins, as Dr. Winford Smith, the superintendent of the Hospital, had informed him that ". . . the two positions of assistant resident surgeons formerly connected with Dr. Cushing's work" had been discontinued (16). Smith subsequently told Dandy that he did not know whether he was on Halsted's staff or not. "I am going to give you," he continued, "a room in the hospital, however, and sometime during the next year you will probably find out from Doctor Halsted what your status is" (17).

Halsted later found a place on his staff for Dandy as an assistant resident surgeon, having meanwhile been much impressed with the originality of the research that the young surgeon and Kenneth D. Blackfan, a resident in pediatrics (18), were doing on hydrocephalus. This fortuitous turn of events proved auspicious for both Dandy and Halsted, as will later be seen.

Dandy was not the only one who had expected to go with Cushing to his new position; for, as Mark M. Ravitch, Professor of Surgery at the University of Pittsburgh, noted in a letter to the writer:

"... [George] Heuer, too, had been told by Cushing that he would go with him to Boston, had similarly been disappointed, had similarly been rescued by Winford Smith that summer (1912), and after a period of limbo, had a place found for him in general surgery. It seems a bit of a coincidence that this should have happened to two men, but I suppose Cushing had given some thought to taking several men up to Boston with him either at once or serially and then changed his mind. What a perceptive man Winford Smith was." And to this episode Ravitch added his own experience of later years: Smith "... contributed to saving my career when Walter, who later became a good friend, refused to have me on the neurosurgical service, which was then an inescapable step on the residency ladder" (19).

Although Cushing and Dandy maintained a gentlemanly civility towards each other, their relations were never to improve. Dandy thought that "the best thing" that every happened to him was his break with Cushing who, in requesting shortly after his arrival in Boston photographs of a Hopkins patient of his, also expressed his pleasure in learning of Dandy's new job. About a year and a half later "Cushing was down to Baltimore & just said 'Hello[,] Dandy.' That was all" (20).

Early in 1912 Dandy, while on Cushing's service, had his first opportunity of performing a craniotomy or, as his father put it, "in fixing up the brain" (21). His operating room experience, both before and after Cushing's departure, was not confined, however, to neurosurgical cases. Actually, by the time he made neurological surgery his specialty Dandy had acquired considerable training and skill in general surgery, which momentarily he considered entering (22). He always felt, as will be discussed later at greater length, that the best preparation for one wishing to become a neurosurgeon "... is to get a thorough training in general surgery first" (23).

While Cushing was abroad with the Society of Clinical Surgery visiting several German clinics early in the summer of 1912, Dandy had the opportunity to operate more frequently. Cushing's brief absence provided, thereby, some compensation to Dandy for having been dropped from his mentor's plans of taking him to Boston.

Busy as Dandy was that summer, he did have time occasionally for relaxation. One day while playing baseball he suffered an accident. Though no bones were broken in jumping after a ball, his watch, which his mother and father had given him some 2 years before (his father had once carried it while working on the railroad), was smashed beyond repair. Upon learning of the accident his mother expressed her maternal concern about the possibility of serious injury as well as the way he played a game. Admonishingly, she suggested:

> Why don't you let the other fellows do the jumping & you look on for a change. If there is any risk to be taken you are always the first to run. The game must not be lost & you are willing to take the chances. Go a little easier & think next time before you make a leap. I am very thankful you escaped without any bones broken, some thing that has always been my greatest anxiety that you not go through the world a cripple (24).

Later in her letter she remarked that his father never had as many accidents on the railroad as he had had in his short life, adding "You made him come off the road for fear of him being killed. I would like to know what we shall do with you for fear you get killed" (24). But at the age of 26, Dandy was unlikely to change, significantly, his behavior; his relentless desire to excel—"the game must not be lost"—whether on or off the field was of prime importance throughout his life.

"Shifting dullness" (a diagnostic term referring to fluid in the thoracic cavity) was the description Hopkins medical students gave to William Steward Halsted's lectures in surgery (25). While he was an indifferent lecturer, he more than compensated for this deficiency by being a brilliant clinician and operator. A rather shy person, Halsted taught by example and quiet encouragement. Dandy was able to identify readily with Halsted, something he could never do with Cushing. In turn, Halsted realized very early that the young surgeon was a man of exceptional talent. He once told Abraham Flexner of the General Education Board and author of the celebrated report on *Medical Education in the United States and Canada* (1910) that Dandy ". . . was the most brilliant pupil he had every had" (26).

There was an interesting contrast in Cushing's and Dandy's relations with "the Professor," as Halsted was known to generations of medical students and hospital staff. Whereas Dandy worked well with and became fond of Halsted, Cushing found his association with Halsted at times irritating and did not develop a friendship with him until after he had left Baltimore (27).

Not only did Dandy consider himself fortunate to be associated with Halsted, he was delighted to work with surgeons such as John

M. T. Finney and Joseph C. Bloodgood, both of whom were senior members of the surgical staff and were encouraging as well as ". . . not afraid to let young men have a little honour that is due them" (28), as Mrs. Dandy wrote in response to her son's comment about them. In several ways, Thomas B. Turner has observed:

Dandy's career probably epitomizes as well as any the extraordinary opportunity The Johns Hopkins Medical Institutions presented to the intelligent, industrious, decent young medical graduate; it also tells a lot about Hopkins in the first part of the twentieth century. With little more than the moral support of Halsted, vital as that might have been, access to the Hunterian experimental laboratory, and the pervading regard for excellence that was in the atmosphere, Dandy little by little sharpened his surgical skill to explore ever deeper into the cranial cavity of man, making at the same time observations of great diagnostic and therapeutic value (29).

Dandy's first major accomplishment in his chosen field resulted from his and Kenneth Blackfan's investigation of internal hydrocephalus (a condition resulting from an abnormal accumulation of cerebrospinal fluid in the brain's ventricular system). As alluded to earlier, their research had begun while Cushing was still at Hopkins, but their results were not published until just before Christmas 1913, more than a year after Cushing's departure for Boston. "Numerous methods have been suggested for the treatment of internal hydrocephalus, none of which have [sic] been productive of satisfactory results," they noted by way of introduction to their preliminary report, the first of 10 papers prepared by Dandy on the subject of hydrocephalus. "So long as the etiology of this condition remains obscure, the treatment must necessarily be only symptomatic" (30).

In their study, Dandy and Blackfan were able to produce experimentally, in dogs, hydrocephalus by obstructing the aqueduct of Sylvius, thereby preventing the exit of cerebrospinal fluid from the third and lateral ventricles. They also were able to demonstrate that this fluid, whose principal function is to protect the brain and the spinal cord, forms in the ventricles (cavities of the brain) and is almost entirely absorbed in the subarachnoid space, which is not really a space but rather a weblike structure lying between the arachnoid and pia mater, the inner two of the three membranes covering the brain and spinal cord. (The dura mater is the membrane immediately beneath the cranium and is the toughest of the three). Moreover, Dandy and Blackfan established in this preliminary report that there are two types of internal hydrocephalus: obstructive, in which the channels are blocked, and communicating, in which the channels are unobstructed but in which a diminished absorption of the fluid in the subarachnoid space develops.

Four years later they published a definitive paper on internal hydrocephalus in *The American Journal of Diseases of Children* in which they reported on 26 cases of internal hydrocephalus, 15 of the obstructive variety and 11 communicating (31). Using intraventricular and intraspinal injections of a neutral solution of phenolsulphonphthalein, the two researchers found by post-mortem examinations ". . . an obstruction in every case in which an obstruction has been shown clinically by this test. The obstruction may be a congenital malformation or inflammatory process or tumor, and occur at any part of the ventricular system, but usually at the aqueduct of Sylvius or the foramina of Luschka and Magendie" (32). In all cases of obstructive hydrocephalus, Dandy and Blackfan determined that the condition resulted from a blockage which prevented the fluid moving from the ventricles where it originates ". . . to the subarachnoid space where it is normally absorbed, and where only it can be absorbed" (33). They found that communicating hydrocephalus results from "a barrier of adhesions at the base of the brain" which prohibits the cerebrospinal fluid from reaching the subarachnoid space. Moreover, both obstructive and communicating hydrocephalus result from an interruption of the normal spinal fluid circulation. The young surgeon and pediatrician further found that obstructive hydrocephalus may spontaneously or by surgery become the communicating variety, and that the reverse may also occur. And sometimes a spontaneous recovery from internal hydrocephalus takes place. Still another interesting conclusion which they reached in this study was the importance of meningitis, ". . . the greatest etiologic factor in both types of hydrocephalus and probably always causes the communicating variety. This may be either prenatal or postnatal. The meningitis may be of a very mild grade and easily overlooked" (33). As a result of their investigations, Dandy and Blackfan had developed a diagnostic test using phenolsulphonphthalein for determining an obstruction in the aqueduct of Sylvius or the foramina of Luschka and Magendie, a test which came to be widely used by neurosurgeons. Moreover, they believed that now a precise anatomical foundation existed on which the surgical treatment of internal hydrocephalus could develop.

So impressed with this work was Halsted that he once remarked to Edwards A. Park, who was later to become professor of pediatrics and director of the Harriet Lane Home in The Johns Hopkins

Hospital, "Dandy will never do anything equal to this again. Few men make more than one great contribution to medicine" (34). Halsted was in error, as later events would show: Dandy's work on hydrocephalus was but the first of several major contributions to medical science.

Following the submission of his and Blackfan's initial paper on hydrocephalus for publication, Dandy wrote a long and revealing letter to his mother and father in which he described the high regard that Blackfan's mentor, John Howland, professor of pediatrics in whose department a part of the research was done, and Halsted had for him:

> Dr. Howland himself was very much pleased with the paper and said it was one of the best ever turned out here and was proud that his department should get the honor of part publication. *Now you won't tell all this stuff will you?* [italics his] If you do have to get it out, tell the milkman, who won't have a burden imposed. Well, Dr. Halsted, from indirect accounts which I received through Dr. Howland's assistant, was tremendously impressed with the practical application which the results portended, that he gave a very glowing account of me to Dr. Howland and even went so far to say this department was very fortunate in having me on the staff & that I was one of the brightest men on the staff. Very unusual for such a reticent person as Dr. Halsted. He even told me that he was very strongly impressed with my last paper, which he took to Germany, and said the Germans were very much pleased with it. I guess [I] had told you that he told Dr. Bloodgood that I was one of the best men on the staff, that was last summer. These things coming from such a high source as Dr. Halsted and from such a hypercritical persona and one with relatively few favorable impressions are very gratifying and make me feel that things may yet be better for me in the long run (35).

At the close of this letter, Dandy indicated that he was sending pictures from *The Baltimore Sun* showing the arrest of the English suffragette Mrs. Emmeline G. Pankhurst. "They have refused," he added, "to let Mrs. Pankhurst land here which I think is just right. How could anybody sympathize with such a fool." Noting that she was at the moment starving herself, Dandy averred, ". . . let her do it[;] everybody would be better off. Think of having her for a wife or mother, from your loving son, Walter" (35). As his comments about Mrs. Pankhurst plainly show, Dandy on occasion had decisive views on the conduct and thought of other people, both within and without the profession, which he was willing to express to members of his family and close friends.

Dandy's work on the pituitary body and on hydrocephalus probably induced him in 1913 to make application to Hopkins for the Doctor of Philosophy degree. On his application he listed physiology as his principal subject, anatomy as his first subordinate, and surgical pathology as his second subordinate subjects. He also indicated that he wished to present himself for examination in the spring of 1914, a request that likely influenced Professor William H. Howell's response. Hopkins' first professor of physiology and dean of the Medical School from 1899 to 1911, Howell had himself received a Ph.D. degree in physiology from Hopkins nearly 30 years before. Although he found Dandy's proposed thesis quite acceptable, he felt ". . . that for a man to pick up a degree of this kind in a semi-incidental way while engaged in other pursuits is not a healthy precedent. On this ground alone, to safeguard the dignity of the degree I should oppose an application coming in this way on any subject. . . ." He added by way of closing that on his "slight knowledge" of the applicant's acquaintance with physiological methods and techniques he could not "certify" him as "a Doctor in the subject" (36). Thus ended Dandy's efforts towards obtaining a fourth academic degree.

Although Dandy meanwhile was concentrating his attention in neurological surgery on Halsted's service following Cushing's departure, he was doing some general surgery, that is, when George J. Heuer, the Associate in Surgery and a former assistant resident of Cushing's, would allow him to operate at all. He felt frustrated, at least for a time. "Heuer," he complained, "is very selfish. He could let me do lots of operations if he would but he just does them all himself. They [sic] are afraid someone will get better than they" (37). Actually, Dandy was getting a variety of surgical experience, performing appendectomies, repair of ruptures and broken backs, excision of brain tumors, and even some plastic surgery. On one occasion in the fall of 1913 he worked on a man who had been ". . . struck by an engine and his face torn to pieces, [his] skull fractured & arm broken. His nose & both his legs were torn wide open and folded back like leaves of a book. Out of these pieces I made him a new nose, like putting parts of a puzzle together and by using alone 100 stitches & spending 2½ hours got him patched up & a good nose and lips again" (38).

Dandy's work in general surgery was reflected by his collaboration with Leonard G. Rowntree of Hopkins' Pharmacology Department on a paper dealing with "Peritoneal and Pleural Absorption, with Reference to Postural Treatment," published in the spring of 1914. In dealing with the influence of gravity on fluids in the pleural and peritoneal cavities, they noted that "from the standpoint of operative treatment it is important to know if, by posture, infectious products can be segregated in selected areas where drainage is easier, the environment is more propitious, and the subsequent complications of less importance" (39). They observed in their conclusion that "gravity has a decided influence upon the localization of fluids—rapid in the pleural cavity, much slower in the peritoneal cavity" (40), with the intestines inhibiting the gravitation of fluids in the latter.

For one of Dandy's ambition and temperament, his research and publications, together with his eagerness to do more surgery, resulted in an anxiety about his future and the desire to make some money. Contributing to these feelings no doubt were Heuer's obstructive presence, the hospital's unappetizing food, and thoughts of marriage and a home. After all, he was now in his late 20s. Dandy had once told his father that if he could find him ". . . an Irish girl as good as the little Boss [John Dandy's term of endearment for Walter's mother], to bring her back" (41). While the Dandys were in Barrow-in-Furness, they met Lena Cranson, an Irish girl, a few times in her own home. As she was 23 years old and quite intelligent, as well as "a fine housekeeper"—"and in the market"— they thought she would be a good catch for the young doctor (42). Nothing, however, came from this trans-Atlantic effort in matchmaking.

As early as the summer of 1913 Dandy considered the possibility of leaving Hopkins for a partnership in Minneapolis, which he subsequently declined (43). Though he owned some Northern Pacific Railroad stock, his general financial condition was reflected in his limited wardrobe, which included but one suit that cost him only $11.50. This sartorial want his father remedied by sending him three school-bond coupons, amounting to $60.00, with which he was to buy himself a couple of suits. "I would hate to see," wrote his mother, "the brightest man in Hopkins with the poorest clothes" (44).

The following February found his prospects unchanged. "I am still on the fence about next year," he confessed. "Osler says to live in 24 hour compartments and never look ahead but I can't do that yet. Guess I am on the flyer which is according to him very bad. Got my new suit—it is a beauty. Also tried on my full dress & it was fine" (45).

Dandy continued to worry about his future, as the following lines from a letter to his mother and father plainly show:

Well [,] I am still wavering very much. I am satisfied and I am not. I want to venture to Chicago & risk Brain Surgery and I want to stay here and I don't know which I want. I think I will see Dr. [John M. T.]Finney and get his advice. I think he likes me very much and he may be able to get me in at Chicago. I will see what he thinks best. Heuer told me the professor (Dr. Halsted) had told him that I was to do the Brain Surgery when he went to Europe in May. That may mean I might keep it permanently which would come in quite right but if Heuer comes back and takes it again, it wouldn't mean so much after all. I think Dr. Halsted likes me very well and Dr. [Henry M.] Thomas I am sure will help me. If Heuer stays another year after he comes back and [Roy D.] McClure (who is next) stays on it will be too long to wait for General Surgery [,] but things may brighten up considerably yet. Still if I went to Chicago and could get started right I am sure I could make money pretty quickly. Here I would get a better reputation. I don't get any but the smaller operations to do now, but they all have turned out excellently (46).

Elsewhere in this letter Dandy remarked how valuable he thought his playing baseball and engaging in outdoor exercise and manual work had been in the development of his surgical ability. "It [sic] has made me quite adept with my hands and I can really operate very skillfully when given a chance" (46).

By the outbreak of World War I, late in July 1914, Dandy had decided that he should remain at Hopkins. He wished, however, that he were resident surgeon, but he would have to wait 2 more years before the coveted appointment would be his, as Roy McClure was ahead of him. Impatient as he was in not advancing more quickly than he had, he did have the satisfaction of having performed ". . . every brain operation which has been done," including cases involving the Gasserian ganglion (the nerve center of the trigeminal or fifth cranial nerve, responsible for the transmission of trigeminal neuralgia or tic douloureux), "Cushing's supposedly hardest operation" (47). Dandy moreover had successfully operated for spinal cord tumor. In 1914 one of his interesting operations—"a bully case"—was on "a little boy with an old brain abscess" who had had 60 to 70 epileptic spells per day before surgery but had had none since (47).

That same year The Johns Hopkins School of Medicine took the important as well as hotly debated step of placing its main clinical chairs on a full-time basis. "As early as 1884, nine years before the School of Medicine actually opened its doors, the University Board of Trustees made it clear that appointments to professorships of the preclinical medical sciences would be made strictly on a full-time basis. This meant that the holders of preclinical chairs would be required to devote themselves entirely to teaching and research without any of the distractions of private practice" (48). The Johns

Hopkins University thus became the first institution in the country to make all its preclinical professorships full-time, a common practice in medical schools today. Thirty years later, the University undertook to do the same for its major clinical chairs—medicine, surgery, and pediatrics—and for obstetrics in 1919 and 4 years later for psychiatry. Halsted, for the most part, favored the plan. "It seemed to reduce itself largely to the question of money, and he realized that there are men who need the stimulus of money-making to compel them to work, but that these are not the desirable men. 'We wish men,' he said, 'who have learned to work for work's sake, who find in it and in the search for truth, their greatest reward'" (49). Dandy, on the other hand, was never drawn to the full-time plan in his later years at Hopkins, as it was not in his interest to do so.

Meanwhile, with Halsted's encouragement he undertook in the Hunterian Laboratory a study of the effects of pinealectomy on young puppies and a description of the procedure he developed for extirpating the pineal body, a cone-shaped endocrine gland about the size of a pea, located almost in the center of the brain (50). What prompted Dandy to make this investigation was the conflicting evidence concerning the effects of removal or partial removal of the pineal body—not infrequently the seat of a tumor— on adiposity and genital and somatic development (51). Contrary to some of the earlier reports he found that the extirpation of the pineal body did not result in sexual precocity or indolence, adiposity or emaciation, somatic or mental precocity or retardation. His experiments revealed ". . . nothing to sustain the view that the pineal gland has an active endocrine function of importance in the very young or adult dogs. "The pineal," Dandy concluded, "is apparently not essential to life and seems to have no influence upon the animal's well being" (51). Dandy's demonstration that removal or partial removal of the pineal body had no adverse effect on the laboratory animals employed was important surgically because pineal tumors, which constitute less than 1% of all brain tumors, could produce internal hydrocephalus by obstructing the aqueduct of Sylvius. The problem of extirpating pineal tumors, however, was one of high risk and high mortality (52).

In 1916, the year following the publication of his article "The Extirpation of the Pineal Body," Dandy joined George Heuer in publishing "A Report of Seventy Cases of Brain Tumor," Dandy's first paper on the subject (53). Like Dandy, Heuer was a graduate of Hopkins (class of '08). He had served as Cushing's first assistant resident (1908 and 1909) and, under Halsted, as resident surgeon (chief resident from 1911 to 1914). "Following Cushing's example, several of his pupils had begun to publish their operative statistics on brain tumors" (54). Heuer and Dandy's paper was the first such report. They indicated that of the 70 cases 62 had undergone surgery. In no instance had the tumor been totally extirpated, and in only 24 of the surgical cases had there been improvement. "This was a candid report, and since Cushing followed the publications of his pupils with close scrutiny, he promptly wrote Heuer (10 Aug. 1916) a friendly letter" (54), an interesting contrast to one he wrote Dandy 6 years later following the latter's publication of a preliminary report on the total removal of acoustic tumors, an incident which will be discussed later.

For Dandy, 1916 was to be a vintage year, as he not only published his first paper on brain tumors, he became chief resident on the surgical service of The Johns Hopkins Hospital, following his friend Roy D. McClure. Two years before, Heuer had told Dandy confidentially that Halsted had almost put the aspiring young neurosurgeon in as chief resident ahead of McClure but had concluded that he would be better trained if this appointment were deferred (55). The waiting and frustration, as well as the further training had finally culminated in the coveted prize, which Thomas B. Turner has so well described:

> In many ways the life of the chief resident on one of the major services was an extremely attractive one, similar in some respects to that of an Oxford or Cambridge tutor. Under the resident were one or more assistant residents, and under them a number of house medical officers, or interns. The individual at the top of the ladder for each service was simply "the resident," never, it should be noted, "the chief resident," a term which has come into common use at Hopkins only in recent years. Paradoxically, he was perhaps closer to his professor than any other member of the faculty or staff; in fact he was the alter ego of his department head, doing his bidding, anticipating his needs and desires and, eventually, if successful, falling heir to all the prestige, professional reputation, and support that were at his professor's disposal. If financial pressures or marriage did not intervene, a Hopkins resident would often hold the post for several years (56).

Dandy, as it turned out, served for 2 years as resident surgeon (1916–1918) while continuing to hold a faculty appointment at a salary of $720.00 per year as instructor in surgery, a position he had held for the previous 2 years. He of course still lived at the Hospital. His close association with Halsted during these years strengthened, no doubt, his affection and regard for him; in turn Halsted reciprocated these feelings, as reflected in a letter he wrote to his resident from High Hampton, the Halsteds' summer home in the mountains of North Carolina, in July 1917:

Dear Dandy:

Our letters must have crossed in the mail. It required about 3 days for a letter to make its journey here from Baltimore.

I am happy to hear that you have had such an interesting service & that everyone is well on our staff. What shall we do if all are called to the colors? I hope that you at least are too old to be conscripted, but I fear not.

As to your paper [on internal hydrocephalus which was previously discussed] I would consult Dr. Howland. He, naturally, will wish you to publish it in the Journ. of Pediatrics [sic], & inasmuch as this paper is in a sense a continuation of the other, I presume it might be best to publish it in Dr. Howland's journal. But if you have a preference for another journal I would say so frankly to Dr. Howland and he surely will take pleasure in advising you & assisting you with its publication elsewhere. The Archives of Int. Med. [sic] might be the next choice; & then, possibly, the Am. Journ. of Med. Sciences [sic] (57).

When Dandy became resident surgeon, President Woodrow Wilson and Charles Evans Hughes, the Republican presidential nominee, were in a close race which Wilson managed to win. The war in Europe was entering its third year, and the following spring the United States was drawn into it on the side of the Allies. With America's entry into the war, The Johns Hopkins Medical Institutions mobilized to serve the nation both at home and abroad. The Hospital's trustees approved the creation of an army hospital unit, Base Hospital No. 18, which subsequently was sent to France. Unsurprisingly it was "... top-heavy with men of unusual ability, who could not all be spared from the Medical School and Hospital" (58). Dandy, however, was to remain at his post in the Hospital and Medical School, thus allaying Halsted's fear that his chief resident would be called "to the colors."

By remaining in Baltimore he was able to introduce in 1918 what Samuel J. Crowe has described as "... the greatest single contribution ever made to brain surgery," (59) ventriculography, a term which Dandy coined for a diagnostic procedure utilizing "... the injection of air or some other gas as a contrast medium into the ventricles of the brain, in order to make the brain tissue visible in contrast to the less opaque gas. In the absence of air or gas, the chambers cannot be seen on an x-ray plate because they are filled with cerebrospinal fluid having the same x-ray opacity as the surrounding brain tissue" (60).

A little less than 6 months following Wilhelm Conrad Roentgen's dramatic discovery of x-rays (1895), Dr. Francis H. Williams of Boston observed that air in the lungs provided a contrast, "a negative shadow," which delineated the ribs, heart, and lungs, as well as lesions of the latter which might be present. Williams discussed the possibilities of using air as a contrast medium in examining various organs of the body in his book, *The Roentgen Rays in Medicine and Surgery*, first published in 1901.

About 12 years later, Dr. William H. Stewart of New York City, in making x-ray plates of the head of a machinist who had been hit by a trolley car, found that the patient had suffered a fractured skull. Subsequently, Stewart made a second set of plates. "To my surprise," he reported, "I found we were dealing with a condition different than [sic] on the former examination" (61). What Stewart saw were shadows that he had never seen before; nor for that matter, had anyone else, so far as we know. "From the shape, location, and of course those shadows," Stewart noted, "their varying density and character simulating gas in the intestines, I was led to conclude that we were dealing with a case of fracture of the skull complicated by distended cerebral ventricles [inflated] with air or gas" (61). Stewart then turned to Dr. Eugene W. Caldwell, one of the outstanding radiologists of the day, for confirmation of his findings. Caldwell agreed with him that the shadows were due to air-filled ventricles. Later, Stewart published an account of this in *The American Journal of Roentgenology* (62). "Thus radiologists, neurologists, and surgeons alike were challenged," as Ruth and Edward Brecher have written in their definitive history of radiology in the United States and Canada, "to take the next step: to introduce air into the ventricles deliberately for diagnostic purposes. But if this crucial idea—the idea of *ventriculography*—occurred to even one reader, there is no evidence he acted on it" (61).

It was not until 1918, some 5 years after Stewart's observation, that Walter Dandy, who was then 32 years old and in his last year as resident on Halsted's service, hit upon the idea of replacing the cerebrospinal fluid with air before making a roentgenogram. Dandy of course knew that the only tumor which could readily be seen on an x-ray negative was one whose opacity had been improved by calcification, and that does not happen very often. Two suggestions set him on the path leading to ventriculography. "It is largely due to the frequent comment by Dr. Halsted on the remarkable power of intestinal gases 'to perforate the bone,'" wrote Dandy in his first paper on the subject, "that my attention was drawn to its practical possibilities in the brain, that is of injecting air into the ventricles" (63).

Meanwhile, in 1917, while examining the roentgenogram of a patient who had a history of intestinal hemorrhages and who was about to undergo an exploratory operation, Dandy confirmed the intestinal perforation previously diagnosed. As the x-ray plate included the upper part of the abdomen, he was able to see that "the liver was widely separated from the diaphragm by a collection of gas" (64). In a paper published 2 years later, Dandy indicated that it was this x-ray plate which suggested to him the injection of air into the cerebral ventricles (65). "If this could be done," as he wrote in his first paper on ventriculography, "an accurate outline of the cerebral ventricles could be photographed with x-rays, and since most neoplasms [tumors] either directly or indirectly modify the size or shape of the ventricles, we should then possess an early and accurate aid to the localization of intracranial affections" (66). Dandy cautioned "that in addition to its radiographic properties, any substance injected into the ventricles must satisfy two very rigid exactions: (1) It must be absolutely non-irritating and non-toxic; and (2) it must be readily absorbed and excreted" (66). Moreover, the exchange of air for cerebrospinal fluid had to be accurately done because if there were a greater volume of air than fluid removed, symptoms of acute pressure would follow. To avoid such consequences Dandy employed a Ricord syringe with a two-way valve attachment, aspirating 20 cc of the fluid and replacing it with an equal amount of air. The procedure was repeated until all of the fluid was withdrawn. By proceeding in this manner, injury to the brain from negative pressure was avoided. Interestingly enough, Dandy did not first try this procedure on laboratory animals but rather on children, from 6 months to 12 years of age, with internal hydrocephalus.

Years later, in evaluating the significance of ventriculography, Gilbert Horrax, Cushing's devoted assistant at the Brigham, wrote: "The importance of this diagnostic method, not only for localization of heretofore unlocalized brain tumors, but also for the more accurate localization of many growths whose situation could not be ascertained with absolute exactness, can hardly be overemphasized. It brought immediately into the operable field at least one third more brain tumors than could be diagnosed and localized previously by the most refined neurological methods" (67).

Yet, there were some, including Harvey Cushing and Adolf Meyer, Professor of Psychiatry at Hopkins and Director of the Phipps Psychiatric Institute, who had misgivings about ventriculography (68). Writing to Dandy in the spring of 1922, nearly 4 years after the first article on ventriculography had appeared, Cushing remarked: "I was glad that you brought the ventrilography [*sic*] matter before the Neurological Association and hope that you don't feel that we were too critical. It has been an important contribution, but you must be very careful not to overdo it, lest you make people expect too much of it, for under these circumstances it is likely to get a black eye" (69). Cushing was reluctant to adopt ventriculography, according to John F. Fulton, his biographer, "because he felt that it would discourage neurosurgeons from becoming adequately trained as neurologists and from doing their own neurological examinations" (70). But deeper, more personal reasons may have underlain Cushing's hesitation to employ ventriculography immediately: he had once been Dandy's mentor, and now his former pupil had made this unequalled—perhaps the greatest single—contribution to brain surgery (71).

Cushing's feelings about the younger man's achievement undoubtedly widened the gulf between them. At the 1922 meeting of the American Neurological Association in Washington, D.C., to which Cushing had referred in his letter to Dandy, he had been critical of his former pupil's statistics concerning ventriculography, surgery following its employment, mortality, and recoveries. Dandy was stung by this criticism, as he had not anticipated that his ". . . veracity would be questioned as it was by Dr. Cushing at Washington" (72). He considered Cushing's attack a petty way "of befogging the main issue . . .," reflecting afterwards that he could have rebutted his former mentor's ". . . statement much more simply by saying that at that time, there had been no failure in the localization in any case of brain tumor; it would then have been irrelevant whether the number had been 50 or 100" (72).

The final episode in the long-standing controversy between Cushing and Dandy came the following fall and will be discussed later. In responding to Cushing's and other criticisms of ventriculography, Dandy was forthright in his assessment of the procedure:

It is very dangerous. There has been a tremendous mortality from its use. However, if judiciously used and only by one thoroughly skilled in intracranial surgery, the danger is minimal. I had three deaths at the beginning of my series. Since then, I have had none. If properly handled, it should carry very little danger to the individual; and certainly the danger in proper hands is small compared to the danger attending cranial operations based upon guesswork (73).

In 1919, a little more than a year after the publication of his article on ventriculography, Dandy introduced encephalography, a companion diagnostic procedure whereby air was injected by lumbar puncture into the spinal subarachnoid space and thus into the cerebral subarachnoid space and ventricles. "Many lesions of the brain affect part of the subarachnoid space directly or indirectly" (74), such as the presence of a tumor on or close to the surface of the brain. Encephalography thus was used in lieu of ventriculography in situations where increased intracranial pressure was not evident.

With the introduction of ventriculography and encephalography and the attendant publicity, Dandy received several invitations in the years immediately following to speak before professional and scientific organizations, including the American Philosophical Society (April 1920) and the New York Academy of Medicine (January 1922). It also brought praise from the noted surgeon and writer W. W. Keen of Philadelphia who, 30 years before, had performed the first brain surgery in this country and began a warm relationship between Dandy and the older man. Shortly after the publication of the article on encephalography, Dandy, in response to a letter from Keen, wrote appreciatively, explaining why he chose not to discuss the question of air sterilization:

> It was very good of you to write me expressing your praise and later your criticism. I assure you that both were appreciated. I was very glad to know that you noted an improvement as a result of our most pleasant conference. I feel that it has been a great benefit to me and really is bearing fruit.
>
> I hesitated to say in the article that the air was not sterilized for I know exactly the impression that this would create with those who are so intolerant of things which are not antiseptic. I reasoned in this way that during every operation large quantities of air fill the exposed parts of the brain and are enclosed after the operation. Similarly in the abdomen and thoracic cavity large quantites are included and for hours at a time the air is in contact with the viscera, but never does any infection occur. Now I have the empirical evidence that in over one hundred cases no infection has developed. However I can readily see that some precautions even though they are of no particular benefit might allay the mind in the procedure (75).

Ten years later Keen, wishing to write on behalf of vivisection an article on Dandy's diagnostic contributions to neurological surgery, asked Dandy to give him the history of "the first things used in inflating the ventricles which proved fatal to dogs or impossible for use with man" (76). Dandy graciously complied with his request, noting that leading up to the use of air sodium bromide, potassium iodide, thorium, and collargol had been tried as contrast media on "perhaps a dozen or fifteen dogs" (77).

Not only was Dandy gaining recognition for ventriculography and encephalography from 1918 to 1919 but for his surgical prowess as well. A newsworthy operation on the 11-year-old son of Harry W. Nice, one of Baltimore's assistant state's attorneys and a future governor of Maryland, was reported early in 1918 by a Dr. Leonard Keene Hirshberg in The American Weekly section of the *New York Sunday American* (78). Hirshberg referred to the surgery as "one of the strangest and most delicate brain operations ever attempted . . . " (78). Dandy removed six small tumors from the meninges in the right hemisphere of the brain which had caused paralysis of the left arm. He then replaced the destroyed membrane (dura mater) with tissue from the upper muscle of the boy's left leg below the hip. As a featured story, the operation was of course a success; young Nice made a good recovery. Such an accomplishment added luster to Dandy's reputation and further renown to The Johns Hopkins Hospital.

The year 1918 was of importance to the world as well as to the Johns Hopkins University and Walter Dandy; for it marked the end of four terrible years of war in Europe, the opening of the School of Hygiene at Hopkins on October 1 and, as already mentioned, the introduction of ventriculography. It also had added significance for Dandy, as it marked the close of an 8-year-period at Hopkins in which he had served, respectively, as an intern, assistant resident, and resident, directly under Cushing for the first two years and under Halsted for the remainder. Now, at age 32, he had completed the arduous training, having demonstrated his abilities both as an investigator and as a surgeon.

END NOTES

1. John Dandy, Sedalia, MO, to W.E.D., letter, April 23, 1910, Dandy MSS.
2. Rachel Dandy, Sedalia, MO, to W.E.D., letter, May 30, 1910, Dandy MSS.
3. Rachel Dandy, Barrow-in-Furness, England, to W.E.D., letter, March 5, 1912, Dandy MSS.
4. John Dandy, Barrow-in-Furness, England, to W.E.D., letter, April 24, 1912; Rachel Dandy, Barrow-in-Furness, England, to W.E.D., letter, April 28, 1912, Dandy MSS.
5. W.E.D., Baltimore, to Mr. and Mrs. John Dandy, London, England, letter, Sept 20, 1914, Dandy MSS.
6. Dandy WE, Goetsch E: The blood supply of the pituitary body. *Am J Anat* 11:137–150, 1910–1911.
7. Dandy WE: The nerve supply to the pituitary body. *Am J Anat* 15:333–345, 1913.
8. Harvey AM: *Adventures in Medical Research: A Century of Discovery at Johns Hopkins.* Baltimore, The Johns Hopkins University Press, 1974–1976, p 68.
9. Fox WL: The Cushing-Dandy controversy. *Surg Neurol* 3:61–66, 1975.

10. Fox WL: The Cushing-Dandy controversy *Surg Neurol* 3:61–66, 1975.
11. Mrs. John Dandy, Barrow-in-Furness, Lancashire, England, letter, Nov 6, 1911, Dandy MSS. Shortly after Dandy's death in 1946, Dr. Helen K. McClure wrote: "I have admired and been fond of Walter ever since those long ago days when he and I both had to endure Dr. Cushing's caustic comments silently." Dr. Helen K. McClure to Mrs. Walter E. Dandy, Baltimore, letter, April 23, 1946. Dandy MSS.
12. W.E.D. to John F. Fulton, New Haven, CT, letter, Nov 26, 1945, Cushing MSS, Yale Medical Library.
13. Howard C. Naffziger, M.D., School of Medicine, University of California, San Francisco, to John F. Fulton, New Haven, CT, letter, Nov 8, 1945, Cushing MSS.
14. Crowe SJ: *Halsted of Johns Hopkins: The Man and His Men.* Springfield, IL, Charles C Thomas, 1957, p 86.
15. W. M. Firor, M.D., Baltimore, to the author, letter, Dec 30, 1975.
16. Winford Smith, M.D., Baltimore, to W.E.D., letter, Oct 8, 1912, Dandy MSS.
17. Crowe SJ: *Halsted of Johns Hopkins: The Man and His Men.* Springfield, IL, Charles C Thomas, 1957, p 86.
18. Blackfan came to Hopkins in 1912 when Dr. John Howland, who had been appointed head of the Pediatrics Department, brought him from Washington University in St. Louis. In time, Blackfan became a recognized pediatrician and in 1923 was appointed Thomas Morgan Rotch Professor of Pediatrics at Harvard. Kenneth D. Blackfan 1883–1941. *Suppl Harvard Med Alumni Bull* vol 16, no 3, April 1942.
19. Mark M. Ravitch, M.D., Pittsburgh, to the author, letter, Feb 13, 1975.
20. W.E.D. to Mr. and Mrs. John Dandy, London, letter, Feb 23, 1914; Harvey Cushing, Boston, to W.E.D., letter, Oct 23, 1912; W.E.D. to Mr. and Mrs. John Dandy, London, March 1, 1914, Dandy MSS.
21. John Dandy, Barrow-in-Furness, Lancashire, England, to W.E.D., letter, Feb 13, 1912, Dandy MSS.
22. W.E.D. to John Dandy, Barrow-in-Furness, Lancashire, England, letter, March 13, 1912, Dandy MSS.
23. W.E.D. to Kenneth D. Blackfan, M.D., Boston, letter, April 6, 1935, Dandy MSS.
24. Rachel Dandy, Barrow-in-Furness, Lancashire, England, to W.E.D., letter, July 16, 1912, Dandy MSS.
25. Harvey Stone, M.D., Baltimore, interview with the author, May 25, 1967.
26. Abraham Flexner, New York, to Mrs. Walter E. Dandy, Baltimore, letter, April 22, 1946, Dandy MSS. Abraham Flexner, *Medical Education in the United States and Canada: A Report to the Carnegie Foundation for the Advancement of Teaching*, Bull. 4, New York, 1910, vol 17.
27. Thomson EH: *Harvey Cushing: Surgeon, Author, Artist* New York, Collier Books, 1961, p 92.
28. Rachel Dandy, London, to W.E.D., letter, Dec 20, 1912, Dandy MSS.
29. Turner TB: *Heritage of Excellence: The Johns Hopkins Medical Institutions, 1914–1947.* Baltimore, The Johns Hopkins University Press, 1974, p 413.
30. Dandy WE, Blackfan KD: An experimental and clinical study of internal hydrocephalus. *JAMA* 61:2216, 1913.
31. Dandy WE, Blackfan KD: Internal hydrocephalus: second paper. *Am J Dis Child* 14:424–443, 1917.
32. Dandy WE, Blackfan KD: Internal hydrocephalus: second paper. *Am J Dis Child* 14:442, 1917.
33. Dandy WE, Blackfan KD: Internal hydrocephalus: second paper. *Am J Dis Child* 14:442b, 443, 1917.
34. Edwards A. Park, M.D., Chief of Pediatrics, Johns Hopkins Hospital. Remarks at the presentation of Dandy's portrait to The Johns Hopkins University, 65th Commemoration Day, Feb 22, 1941.
35. W.E.D. to Mr. and Mrs. John Dandy, London, letter, Oct 20, 1913, Dandy MSS.
36. W. H. Howell, Baltimore, to W.E.D., letter, Oct 20, 1913, Dandy MSS.
37. W.E.D. to Mr. and Mrs. John Dandy, London, letter, March 1, 1914, Dandy MSS.
38. W.E.D. to Mr. and Mrs. John Dandy, London, letter, Oct 20, 1913, Dandy MSS.

39. Dandy WE, Rowntree LG: Peritoneal and pleural absorption, with reference to postural treatment. *Ann Surg* 59:595, 1914.

40. Dandy WE, Rowntree LG: Peritoneal and pleural absorption, with reference to postural treatment. *Ann Surg* 59:595, 1914.

41. John Dandy, London, to W.E.D., letter, Oct 3, 1913, Dandy MSS.

42. John Dandy, London, to W.E.D., letter, Oct 3, 1913, Dandy MSS. Rachel Dandy, London, to W.E.D., letters, Oct 9, Nov 13, Dec 3, 1913; John Dandy, London, England, to W.E.D., letter, Dec 3, 1913, Dandy MSS.

43. John Dandy, London, to W.E.D., letter, July 18, 1913, Dandy MSS.

44. Rachel Dandy, London, to W.E.D., letter, Nov 13, 1913, Dandy MSS.

45. W.E.D. to Mr. and Mrs. John Dandy, London, letter, Feb 23, 1914, Dandy MSS. Osler W: *A Way of Life and Selected Writings of Sir William Osler 12 July 1849 to 29 December 1919*, with an introduction by G. L. Keynes, M.D. New York, Dover, 1958, pp 237–249.

46. W.E.D. to Mr. and Mrs. John Dandy, London, letter, March 1, 1914, Dandy MSS.

47. W.E.D. to Mr. and Mrs. John Dandy, London, letter, Sept 20, 1914, Dandy MSS.

48. Sharkey RP: *Johns Hopkins: Centennial Portrait of a University*. Baltimore, The Johns Hopkins University Press, 1975, p 9.

49. MacCallum WG: *William Stewart Halsted: Surgeon*. Baltimore, Johns Hopkins Press, 1930, p 184.

50. Dandy WE: Extirpation of the pineal body. *J Exp Med* 22:237–247, 1915.

51. See references in article in note 50.

52. Thomson AF: Surgery of the third ventricle. In: *A History of Neurological Surgery*. Baltimore, Williams & Wilkins, 1951, pp 137–141.

53. Heuer GJ, Dandy WE: A report of seventy cases of brain tumor. *Johns Hopkins Hosp Bull* 27:224–237, 1916.

54. Fulton JF: *Harvey Cushing: A Biography*. Springfield, IL, Charles C Thomas, 1946, p 489.

55. W.E.D. to Mr. and Mrs. John Dandy, London, letter, Sept 20, 1914, Dandy MSS.

56. Turner TB: *Heritage of Excellence: The Johns Hopkins Medical Institutions, 1914–1947*. Baltimore, The Johns Hopkins University Press, 1974, p 233.

57. W. S. Halsted, High Hampton, Cashiers, NC, to W.E.D., letter, July 25, 1917, Dandy MSS.

58. Turner TB: *Heritage of Excellence: The Johns Hopkins Medical Institutions, 1914–1947*. Baltimore, The Johns Hopkins University Press, 1974, p 233.

59. Crowe SJ: *Halsted of Johns Hopkins: The Man and His Men*. Springfield, IL, Charles C Thomas, 1957, pp 88–89.

60. Ruth and Edward Brecher, draft of *The Rays: A History of Radiology in the United States and Canada*, p 78. This quotation does not appear in the published book (Baltimore, Williams & Wilkins, 1969).

61. Brecher R, Brecher E: draft of *The Rays: A History of Radiology in the United States and Canada*, p 221. This quotation does not appear in the published book (Baltimore, Williams & Wilkins, 1969).

62. Stewart WH: Fracture of the skull with air in the ventricles. *Am J Roentgenol* 1(2):83–87, 1913.

63. Dandy WE: Ventriculography following the injection of air into the cerebral ventricles. *Ann Surg* 68:6, 1918.

64. Dandy WE: Pneumoperitoneum: a method of detecting intestinal perforation—an aid in abdominal diagnosis. *Ann Surg* 70:379, 1919.

65. Dandy WE: Pneumoperitoneum: a method of detecting intestinal perforation—an aid in abdominal diagnosis. *Ann Surg* 70:378–383, 1919.

66. Dandy WE: Ventriculography following the injection of air into the cerebral ventricles. *Ann Surg* 68:5, 1918.

67. Thomson EH: *Harvey Cushing: Surgeon, Author, Artist*. New York, Collier, 1961, p 194.

68. Fulton JF: *Harvey Cushing: A Biography*. Springfield, IL, Charles C Thomas, 1946, p 490. W. M. Firor, M.D., Baltimore, to the author, letter, March 15, 1976. In this letter Dr. Firor, who served a part of his residency under Dandy, reported that Meyer did

not realize the importance of ventriculography and that "Dandy thought psychiatrists were mostly 'nuts.'"

69. Harvey Cushing, Boston, to W.E.D., letter, May 12, 1922, Cushing MSS.
70. Fulton JF: *Harvey Cushing: A Biography*. Springfield, IL, Charles C Thomas, 1946, p 490.
71. Thomson EH: Harvey Cushing: *Surgeon, Author, Artist*. New York, Collier, 1961, p 194. Frank J. Otenasek, M.D. "Tribute Proposed for the Semi-annual Staff Meeting of The Union Memorial Hospital (Baltimore), April 10, 1947, on the death of Doctor Walter Edward Dandy," Dandy MSS.
72. W.E.D. to Dr. Israel Strauss, New York City, letter, May 15, 1922, Dandy MSS.
73. Dandy WE: Localization of brain tumors by cerebral pneumography. *Am J Roentgenol Radium Ther* 10(8):611, 1923.
74. Dandy WE: Roentgenography of the brain after the injection of air into the spinal canal. *Ann Surg* 70:397, 1919. Several years later, in response to a query from Dr. Lewis J. Friedman about the origin of encephalography, Dandy noted that he had introduced it in 1919 as reported in the *Annals of Surgery*. "The next report was by Bingel of Germany two years later. Most American writers never fail to give Bingel the credit for reasons I have not been able to understand. The Germans have been much more fair. It is, of course, no question as to where the priority belongs." W.E.D. to Dr. Lewis J. Friedman, New York City, letter, Jan 14, 1935, Dandy MSS.
75. W.E.D. to Dr. W. W. Keen, Philadelphia, letter, Nov 6, 1919, Dandy MSS.
76. W. W. Keen, M.D., Philadelphia, to W.E.D., letter, Dec 21, 1928, Dandy MSS.
77. W.E.D., to Dr. W. W. Keen, Philadelphia, letters, Dec 28, 1928, and Jan 26, 1929, Dandy MSS.
78. Hirshberg LK: How Little Harry's Leg Muscle Helped Restore His Brain, The American Weekly section of the *New York Sunday American*, Jan 6, 1918. See also the same article in *The Pittsburgh Sunday Post*, Jan 6, 1918.

CHAPTER 5

To Leave or Not to Leave

For 8 years Dandy had lived at the Johns Hopkins Hospital. He had frequently found the meals unappetizing, a common complaint of institutional food and a dismal contrast to his mother's cooking. Upon the completion of his service as chief resident, he gladly moved into his mother and father's home at 3021 Arunah Avenue in northwest Baltimore where he was to live for the next 6 years.

Like everyone else associated with the clinical departments of the Johns Hopkins Hospital and the School of Medicine in 1918, Dandy wore two hats and therefore had twin titles. Having finished his residency, he now became, with Halsted's approbation, Associate Surgeon in the Hospital and Associate in Surgery on the medical faculty, at a salary for the latter of $2,500 per year. These were but two among several different titles which he was to have during his 36 years of service at Hopkins.

In discussing this dual arrangement under which Dandy and his colleagues worked, Turner observed that members of the clinical departments ". . . went about their daily tasks largely unaware of the distinctions and impatient of them when they reached the level of consciousness" (1). This was certainly true of Dandy who by early 1919 was shouldering much of the responsibility for the Department of Surgery because of Halsted's declining health and advancing years.

At this time Abraham Flexner, assistant secretary of the General Education Board and author of the famous 1910 report on medical education in the United States and Canada (2), was a patient on Halsted's service. The Board was then contemplating the funding of a full-time professorship of surgery at Hopkins. Flexner was quite impressed with Dandy, as he noted in a letter to his brother Simon, who was director of the Rockefeller Institute of Scientific Research (now Rockefeller University):

The general sentiment hereabouts is that Dandy is the man for surgery. I should myself prefer to see him a few years in a full-time post with entire responsibility at Nashville or Chicago for he is only thirty-two; but, as Dr. Halsted comes about very little now, Dandy is carrying the whole thing, and, as far as I can judge, does it admirably. He has the devotion and confidence of all his associates and treats them in a really beautiful way. I have never seen a young man who is so little intoxicated by his position and who is so easy and helpful and cooperative in dealing with others in his department, some of them older than he. He has as well natural sense. He is, as compared with Dr. Halsted and Dr. Welch culturally crude, but he knows it and he is working pathetically in odd minutes to build himself out. Of all the persons I have met here, he strikes me as having the largest possibilities in a scientific way. I wish I felt equally sure on the score of medicine. I have talked with young medical men, too, but have found none of them who are in his class (3).

Actually no successor to Halsted was appointed until Dr. Dean Lewis was tapped for the post 3 years after Halsted's death (1922). Meanwhile, in November and December 1919, Dandy was laid up with what he described as "an intractable neuralgia" (4). His illness brought expressions of sympathy from several associates, including Howard A. Kelly, professor of gynecology and one of the Hopkins "Big Four," and Halsted. Their notes reveal their regard for the young surgeon as well as something of themselves. Kelly wrote:

Dear Dr. Dandy:
    I have been much distressed to hear of your enforced rest but trust sincerely that it is nearing an end. I know how irksome it must seem to your active mind with so much work simply waiting for you. May the New Year bring you the blessing of an established health. It is a great thing I am sure from my own observation if we can learn the lessions of adversity which tho' so bitter are ever more fruitful than success. I feel as I look back that while God is in all our life [sic] He is most of all in its trials [,] one great use of which is to reveal true values and to draw us to Himself. Then too when we trust in Our Lord Jesus Christ we have closer fellowship with Him. Ask Him to show you what there is in it of blessing and He will do it. Life is but a poor experiment without God, is it not?

Faithfully yours,
Howard A. Kelly (5)

On Christmas Eve Halsted penned a few lines to Dandy:

My dear Dandy:
    I wish you great happiness and prosperity for the years to come & trust that you may never again suffer from sciatica[,] the cause of which is so obscure & certainly not due to "top heaviness."

Faithfully,
W. S. Halsted (6)

This illness—sciatic neuralgia—was one of the few times in Dandy's life that he was indisposed. Apparently he was never bothered again by this painful condition.

The postwar years were indeed a time of transition for the Hopkins medical faculty. A second generation was coming on the scene, and ". . . old departments and newly formed ones were acquiring new heads who in turn assembled younger men around them. New people brought new ideas and new approaches to old problems" (7). The flow of talent, moreover, was not simply one way. When, for example, Vanderbilt University opened its medical school in 1920, no less than the heads of four major departments were drawn from Hopkins.

In addition to the changes in staff, an impressive building program at The Johns Hopkins Medical Institutions was undertaken in the early 1920s. The General Education Board presented to the Medical School in 1921 a grant of $3,000,000 for its expansion. By the end of the decade, buildings amounting to $10.6 million had been raised, including the Wilmer Ophthalmological Institute and the Welch Medical Library. Such developments may have influenced in some measure the decision Dandy ultimately made about his career at Hopkins.

Not surprisingly, Dandy was among those who received offers from other medical institutions. Early in January, 1919, Dean Edward M. Cary offered him a post at the Baylor University School of Medicine in Dallas (8). Later that year he was unofficially asked if he would be interested in going to the University of Michigan as the professor of surgery on a full-time basis (9). And during the following year Chancellor J. H. Kirkland tendered Dandy the chair in surgery at Vanderbilt, an offer he seriously considered at the urging of Dr. Buttrick and Dr. Flexner of the General Education Board, as his reply to Kirkland attests: "I have thought a great deal about Vanderbilt since leaving you but have now definitely come to the conclusion that is it wiser for me to decline your offer. Needless to say, I regard the position as one of very great opportunity, and realize the important part which Vanderbilt is going to play in medicine of the future. I surely hope you will obtain the services of the very highest type of men, of which there can be little doubt" (10). All of these offers as well as an invitation to join a partnership in Kansas City, Missouri (11), Dandy turned down. But in 1921 he was considerably tempted to accept the offer of Colonel Henry Page, the dean of the University of Cincinnati

College of Medicine, to become head of the department of surgery. Page told Dandy that he did not want him ". . . to do the small things. I want you as the 'big boss' to develop the surgical situation. I don't want you to be a pedagogic hack (12). After visiting Cincinnati, Dandy wrote to Page that the more he thought of it the better the opening appealed to him, adding "of course, if I should take it, I should want to build the best surgical department in the east, and I think your opportunities will put the burden of this up to the surgeon" (13). So concerned was Dandy about the Cincinnati offer, he made a special trip down to High Hampton, North Carolina, Halsted's summer home, in order to discuss it with him. More than likely Halsted urged him to remain at Hopkins. As with the earlier offers, Dandy declined Colonel Page's invitation, stating as his reason what turned out to be the key to his remaining at Hopkins for the rest of his life: "It was only because I have things here so thoroughly fitted to my needs and desires that I finally found it wiser not to make the change" (14). Page then tendered the position to George Heuer, who had been ahead of Dandy on Halsted's service; Heuer readily accepted.

Though Dandy elected to remain at Hopkins in 1921, his titles were changed again. He now became an Associate Professor of Surgery in the medical school, a rank he was to hold for the next 10 years, and Assistant Visiting Surgeon in the hospital. These titles reflected Dandy's part-time status, a situation which he very much preferred as his income was not restricted. The distinction between part-time and full-time staff as reflected in the titles became a rather thorny issue (15) but did not appear to bother Dandy. There were more important things to think about.

In the years following the war Dandy continued to be interested in the causes, diagnosis, and treatment of hydrocephalus, preparing no fewer than five papers on the subject (16). "Hydrocephalus," he wrote in 1920, "is always secondary to a primary cause and it should now be possible in every instance to locate the primary lesion, though its discovery, while at times simple, is usually sufficiently difficult to exhaust all the newer methods at our command. Moreover, in the chronic form of the disease (which is practically always referred to), there is but slight hope of spontaneous cure; there is no hope whatever from any medicinal therapy; the only hope lies in surgically correcting the cause of the disease, which is almost always an obstruction in the cerebrospinal spaces. The maximum results of surgical treatment, when this becomes proficient, and it is rapidly becoming so, will always be dependent on an early and accurate diagnosis" (17).

Dandy found that the most common lesion in congenital hydrocephalus, particularly in infancy and early childhood, is cicatricial stenosis (a narrowing or stricture of a duct or canal due to scar tissue) of the aqueduct of Sylvius. If the aqueduct is occluded, hydrocephalus always results. Dandy's response to the problem was to attempt the construction of a new aqueduct.

He also found that blockage of the two foramina (natural openings or passages) of Luschka and the foramen of Magendie regularly results in hydrocephalus, as these three openings connecting the fourth ventricle with the cisterna magna (subarachnoid space) provide "the balance between the formation and the absorption of cerebrospinal fluid . . ." (18). Again Dandy's solution to the problem, where possible, was construction of a new foramen. In diagnosing the origins of hydrocephalus he employed ventriculography as well as the intraspinous phenolsulphonphthalein test, which Blackfan and he had developed some years before.

Hydrocephalus was, however, only one of Dandy's concerns during the postwar years. The pathological and therapeutic study of epilepsy was another. In June, 1920, he made application for a grant of $3,000 from Hopkins which was to be used ". . . to study epilepsy intensively at an epileptic colony, the privilege of which I think can be arranged. The expense would be that incident to weekend trips to this colony with an assistant, an artist, and a stenographer. The cases would be studied by careful analysis of the history for possible etiological factors. They would be studied by the newer methods of absorption from the spinal canal, by operations, and drawing the pathological picture which is found at the operation. It may also be necessary to procure a few instruments for the operative procedure" (19). Dandy subsequently received a grant to do research on epilepsy at the Craig Colony for Epileptics at Sonyea, New York, some 40 miles south of Rochester. There he amassed material, including information from postmortem examinations, for an elaborate chart which his secretary spent 2 weeks completing (20).

Historically, epilepsy was classified as an idiopathic disease; but Dandy, after experiments on animals and observations during surgery on the brains of epileptic patients, concluded otherwise. In

1925 he published with Robert Elman an article on "Studies in Experimental Epilepsy," which contained an excellent summary of previous research done in experimental epilepsy by such people as Victor Horsley, Hughlings Jackson, and Charles-Edouard Brown-Séquard, as well as a summary of the investigation of the effects of absinthe on cats both with and without brain lesions. "The most striking fact contained in these experiments is that one-third to one-seventh of the dose of absinthe required to produce convulsions in normal cats will incite attacks when the motor cortex has been injured several weeks previously. The experiments show conclusively that injury to the cerebellar and occipital lobes is far less effective in making the animal susceptible to convulsions than is injury to the motor cortex" (21). Dandy and Elman found that the convulsant drug attacked the injured area and that in cats with healed motor defects convulsions occurred suddenly without preliminary irritability which normal cats experienced. Furthermore, in both animals and human beings "the margin of safety which is the difference between the normal and the epileptic condition is permanently lost when a cerebral lesion of long standing exists" (22).

In the early twenties, Dandy was much more confident about the prospects of curing epilepsy than he was later in his career. To an inquiring brother of an epileptic he wrote in the summer of 1920: "The treatment for epilepsy is an operation upon the brain. It has been used on certain types of epilepsy only, and in all of those it has apparently produced a cure. If your brother should care to come to see me, I should be very glad to tell him whether it would be worthwhile to operate" (23). And a few months later the young neurosurgeon was quoted in the *Syracuse Herald* on the prospects for treating epilepsy: "From observations made at numerous operations upon the brains of epileptics I have come to the conclusion that epilepsy is due to a definite injury of the brain, and I am now encouraged to a hopeful outlook for its treatment" (24).

Having found that there is a close analogy between epilepsy and trigeminal neuralgia, Dandy later concluded that:

1. The attacks of epilepsy are precisely similar to the paroxysmal attacks in trigeminal or glossopharyngeal neuralgia and Ménière's disease.
2. It is impossible to produce recurring spasmodic attacks of convulsions, of dizziness, or of pain, except by a lesion in the upper neurons.
3. Involvement of a higher neurone is essential for the production of any paroxysmal attacks. Epilepsy cannot be produced by any lesion along the

peripheral nerves. It can only result from a lesion in the cerebral hemisphere (25).

Thus epilepsy, which stems from a lesion in the cerebral hemispheres and never from one in the cerebellum, is "a disease with a specific character," one whose cause with few exceptions can be identified. "Epilepsy may occasionally be due to lesions along the brain stem, but when that is true, it is always a lesion that affects directly or indirectly the same motor tracts that are affected in the cerebral hemispheres" (26).

Dandy's research and clinical studies consequently established a pathological foundation for epilepsy, removing it from the catalog of idiopathic diseases (27). He realized that ". . . it must test one's credulity to be told that the cause of epilepsy is determined. Unfortunately, however, the determination of the cause has not resulted in any change of treatment, except in so far we are much more alert in ferreting out tumors by ventriculography" (28).

Though Dandy maintained an interest in epilepsy throughout his career—"epilepsies are always fascinating studies" (29)—he never conducted the extensive laboratory and clinical research that Wilder Penfield did at the Montreal Neurological Institute (30). "Penfield," as D. W. C. Northfield has written, "was the first of modern neurosurgeons to resurrect interest in epilepsy and he is largely responsible for establishing the value of operation for the relief of this particularly unpleasant disorder of central nervous function" (31).

In the summer of 1921, Penfield, who had graduated from The Johns Hopkins School of Medicine in 1918 and now was starting to do the neurological surgery at The Presbyterian Hospital in New York City, asked Dandy if as a former student of his he could visit his clinic to learn the procedure of ventriculography. Dandy he ". . . found to be both hospitable and helpful . . ." (32). As a result of this visit Penfield learned ". . . some of the dangers of ventriculography as well as its advantages" (33).

The following year Penfield was approached by Lewis Weed, who was shortly to become the dean of the Hopkins School of Medicine, about the possibility of becoming a member of an enlarged department of neurology which would include neurosurgery. In his interesting, though truncated autobiography, Penfield, recalling this overture, observes: "If Walter Dandy . . . had wanted to welcome me I suppose I might have moved to Baltimore. But no. He was not interested in the dean's plan to cut across the departmental lines and thus create a new enlarged department" (34). As Penfield notes elsewhere in his autobiography, Dandy had no need for a beginner in neurosurgery (35). And understandably so, for at that time Hopkins hardly required the skills of another neurosurgeon. More than likely Dandy also had reservations about a department wherein he would play a lesser role, inasmuch as it would have included Weed, an anatomist, William G. MacCallum in pathology, and Adolf Meyer in psychiatry (36).

Actually, in later years Dandy expressed a desire to establish a neurological institute in Baltimore, if only a wealthy patient would provide an endowment as Diamond Jim Brady had done for the Hopkins urological institute bearing his name (37). But perhaps the reverse was a closer reflection of his true feelings, as a member of his family has suggested (38). Following World War II, a representative committee in dealing with the construction needs of The Johns Hopkins Medical Institutions considered the establishment of a neurological institute, but the proposal never materialized (39). This goal was finally met in the fall of 1982 with the opening of the Adolf Meyer Building that includes a Center for Neurological Diseases and the Henry Phipps Psychiatric Service, thus making Hopkins one of the few medical institutions to place research and patient care in neurology, neurosurgery, and psychiatry under one roof.

"It is amazing how well one can be and still have a [brain] tumor which is approaching the last stages of pressure. It seems a straw breaks the camel's back" (40). An accurate, though perhaps to the layman strange, observation, which Dandy made to a Hopkins colleague after some 15 years of involvement with brain surgery. His reference was to the exceptional rather than to the usual condition found with brain tumors, as certain clinical symptoms generally manifest themselves.

The early 1920s found Dandy heavily involved in the perfection of his surgery for the extirpation of tumors in various areas of the brain. He reported in 1920 "the first primary benign tumor in the lateral ventricle to be found at operation and completely removed" (41). Shortly after he had published his paper on ventriculography he had localized this tumor by the new diagnostic procedure after three previous unsuccessful attempts. One important result of Dandy's work in this area was to show that not all tumors within the brain are gliomas (malignancies arising from the neuroglia, the connective tissue of the nervous system), which had been commonly believed among surgeons. His experience with benign tumors of the lateral ventricles led some years later to the publication of one of his five books, *Benign, Encapsulated Tumors in the Lateral Ventricles of the Brain: Diagnosis and Treatment* (42).

Until 1921 tumors of the pineal body (epiphysis cerebri) had seldom been diagnosed. Because precise localization had not been possible before the introduction of ventriculography, surgery had been precluded. But Dandy had demonstrated in the Hunterian Laboratory, as was discussed earlier, that the removal of the pineal body from grown dogs and puppies did not inhibit their normal growth nor affect in any way their sexual activity. After 6 years of experimental work he began, in 1921, extirpating pineal tumors from patients, insisting that only with ventriculography could an exact diagnosis be made. He believed that bilateral ptosis (drooping of both upper eyelids) was the most important single sign for this tumor (43). For his first 20 cases of pineal tumor he had a mortality rate of about 20%, which was considered very good.

Late in 1921, Dandy published in *The Journal of the American Medical Association* an article on "The Treatment of Brain Tumors," in which he succinctly summarized in the final section his thinking about the diagnosis and treatment of brain tumors. His position on these interrelated subjects was to remain essentially unchanged during the rest of his career. In clear, concise prose, which had become a hallmark, he stated that:

1. Brain tumors are among the most frequent neoplastic lesions; their growth is always progressive and almost always leads to a train of terrible sequelae and eventually to death.
2. There is only one form of treatment for tumors of the brain—operative removal, and this must be complete.
3. To obtain the best operative results, brain tumors must be diagnosed and localized in the earliest stages.
4. It is now possible to diagnose and localize practically every tumor, and in the early stages. When all other signs and symptoms fail in the localization, cerebral pneumography will make the diagnosis and localization with precision and without equivocation. And when a tumor is not present, it can be excluded by the same method.
5. The operative approach will be dictated by the precise localization. The approach should afford adequate room, and it should be directly over the tumor.
6. After correct localization, all brain tumors should be disclosed at operation.
7. Every effort should be made to cure the patient by complete extirpation of

the growth. There is less mortality from carefully performed tumor extirpations than from unsuccessful exploration for tumors. When, for any reason, it is impossible or unjustifiable to remove the tumor, the maximum palliative relief should be given at the same operation.

8. Decompressions [removal of a flap of the skull and incision of the dura mater so as to relieve intracranial pressure], routinely performed, are among the most harmful and indefensible operations in surgery. They should never be performed for unlocalizable tumors. They are the exact equivalent of giving morphine for abdominal pain; the symptoms are masked until it is too late.

9. Decompressions should be performed only as a last resort—when the tumor cannot be removed; and then only after the location of the tumor is known, for in half the cases of brain tumor, no good can possibly be derived from a decompression.

10. Exploratory craniotomies for brain tumors are now scarcely ever indicated. The tumor should be precisely localized before any operative procedure is attempted.

11. Scientific accuracy must supplant guesswork in diagnosis and in directing the treatment. Early and accurate localization and thorough operative treatment will eliminate all unnecessary and harmful operations. The treatment of brain tumors can only be a direct eradication of the cause—prompt and efficient (44).

The article produced repercussions, as Dandy indicated in a letter written a month later to his friend Dr. Caroline McGill of Murray Hospital, Butte, Montana: "It is certainly a great sensation to be an iconoclast. It is a good time to test one's friends, also. Really, I did hesitate a great deal about publishing this thing, for it is rather below one's dignity, but, as you know, people with brain tumors have had very poor treatment in the past and I have been up against the proposition of being banged by all the neurological surgeons to such a degree that I have been forced to paddle my own canoe. It is useless to try to change people who have been trained in the old way, so that it seemed best to let the family physicians know directly, for they are more susceptible to progress than are the hide-bound members" (45).

Besides his work on benign encapsulated tumors of the lateral ventricles and on pineal tumors as well, Dandy, in the meantime, had been perfecting an operation for the total removal of an acoustic tumor in the cerebellopontine angle. ". . . This type of tumor," he noted in a letter to a Houston physician "is among the most difficult in brain surgery, the type which Cushing and others say cannot be removed" (46). The history of total extirpation of this tumor had been bleak for several reasons, including a lack of detailed knowledge on the function of various areas of the brain, the problem of controlling hemorrhage, and the need for specially designed instruments for this demanding surgery. "At the beginning of the twentieth century it seems probable that there had been but one tumor of this kind completely and successfully extirpated—one removed by [Charles A.] Ballance in 1894 and reported in 1907" (47). Dandy's success in meeting this surgical problem and the attendant attack made upon him by Cushing will be dealt with in the following chapter.

By 1921, when Dandy was 35 years old, his reputation as a neurosurgeon was firmly established. His studies of hydrocephalus and epilepsy, his introduction of ventriculography and pneumoencephalography, together with his operating skills placed him among the leading neurosurgeons of the country.

END NOTES

1. Turner TB: *Heritage of Excellence: The Johns Hopkins Medical Institutions, 1914–1947.* Baltimore, Johns Hopkins University Press, 1974, pp 75–76.
2. Flexner A: *Medical Education in the United States and Canada: A Report to the Carnegie Foundation for the Advancement of Teaching.* New York City, Bulletin Number Four, 1910, 17, 346 pp.
3. Abraham Flexner, Baltimore, to Simon Flexner, New York, letter, Jan 30, 1919, Simon Flexner MSS, American Philosophical Society Library.
4. W.E.D. to W. W. Keen, M.D., Philadelphia, letter, Nov 6, 1919, Dandy MSS.
5. Howard A. Kelly, M.D., Baltimore, to W.E.D., letter, Dec 21, 1919, Dandy MSS.
6. W. S. Halsted, Baltimore, to W.E.D., letter, Dec 24, 1919, Dandy MSS.
7. Turner TB: *Heritage of Excellence: The Johns Hopkins Medical Institutions, 1914–1947.* Baltimore, Johns Hopkins University Press, 1974, p 99.
8. Edward H. Cary, M.D., Dallas, to W.E.D., letter, Jan 8, 1919, Dandy MSS.
9. Udo J. Wile, M.D., Department of Dermatology and Syphilology, University Hospital, University of Michigan, Ann Arbor, to W.E.D., letter, July 11, 1919, Dandy MSS.
10. W.E.D. to J. H. Kirkland, Nashville, TN, letter, June 1, 1920, Dandy MSS.
11. W.E.D. to William W. Duke, M.D., Kansas City, MO, letter, June 22, 1920, Dandy MSS.
12. Henry Page, Cincinnati, to W.E.D., letter, July 27, 1921, Dandy MSS.
13. W.E.D. to Col. Henry Page, Cincinnati, letter, July 25, 1921, Dandy MSS.
14. W.E.D. to Henry Page, Cincinnati, letter, Aug 8, 1921, Dandy MSS.
15. Turner TB: *Heritage of Excellence: The Johns Hopkins Medical Institutions, 1914–1947.* Baltimore, Johns Hopkins University Press, 1974, pp 20–21.
16. See the bibliography of Dandy's writings.
17. Dandy WE: The diagnosis and treatment of hydrocephalus resulting from strictures of the aqueduct of Sylvius. *Surg Gynecol Obstet* 31:340, 1920.
18. Dandy WE: The diagnosis and treatment of hydrocephalus due to occlusions of the foramina of Magendie and Luschka. *Surg Gynecol Obstet* 32:112, 1921.
19. W.E.D. to William G. MacCallum, M.D., Johns Hopkins Hospital, Baltimore, letter, June 10, 1920, Dandy MSS.
20. Mrs. Miriam C. Benson, Arlington, VA, interview by telephone with the author, Nov 25, 1967. A 1918 graduate of Goucher College, Mrs. Benson, née Connet, went to work for Dandy in the spring of 1920, worked for him for only 4 months, and then went abroad for a year. Upon her return she again went to work for him as he had not found another secretary, and she remained with him for 4 years. She found him very considerate and easy to work for and recalled that he was just as interested in his charity patients as he was in those who were millionaires. Her first task upon going to work for

Dandy, she recalled, was to take care of a drawer full of letters of inquiry concerning his recent work on epilepsy.

21. Dandy WE, Elman R: Studies in experimental epilepsy. *Bull Johns Hopkins Hosp* 36:47, 1925.

22. Fairman D: Evolution of neurosurgery through Walter E. Dandy's work. *Surgery* 19:590, 1946.

23. W.E.D. to L. Barnaby, Newark, NJ, letter, July 2, 1920, Dandy MSS.

24. *Syracuse Herald*, Sept 19, 1920, p 7.

25. Fairman D: Evolution of neurosurgery through Walter E. Dandy's work. *Surgery* 19:590, 1946.

26. Dandy WE: Epilepsy. Annual Meeting of the Medical and Surgical Section, American Railway Association, New York City, June 8, 1931; published in the proceedings of the Association in the Fall of 1931.

27. Penfield W: Epilepsy—can science find a cure? *No Man Alone: A Neurosurgeon's Life.* Boston, Little, Brown, 1977, ch 12.

28. W.E.D. to W. W. Keen, M.D., Philadelphia, letter, Jan 14, 1929, Dandy MSS. For a passing reference to Dandy's attitude toward unorthodox epileptic surgery, see *Life*, 1:2–3, Nov 30, 1936.

29. W.E.D. to Ralph Greene, M.D., Jacksonville, FL, letter, July 19, 1927, Dandy MSS.

30. In the later years of his career Dandy would expose the area of the brain he thought affected the epileptic condition and paint it with iodine. Hugo V. Rizzoli, M.D., Washington, DC, interview with the author, March 21, 1979.

31. Northfield DWC: *The Surgery of the Central Nervous System: A Textbook for Postgraduate Students.* Oxford, Blackwell Scientific Publications, 1973, p 538.

32. Wilder G. Penfield, M.D., New York City, to W.E.D., letter, July 15, 1921, Dandy MSS. Penfield, p 67.

33. Wilder G. Penfield, M.D., New York City, W.E.D., letter, Aug 4, 1921, Dandy MSS.

34. Penfield W: *No Man Alone: A Neurosurgeon's Life.* Boston, Little, Brown, 1977, p 75.

35. Penfield W: *No Man Alone: A Neurosurgeon's Life.* Boston, Little, Brown, 1977, p 77.

36. Lewis Weed later did work on the origin and circulation of the cerebrospinal fluid. In a lecture given in the 1930s on the subject, according to Dr. W. M. Firor, "he made no mention of Dr. Dandy's epochal earlier work with Blackfan. Weed's theory was all wrong. Dandy saw through him [and] loathed him. Weed's work was later found erroneous." Firor believes that Weed was "jealous of Dandy." W. M. Firor, M.D., Baltimore, to the author, letter, Dec 30, 1975.

37. Mrs. Walter E. Dandy, Baltimore, interview with the author, March 24, 1975.

38. Sometime in the spring, 1976, Dr. Walter E. Dandy, Jr., indicated to his mother that he thought his father never really wanted a neurological institute as he occasionally stated because he was able to do as he pleased under the existing arrangements. Mrs. Walter E. Dandy, Baltimore, interview with the author, June 10, 1976.

39. Turner TB: *Heritage of Excellence: The Johns Hopkins Medical Institutions, 1914–1947.* Baltimore, Johns Hopkins University Press, 1974, p 506.

40. W.E.D. to Lewellys F. Barker, M.D., Baltimore, letter, Feb 24, 1927, Dandy MSS.

41. Fairman D: Evolution of neurosurgery through Walter E. Dandy's work. *Surgery* 19:590, 1946.

42. See Dandy's bibliography.

43. Dandy WE: An operation for the removal of pineal tumors. *Surg Gynecol Obstet* 33:113–119, 1921.

44. Dandy WE: The treatment of brain tumors. *J Am Med Assoc* 77:1858–1859, 1921.

45. W.E.D. to Caroline McGill, M.D., Butte, Montana, letter, Jan 10, 1922, Dandy MSS. Dr. McGill had written to Dandy in jest earlier: "You are a jolly old image breaker. If there was an idol left in the camp you have smashed it. All their Lares & Penates, all their icons and their pet Teddy-bears—of the whole generation of neuro-surgeons you have smashed and thrown Chaplin-like at their own heads. They can help themselves not at all for you have the data and they have not. To take away their decompression, their colossal puncture & other pet operations and to hold them to rigid pre-operation diagnosis is cruel beyond measure. To tell them that the diagnosis can be made before

the scalpel goes thorugh the scalp if they are only clever enough puts the burden on them." Caroline McGill, M.D., Butte, Montana, to W.E.D., letter, n.d., Dandy MSS.

46. W.E.D. to Dr. E. W. Bertner, Houston, letter, Aug 2, 1922, Dandy MSS.
47. Dandy WE: An operation for the total removal of cerebellopontile (acoustic) tumors. *Surg Gynecol Obstet* 41:129, 1925.

CHAPTER 6

In Demand

Except for the last weeks of his life, Dandy enjoyed relatively good health. Rarely was he confined by illness. During the year after his residency he was laid up for several months, as noted earlier, with sciatic neuralgia and with what he later described as a bad knee. He put the enforced idleness to good use by extensive reading, including the *Encyclopedia Britannica.* In looking back on this period, Dandy considered it ". . . the most valuable time I have spent for my whole outlook on life was changed and it was possible to continue on in a way that was more satisfying and at the same time more profitable" (1). He did not elaborate as to how his "whole outlook on life was changed"; thus we are left to speculate about the nature of this changed outlook. His remarks were made to a friend who was convalescing from a serious illness and so may have been made in order to help the friend through a difficult adjustment.

As intense as his schedule was during the years following the war, Dandy found it both necessary and profitable to take extended winter vacations at Jekyll Island, near Brunswick, Georgia, a refuge of the wealthy, including William Rockefeller, from freezing weather and snow. They wished to have on hand a reputable physician. Consequently Dandy was but one of several Hopkins men who enjoyed the delights of rest and recreation amidst affluence in a lovely setting. Typical of Dandy's six winter vacations was that of 1921 when he stayed at the Jekyll Island Club from mid-February to the first of April, enjoying the golf, swimming, and tennis.

During this season Cushing and his wife, together with friends, vacationed at the Island. Learning that Dandy was there at the same time, Cushing ". . . took delight in challenging him once again on the court" (2). It was said that while Cushing had the form,

Dandy won the game, a remark attributed to Mrs. Harry R. Slack, Jr., who following a match took a picture of the two men dressed in blazers and white flannels while casually holding their racquets. In later years this picture became well known as it was reproduced in several professional publications. Interestingly enough, a copy of it hung in Dandy's bedroom, as Frank J. Otenasek, a resident of his, learned many years later during a stay in the Dandy home while the family was away on vacation (3).

It was Ernest G. Grob, the superintendent of the Jekyll Island Club, who was instrumental in arranging for Dandy and his residents to come to the Island for vacations and at the same time to provide professional care at a fee for the wealthy patrons. (By the end of his winter sojourn in 1921, Dandy expected ". . . to make $1800 or $2000 possibly") (4). There developed over the years a warm friendship between Grob and Dandy who regarded him as ". . . a wonderful friend to all of us in our days of poverty. We shall never forget him. I do not see how I could have existed had I not had Jekyll" (5).

Though still a bachelor in the early 1920s, Dandy was not indifferent to women and marriage. In letters to his mother and father from Jekyll Island during the winter of 1921, he wrote that he had heard from his girl—we don't know her identity—and that "she is appealing to me more and more. I think she is a *real* [emphasis his] type of girl and one who will meet all your requirements" (6). He indicated in another note that he would send them ". . . one of her letters—the last one. I don't know what you will think but you can tell me. I think she is a wonderful girl though— very sensible and very sweet, unless I am mistaken. Will let you see her when I come home" (7). Nothing, however, came of this romance.

As a young surgeon who had already achieved professional recognition and public acclaim, Dandy must have appeared to more than a few young women at the Hospital and elsewhere as "a good catch." But it was not until the fall of 1923 that he met the woman who a year later was to become his wife.

By the early 1920s no one other than his mother and father had exerted a greater influence on Dandy's life than William Stewart Halsted, known fondly to colleagues and students as "the Professor." Halsted, it will be recalled, had found a place for the aspiring young neurosurgeon on his service after Cushing had announced on the eve of his departure for Boston in 1912 that he was not taking Dandy with him. Dandy was forever grateful for the opportunity to become an assistant resident and later (chief) resident under Halsted, who in turn quickly realized Dandy's exceptional promise and gave it encouragement. A warm friendship developed between the two men. On occasion, in later years, Dandy would take Halsted for a drive around Baltimore. And on at least one occasion Dandy accepted Halsted's invitation to visit High Hampton, the Halsted summer home at Cashiers in the mountains of North Carolina.

Meticulous in his dress, Halsted undoubtedly influenced Dandy in giving proper attention to his attire (8). Consequently it is not surprising that Dandy always insisted to his interns and residents on the importance of a neat appearance, including polished shoes.

In the spring of 1921, Halsted indicated that he would like to propose Dandy for membership in the prestigious American Surgical Association and asked him to provide a list of his publications. Such consideration was an honor which the young surgeon much appreciated (9). Yet for some unapparent reason it was not until 4 years later that he was elected to membership in that association.

Another instance of Halsted's warm regard for Dandy is reflected in the following letter written from High Hampton in August 1921:

Dear Dandy:
  I have just this moment read your welcome and most kind & cheerful letter. Thank you for all the news of the J.H.H. & for assuring me that you enjoyed your visit more than you had reason to expect from the accounts that others had given you of this quiet retreat for the aged. It was a shame that your sojourn had to be so brief. I was positively shocked to hear you say that you must escape at the first possible moment. I saw Miss Hanna today at the girls camp at Lake Fairfield. She told of the pleasant encounter she had with you on the train. She seems to be a particularly nice person & seems very happy at the camp. I was summoned to see one of the girls who seems to have torn the capsule of a hip-joint—or torn something in the neighborhood of this joint. I am glad to know that [George] Heuer has been offered the position at Cincinnati but we shall miss him dreadfully if he accepts; & I presume he will. He has not written to me about it. I am sorry that [Mont] Reid's brief vacation seems to have benefited him so little. Do beg him to go away again. [Frederick] Reichert is, as you say, a fine fellow [Dandy's first resident]. He has the true spirit of the research worker & is also a good operator already. With love to all the chirurgs I am ever sincerely yours,

W. S. Halsted (10)

Knowing the Halsteds' love of flowers, Dandy sent to Mrs. Halsted the following spring a two-volume work on the *Wild Flowers of New York*, for which she was most grateful and which prompted

Halsted to respond in part as follows:

Dear Dandy:
    I have just passed a delightful hour with the "Wild Flowers of New York,"
& must tell you how much I appreciate your kindness in sending these
superb volumes to Mrs. Halsted and congratulate you on selecting a gift so
appropriate & so welcome. We consult it almost every day, for most of our
flowers are portrayed in this remarkable production of the University of the
State of New York.
    Illustrations so fine as these are far more useful for general purposes than
fine herbarium such as they have at Ashville on the Biltmore Estate of
George Vanderbilt (11).

Meanwhile, the Maryland State Dental Society arranged a dinner
for Halsted at the Belvedere Hotel, Baltimore, on April 1, 1922, at
which he was presented the gold medal of the National (now
American) Dental Association in recognition of his work on local
or nerve block anesthesia, an achievement which by that date
dentists universally employed. Dandy was present at this occasion
honoring Halsted for the research which he had done on nerve
block anesthesia before coming to Hopkins.

Six months later, Halsted died at The Johns Hopkins Hospital
while Dandy was away giving a paper at the annual meeting of The
State Medical Society of Wisconsin (12). Dandy had passed up
earlier a fishing trip in order to remain in Baltimore during what
turned out to be Halsted's final illness, but having made a commitment to The State Medical Society of Wisconsin he decided to
proceed as planned. Halsted's death was deeply felt by Dandy as
he indicated in the following lines he wrote to Mrs. Halsted: "Dr.
Halsted's loss is felt more keenly every day. I find myself constantly
wishing to run up to his office to consult with him on new problems[,] a source from which I could always receive stimulation and
at the same time modulation. His services can never die and to men
who have worked with him, the stimulus will go on as long as they
live" (13). In this letter he also mentioned that he had just received
a little volume entitled *Synonyms Discriminated* which Halsted had
ordered for him several months before. "It was good of Dr. Halsted,
like so many things he had done for us" (13).

Dandy's affection and regard for Halsted were reciprocated, as
was evident by the older man's letters, his thoughtfulness, and his
observation that Dandy was ". . . the most brilliant pupil he had
ever had " (14). When, 20 years after Halsted's death, George
Heuer undertook to prepare a biography of Hopkins' first professor
of surgery, which ultimately appeared in the *Bulletin of The Johns*

Hopkins Hospital (15), Dandy readily responded when the biographer called upon him for information and suggestions.

Within a few weeks of Halsted's death, John M. T. Finney, whom Halsted had appointed to his service when the Hospital opened in 1889, was made acting head for 2 years (so as to allow enough time to select a successor to Halsted) and was asked to sit on both the Advisory Board of the Medical School and the Medical Board of the Hospital. Dandy, who ". . . was indifferent about departmental organization and affairs" (16), liked Finney. During the years that Finney served as acting head of the Department of Surgery, the esprit de corps deteriorated, according to Warfield M. Firor, who was then a house officer. Bitter contention arose among the house staff, the new appointments were said to be based on favoritism. ". . . The most experienced house surgeons, [Emile] Holman and [Karl] Schlaepfer, left. In retrospect one realizes that the giant of the situation was Dr. Dandy. His incessantly active mind, his masterful operating, and the rigid discipline he imposed upon his staff exerted a solid influence, and maintained Dr. Halsted's standard of excellence. The stage was set for the arrival of a vigorous chief" (17). It was nearly 3 years after Halsted's death, however, before the new chief took charge.

Meanwhile, Dandy through his work and association with Halsted, was making friends with some of the leading men in American medicine, such as J. Chalmers Da Costa of Philadelphia, Alexis Carrel of The Rockefeller Institute for Medical Research (now Rockefeller University), New York City, and George W. Crile of Cleveland, Ohio. In response to Dandy's desire to attend one of his Wednesday afternoon clinics at the Jefferson Hospital, Dr. Da Costa replied that he would ". . . feel personally honored" (18). By the time of Da Costa's death a dozen years later Dandy considered it a privilege ". . . to have had his acquaintance and particularly to have felt that I retained his confidence" (19).

In December 1922 Dandy spent a "very stimulating day" with Carrel in his laboratory at the Rockefeller Institute. "It is the real inspiration centre of research," wrote Dandy following his visit, "and I carried away many ideas which are so fundamentally important to surgery. I shall always hope to take as keen interest in your work as did Dr. Halsted, for I know how fundamental and accurate it is" (20).

A few months later Dandy visited Crile, who had recently

founded the Cleveland Clinic Foundation. Dandy was much impressed with what he saw. "I learned," he later wrote to Crile, "a great deal from your details and principles of which I hope to make use in the finesse of handling brain surgery. Nowhere will one get such an impression of delicacy in operating and handling patients and preventing complications which are taken more or less as a matter of routine expectation. It is the difference between accuracy and guesswork" (21).

Though Dandy was eager to become acquainted with outstanding surgeons and to visit their clinics, he was reluctant to join the American College of Surgeons (ACS), unless it was on his own terms. Founded in 1913, the "ACS" as early as 1921 invited Dandy to become a member. But Dandy did not want to be bothered fulfilling the requirements for membership. "It goes without saying," wrote the College's director general, Dr. Franklin H. Martin, to Dandy in 1925, "that we are all extremely anxious to have you numbered among the Fellows of the American College of Surgeons." Martin went on to explain why no exceptions to the College's requirements could be made, a question which Dandy apparently had raised:

I know you will appreciate that the Regents would be subjected to severe criticism if they did not in every instance follow the rules and regulations of the College as set forth in the requirements for Fellowship, which specify that each candidate shall be required to submit in complete detail the case records of fifty major operations which he has performed himself, and in addition a brief abstract report of at least fifty other major operations in which he has acted as assistant or which he has performed himself. Considering the large service that you have at The Johns Hopkins Hospital, it should not be a difficult matter for you to have the one hundred case histories copied and sent to us within the next month (22).

Dandy was not immediately persuaded by Martin's argument. It was not until 1930, 5 years later and nearly 10 years after he had been invited to join, that he became a member, which, despite some irritations, he remained till his death (23). While the College's records reveal that Dandy never gave up his membership, he indicated in a letter to the chairman of the ACS dinner committee in 1938 that he had ". . . dropped out of the American College of Surgeons a year ago" (24). Perhaps he really thought that he had dropped his membership; perhaps his secretary had paid his dues, or possibly he confused ending his subscription to *Surgery, Gynecology and Obstetrics* with withdrawal from the College. Although he never gave up his membership in the College, he never had the interest in it that he had in the American Surgical Association and the Southern Surgical Association.

One organization which Dandy never joined was the source of a minor irritation between Cushing and him. Dandy was unwilling to join Cushing's "Neuro-Surgical Club" (Dandy's reference to the Society of Neurological Surgeons) as a charter member, for as he stated to Cushing he had always been ". . . very averse to joining societies of all kinds because I feel they are more social than beneficial and I cannot spare the time for them" (25). Dr. Ernest Sachs of St. Louis, who was the new society's secretary, was to write again to Dandy and again Dandy declined. "This happened three times in succession, whereupon I declined to approach him another time. As a result, Walter Dandy never became a member, which was due entirely to some long-standing disagreement he had had with Dr. Cushing" (26). Sachs' explanation for Dandy's refusal to join the Society of Neurological Surgeons (known today as the "Senior Society") came closer to the truth than Dandy's reply to Cushing.

Late in 1921, 6 months after Dandy had responded to Cushing's query about joining the Society of Neurological Surgeons, Cushing learned that his former pupil was handling two cases which had been his "and possibly more . . . ." Caustically he asked Dandy: "Don't you think it would be a good thing if you and I could have a mutual agreement always to notify one another in case a former patient in the care of either of us changes hands for one reason or another? [Charles H.] Frazier, [Charles A.] Elsberg, [Alfred W.] Adson, and [Ernest] Sachs almost invariably do so, and I endeavor to be as punctilious as possible in the matter myself" (27). Having meanwhile been to the Pacific Coast, Dandy, nearly a month later, replied that he would ". . . be only too glad to cooperate with you in any way and I will notify you if I have any of your cases" (28). He then reported on the two patients Cushing had inquired about.

What was to be the final episode in the Cushing-Dandy quarrel occurred the following September when Dandy published in the *Bulletin of The Johns Hopkins Hospital* a preliminary report on "An Operation for the Total Extirpation of Tumors in the Cerebellopontine Angle" (29). This was a rather dramatic breakthrough as the generally accepted procedure, advanced by Cushing in 1917, involved only a partial intracapsular enucleation of these acoustic tumors (30). Whereas Cushing recommended subtotal extirpation of tumors in the cerebellopontine angle, Dandy ". . . completely removed such a growth from a patient . . ." who during the ensuing 5 years had remained well (29). Dandy's procedure called for "a sub-occipital exposure of the cerebellum . . . with as much exposure of the affected angle as possible" (29). The interior of the tumor was then removed with a curette. In turn the capsule was . . . carefully drawn away from the medulla, pons, and mid-brain." Thus the whole tumor was painstakingly extirpated ". . . without bleeding and without trauma to the brain-stem" (29). The cranial nerves which the tumor had stretched were now freed with the removal of the capsule.

With Cushing's procedure the capsule was not excised, thus allowing for the tumor's recurrence. Total extirpation, Cushing believed, was too dangerous. But his former pupil declared otherwise in an article which made no reference to his monograph on acoustic tumors. Dandy felt that it was unnecessary to list references in a preliminary report as they would be included in a later, definitive monograph on the subject. Cushing was greatly annoyed by the publication of Dandy's preliminary report, as he believed that Dandy desired the credit for an operative approach which Cushing had earlier described. He vented his feelings in the following letter to Winford H. Smith, the director of The Johns Hopkins Hospital, but decided to send the letter to Dandy:

My dear Smithie:

I assume that you are the Editor of the Bulletin but if not, you will know to whom this letter should be referred. I have been very much disturbed by seeing an article by Dr. Dandy in the last issue which, in the shape of a preliminary report, consists of nothing more than a promise, so far as I can see, that he is going to describe in the future an operation for a certain kind of brain tumor. It is exceedingly bad for me, inasmuch as many people know that I had something to do with Dr. Dandy's training; it is equally bad for Dr. Dandy himself, insofar as general professional esteem is concerned; but what affects all of us still more is that it is very bad for the Hopkins to have the Bulletin accept and permit the title of such an incomplete and promissory article to get into the literature.

Leaving all else aside—the tumors he evidently has in mind are not endotheliomas; that the operation he outlines is the same operation which has been fully detailed by another person who had made clear that though one may occasionally succeed in removing a small tumor of this kind in toto, the effort to do so in most cases is attended by unjustifiable risks—leaving all this aside, as I say, it is not the sort of article that a member of the surgical staff of the Johns Hopkins Hospital, at least in former days, would have written.

Cushing closed this letter with the following suggestion:

If the editorial board of the Bulletin sees nothing out of the way with Dr.

Dandy's article, there is nothing more to be said; but now that the article has
been published, I feel that Dr. Dandy should be requested to report in full, with
due reference to the literature of the subject, his cases of cerebello-pontine
angle tumors, giving the operative mortality figures and end results for the
entire series. It is the only possible way for him to square himself. I grieve to say
it is by no means his first offense.

Having decided to address his letter to Smith to Dandy, Cushing
added a postscript in his own hand:

Dear Dandy,
    I have cogitated over this letter a good deal. I think I will send it to you
instead of Dr. Smith. Perhaps you will wish to show it to him and get his advice.
After all it is as important for you as it is for me that you stand in a high plane of
professional ethics.
    I think you are doing yourself a great deal of harm by the tone of some of
your publications. You are an independent thinker and worker, and that is not at
all a bad thing. But you must not forget your manners, and this last note of yours
is in extremely bad taste.

                                                    Always your friend,
                                                    Harvey Cushing (31)

Understandably, Dandy was offended by this attack on his professional conduct and manners. He had felt, as was mentioned earlier,
that in making a preliminary report on the total extirpation of
acoustic tumors, using the Cushing approach, it was unnecessary
to cite the literature; that would come later in a definitive paper.
He wasted no time in replying to Cushing's attack. In a direct,
forthright letter to his former mentor, Dandy wrote:

    I have read and considered your letter. I don't think I shall show it to Dr.
Smith or anyone [else]. It would surely do you an injustice. You can do it if you
wish. While of course I am not unmindful of your inferences and taunts of
dishonesty and your invidious generalizations at various times, it has seemed far
better to ignore them. It must be clear that they never seriously harm the
intended victim, but they do reflect on you a great deal and in your position you
can ill afford it.
    However, if you really believe them to be facts, the Hospital, University and
Medical profession will be most grateful for them; indeed, they are entitled to
them and you are shirking a most important responsibility if you neglect to make
them known—but they will want facts—and not invective propaganda.

Towards the end of this letter, Dandy, with perhaps more of a
touch of sadness than of resentment, observed:

    Doubtless I should feel a keen resentment from such a letter, but I do not;
I feel very sorry for one who is laboring under such an obsession and
particularly as it is from one to whom I should now be feeling the deepest

debt of gratitude and upon whom I should look with the greatest adoration and consider my friend, guide and master.

I trust I have not been discourteous; such is not intended, you may be assured. It all seems so unnecessary. It should all be so different (32).

Dandy did submit Cushing's letter to the Board of Editors of the *Bulletin of The Johns Hopkins Hospital*, confessing in a covering letter that he was "absolutely at a loss to discover the point for such a letter other than personal animus" (33). The only reason why he submitted the preliminary report, he noted, "was to establish priority for a procedure which is directed towards the total enucleation of these tumors" (33). No one else, Cushing included, had published to date, said Dandy, a procedure for the safe, total extirpation of acoustic tumors.

Cushing's caustic attack and Dandy's hardhitting reply comprised the last episode in their longstanding quarrel. An interesting sidelight to this clash may be found in a letter among the Cushing Papers which Cushing wrote but never sent to Dandy. It is revealing for the admission which Cushing, a proud man, made at one point: "Everyone knows that you were once a pupil of mine, and though most of them know that you have far surpassed your teacher, there are at the same time certain amenities which most of us try to observe" (34).

Cushing's vitriolic assault on Dandy for his alleged lack of professional ethics and attendant bad manners compels one to agree with John F. Fulton, Cushing's official biographer, that "there can be no doubt that Cushing's reproach of Dr. Dandy was uncalled for . . ." (35). Having been offended by Cushing's earlier treatment of him, Dandy never forgave his former mentor for his searing comments about the publication of the preliminary report on the total excision of tumors of the cerebellopontine angle. Yet the two men in the years that followed maintained a gentlemanly civility towards each other, as when Dandy wrote to Cushing 2 years after the acoustic tumor episode: "Would you be good enough to tell me if you ever have serious infections; I do not mean skin infections, but those deep in the brain" (36). Cushing, meanwhile, had written to his former pupil at Hopkins in a friendly vein: "Dear Dandy: I am glad to know you are going to get away for a trip abroad. You are so well known that you will not need any letter of introduction"; and in a postscript added: "So glad to have seen your young assistant [Frederick Reichert] who was on here for the Neurological meeting. Such a nice fellow. Too bad you did not join that band. We all need your experience in our discussions. I hope you may think better of it some day" (37).

Four years later Dandy began a letter to his erstwhile teacher with: "Dear Doctor Cushing: I have just read with much interest your Macewen lecture. The beauty of its introduction particularly thrilled me. For sometime I have been playing with electric cautery but with rather indifferent enthusiasm. I wonder if sometime I might run up to see you use it" (38). Cushing answered Dandy's letter immediately, saying that if he had had his letter a day or two before, he would have sent for him (39).

In the meantime, Cushing's son Bill was killed while a student at Yale in an automobile accident. Dandy promptly sent his condolences, to which Cushing replied: "Thanks[,] dear Dandy[,] for your message of sympathy" (40).

These courtesies not withstanding, the mention of Cushing's name to Dandy often brought the conditioned response: "That son-of-a-bitch!" (41). And anyone who came to see Dandy with a letter of introduction from Cushing was generally not kindly received (42).

In the closing lines of a rather lengthy letter which Dandy wrote to John Fulton on November 26, 1945, about his relations with his former teacher, he said of Cushing: "I think he realized his unfairness in later life and in some slight way tried to make amends, to which I did not at all reciprocate. You can use your own judgment about publishing this. You have my permission to do so, but I do not think anything would be gained and I think it would be better left out. Cushing certainly was not a big man; he was a very selfish one and certainly not the type who wished his pupils to excel, and I have never felt that his scientific contributions were trustworthy." Earlier in the letter, Dandy noted his gratitude to Cushing: "He gave me my start in neuro-surgery and I, of course, owe a great debt to him for that. He certainly was far and away above all others in neuro-surgery at that time and it was particularly fortunate for me to have been associated with the Master" (43).

Perhaps Cushing learned something from his quarrel with Dandy. Fulton, who knew Cushing well, seemed to think so: ". . . I have always had a sneaking suspicion that Dandy's differences with H.C. caused Dr. Cushing to be more considerate thereafter with his assistants. I think it also made him more interested in his own operative statistics" (44).

A little less than 3 months after his attack on Dandy over the issue of total excision of cerebellopontine angle tumors, Cushing was tendered the chair of surgery at Hopkins by Lewis H. Weed, professor of anatomy and spokesman of the search committee. Weed, who had gone with Cushing to Harvard but had returned to Hopkins 2 years later as a permanent member of the Department of Anatomy, was to become, the following year (1923), dean of the Medical School. Cushing promptly declined the invitation stating ". . . that he could not possibly face another transplantation" (45). Dandy was greatly relieved that Cushing had declined the Hopkins chair (46). Unfortunately for The Hopkins Medical Institutions, however, nearly 3 years were to elapse before a permanent chief of surgery was appointed.

A fitting postscript to the final episode of the Cushing-Dandy quarrel was reflected in a comment which Dandy, perhaps having in mind Cushing's attack, made to Dean Marvin T. Sudler of the University of Kansas School of Medicine. Some prominent members of the medical profession of Kansas City, Kansas, had attacked Sudler who had written to Dandy for permission to use a letter which Dandy had earlier written in his defense. Dandy replied: "While I am very sorry to know that you are subject to adverse comment, I usually look upon such as an asset rather than a liability. One only has to look at the careers of the great Lister and Pasteur to realize that it is only the best things which receive the strongest and most persistent attacks. It would, of course, be a pleasure to have you use the letter in any way you wish" (47). Such a thought may well have been a balm to the recipient as well as to the writer. Yet, as noted earlier, the hurt and resentment resulting from Cushing's accrued sharp criticisms never really left Dandy (48).

In the annals of American medicine the Cushing-Dandy controversy was a most unfortunate episode, reminding one of Sir William Osler's observation: "No sin will so easily beset you as uncharitableness toward your brother practitioner" (49).

From the early 1920s, Dandy was in demand as a speaker at a wide variety of professional meetings. During the course of that decade he addressed the Cleveland Academy of Medicine, the Norfolk County (Virginia) Medical Society, the West Virginia Medical Association, the Medical Society of the State of New York, the Association for Research in Nervous and Mental Disease, the Surgical Research Society, of which he was a member of the Baltimore delegation, and the Pan-American Medical Association in Panama.

And on several occasions Dandy spoke before the Inter-State Post Graduate Assembly of the Tri-State District Medical Association. He was so impressed with the work of this organization that late in 1926 he wrote to its managing director, Dr. William B. Peck: "You have performed a great service to the medical men of this country. The growth of your Tri-State is one of the most amazing things in contemporary medicine" (50). A few weeks before, George Crile of the Cleveland Clinic, expressed his gratitude to Dandy for his discussion of ventriculography, along with a diagnostic clinic, at the most recent meeting of the Inter-State Post Graduate Assembly: "Before finally filing away the material connected with the recent Inter-State Post Graduate Assembly held in Cleveland, I want to tell you how very much your contribution was appreciated. It will be a pleasure to have the privilege of reading your paper in the 'Proceedings' . . ." (51).

An interesting sidelight to Dandy's numerous speaking engagements was his practice of "talking his papers" instead of reading them. "He never read his papers because he . . . wished to watch the faces of his audience to see their reaction" (52). It was not only what Dandy had to say but his manner of delivery that made him a popular speaker at medical meetings.

Although he attended and participated in countless professional meetings, Dandy did not, so he told his Missouri and Hopkins classmate, R. Eustace Semmes, ". . . get anything out of meetings or societies other than social contacts. I should much rather spend a few days in a chosen clinic than to waste so much time in a standardized meeting" (53).

In addition to addressing various medical organizations, Dandy spoke on occasion to medical students, other than those whom he instructed at Hopkins. An instance of his interest in medical students occurred late in 1930 when he readily accepted Owen H. Wangensteen's invitation to speak to the junior and senior students at the University of Minnesota Medical School while he was filling a speaking engagement in Minneapolis (54).

Under Halsted's progressive residency system in surgery, which spanned a period of 6 to 8 years, "most of the assistant residents climbing up the ladder to the surgical residency spent the last year but one with Dandy. An occasional one met his Waterloo there, but most profited by the experience and a few became neurosurgeons . . ." (55), such as Fred W. Geib, M. Barnes Woodhall,

Eldridge H. Campbell, Jr., Francis J. Otenasek, John W. Chambers, Irving J. Sherman, Hugo V. Rizzoli, Charles E. Troland, and Arthur B. King. Until September 1922, Dandy, though his practice was growing, had only the part-time services of an assistant resident. After Halsted's death, John M. T. Finney, the acting chief of surgery, realizing that Dandy needed a full-time assistant resident, made provision for such an arrangement. In effect, this meant that the individual selected became Dandy's resident.

Frederick L. Reichert, a graduate of The Johns Hopkins Medical School, thus became Dandy's first resident (September 1, 1922 to July 5, 1923) (56). The two men became very fond of each other, as was reflected in their later correspondence. By way of a post-script to a letter to Reichert, who had meanwhile accepted a post at Stanford University following the completion of his (chief) residency in 1926, Dandy expressed his feelings about his first resident as follows: "I forgot to tell you that, of course, you are always my first associate in brain surgery and I am always interested in your future" (57). Another evidence of his interest in Reichert may be found in a strong letter of recommendation he wrote on behalf of his first resident for a Guggenheim fellowship: "I think he is one of the outstanding young men in surgery in this country and is destined to a very bright future" (58). Dandy also proposed Reichert for membership in the American Neurological Association, noting that if his former pupil ". . . could have a better proposer, I am sure your entry would have been more expeditious" (59).

Reichert, in turn, was most appreciative of "the training and close association . . ." which he had enjoyed with Dandy (60). In 1933 he demonstrated his regard for his friend and former mentor by proposing his name for the Nobel Prize in physiology and medicine (61), an honor which Dandy never received.

Meanwhile, the two men collaborated in publishing over a 13-year period three articles dealing with their research on the hypophysis (pituitary body) and the effect of its total excision on laboratory dogs. In the first article they presented a procedure ". . . for the safe removal of the canine hypophysis." They ". . . found no evidence to support, and every evidence to refute, the assumption that the hypophysis is essential to life, or that the group of symptoms which have been described is essential to life, or that the group of symptoms which have been described by others as preceding death in hypophysectomized animals are of hypophyseal origin" (62). Their research centered on the quest to clear up the mystery of diabetes insipidus as to ". . . either the manner or the exact site of its production" (63).

In their second report, Dandy and Reichert concluded that "since polyuria [excretion of abnormally large amounts of urine] and polydipsia [excessive thirst] follow injuries to the hypothalamus, after the hypophysis has been removed, the conclusion is inescapable that diabetes insipidus is not due to the absence of a hypophyseal hormone" (64).

Two years later they published their final report of this series entitled "Studies on Experimental Hypophysectomy in Dogs, III. Somatic, Mental and Glandular Effects" (65). They found that the hypophysectomized dogs were more prone to disease and less resistant to the effects than were normal dogs. They also found that "dogs without a hypophysis definitely show signs of senility much sooner; indeed they very closely suggest the well known human state of progeria [premature old age]" (66). The hypophysectomized dogs, furthermore, showed a cessation of both skeletal development and growth, most especially of the endocrine group of glands (67). Their results corroborated fully the views of Bernard Aschner of Vienna whose ". . . conclusions [in 1912] were always under a cloud because it was felt that the operative route through the nose [for hypophysectomy] had influenced his results" (68).

In the meantime Dandy admonished Reichert to publish his report on pituitary feeding experiments because "it is always wise to protect one's self for tales spread so rapidly that priority is lost so unjustly" (69). And with a touch of presumably unintended humor, he added: "Publish it wherever you prefer. I should think *Endocrinology* might be very good, except that I always look upon it as a quack journal and like to stay away from such as far as possible" (69).

Although Reichert and Dandy were separated by the breadth of a continent after Reichert left Baltimore, they remained in touch with one another through correspondence and the exchange of gifts at Christmas (70). They, of course, occasionally saw one another at professional meetings.

It was during Reichert's residency in neurosurgery that Dandy made a serious, though rectifiable, error in performing a craniotomy. Helen Douw (later Mrs. Alfred H. Richards) was in her last year at The Johns Hopkins School for Nurses (in 1935 the name was changed to The Johns Hopkins School of Nursing) when one day in January or February 1923 she was assigned as the "clean nurse" to Dandy's "brain team." "She was 'scared to death' as she put it. Dr. Dandy was someone you only looked at from afar. *Never* had a student nurse worked on his team[,] particularly one who had not had the full training. She was the first student to get this assignment." Miss Douw rehearsed her role as much as time permitted. Dandy, as scheduled, proceeded with the craniotomy, ". . . layed [*sic*] back the flap, etc. Everything had gone perfectly, when Dr. Dandy said, "My God, I went in on the wrong side!" According to Helen Douw, ". . . he was completely crushed, tears streamed down his cheeks (under his mask) as he stood back and said, 'Come, come, let's get on with closing it up.' " Later, after paying all of the patient's hospital expenses for 6 to 8 weeks, Dandy ". . . repeated the operation on the 'right' side, and the (brain) tumor was removed successfully" (71). Perhaps the only worthy comment to make of this embarrassment is that of Joseph Addison: "The best may err" (72).

Following Reichert, Warfield M. ("Monty") Firor became Dandy's second resident (July 5, 1923 to January 29, 1925). Like his predecessor he was a graduate of the Hopkins Medical School. Dandy came to have a high regard for his second resident who was instrumental in preparing a manual of procedural details for the interns to follow in the neurosurgical operating room. This had not been done before (73).

In 1923, while Firor was resident in neurological surgery, Dandy introduced what may well have been the first postoperative recovery room in the history of surgery for this century. "The direct antecedent of the intensive care unit was the postoperative recovery room," according to Mark Hilberman. "Recovery rooms have only become common in the last 25 years, but in 1863 Florence Nightingale observed: 'It is not uncommon, in small country hospitals, to have a recess or small room leading from the operating theatre in which the patients remain until they have recovered, or at least recovered from the immediate effects of the operation' " (74). Dandy arranged to have a three-bed unit which was staffed by specially trained nurses day and night. It was adjacent to the operating room on the fourth floor of the Department of Surgery (75). With the completion of the new surgery clinic, the neurosurgical recovery room was moved to Halsted 7. "This was the beginning of careful attention to airway care, temperature control, circulatory monitoring, fluid and electrolyte balance and observation of the state of consciousness of the patient. Interestingly, the new surgical intensive care unit is at present on the site of the old neurosurgical intensive care unit" (76).

During Firor's residency with Dandy he had occasion to witness his chief's sense of humor and the strange twist it once in a while took. In walking down a hospital corridor with an associate Dandy would occasionally give him a Missouri mule-kick. He did that once when a nurse came along and in turn told her that she should watch out or the fellow whom he kicked would kick her (77)!

In another instance (77), Dandy suggested to Firor that they go in to watch Reichert operate on a nurse with a sebaceous cyst. As they entered, Dandy quietly took a can of ether, punctured it, and slipped it into Reichert's pants pocket. Of course Reichert began to dance!

Firor also experienced Dandy's hot temper, as Dandy sometimes would bawl him out unmercifully. Once Dandy bellowed, "You've killed the patient!" To which Firor promptly responded (77), "She's not dead yet!"

Yet, as with Reichert, Dandy was effusive in his praise of Firor. In response to a query in 1926 from Barney Brooks, who was professor of surgery at Vanderbilt University, about his need for a good associate professor of surgery, Dandy answered ". . . that there will be available probably in a year one of the best boys we have ever turned out—Doctor Firor. There is no question that he would make a wonderful associate. He is an indefatigable worker and as keen as anyone I have ever seen. He is a live wire, thoroughly interested and thoroughly loyal" (78). To Firor and other residents of superior ability and steadfast dedication, Dandy gave his lifelong loyalty and unremitting support.

By the early 1920s the automobile had become an important symbol of American life and its mobility. Dandy especially liked big cars, not only for their size and comfort but because they cut down on head and other injuries in the event of accident (79). In the winter of 1923, having sold his air-cooled Franklin, he bought a Wills Sainte Claire, which his friend and immediate predecessor as resident surgeon at Hopkins, Roy D. McClure of the Henry Ford Hospital, Detroit, had told him about. "It (the car manufacturer) was in the hands of the receiver when I bought it, but I could not imagine such a wonderful car going out of business" (80). In later years Dandy owned another Franklin as well as a Packard. It was the trouble that he had with the later Franklin which caused him to write the following blistering letter to the Franklin Automobile Company of Syracuse, New York:

> I think it is only fair to let you know that the Franklin car which I now have has a very gross mechanical defect. The gear frequently shifts from high into neutral when driving. I am advised that it is a defective gear and that such has been found in other cars of the same vintage, and that the only remedy is to replace the gears at a cost around $90.00.
>
> I am prepared to trade in the car for one of the General Motor types, but if you feel inclined to replace the defect I could carry on with a better feeling for the Franklin car. I do not know that I care particularly whether or not you do it, but I thought I could give you the chance. This is my second Franklin car, and, of course, will be the last unless I obtain satisfaction.
>
> The car is a 1930 Model; was purchased through your agent here, Scott, and has been driven three thousand miles, but I will have no dealing whatever with Scott so that there is no use to have him communicate with me in any way. The car now registers 12,000 miles (81).

Two weeks later the service manager of the Franklin Automobile Company responded with an offer of a new transmission for $75.00—Dandy called it "pseudo-generosity"—and a report showing that Dandy's car was bought as a used automobile and had been in service for more than three years. In his rejoinder Dandy noted that he had meanwhile obtained a transmission for considerably less than $75.00, ". . . without your help" (82). He added caustically that it had always been his ". . . impression that when there were gross defects the manufacturers were anxious to make the defects good, but apparently that is not true" (82).

As a motorist Dandy had other problems besides mechanical failures. Shortly after his purchase of the Wills Sainte Claire, he was charged with speeding and was ordered per summons to appear in traffic court, which, as he explained in a note to the judge, would have been difficult for him to do. He readily admitted the accuracy of the charge, which he asked to have sent to the Hospital so that he could forward his check ($5.00) (83). This was not the last traffic ticket he ever received.

Once when a motorcycle policeman started to write out a ticket, Dandy told him (84), "Look here; I'm a brain surgeon. Someday you're going to fall off that motorcycle. What do you think I'm going to do when I get you into the hospital?" The police officer tore up the ticket!

As a driver Dandy did not always exercise patience. In handling the problem of cars parked immediately in front of and behind his, he would not hesitate to bang into them until he was able to get his car out (85). And frequently he would park his car at the hospital in front of a fire hydrant! Perhaps he felt that it was wasting time to look for a place to park; perhaps he was "asserting" himself, for he was not hesitant about using his status at times (86).

1923 was an important year in Dandy's life, not only because of his introduction of the postoperative recovery room and a dye test for studying the flow of cerebrospinal fluid, but because of his meeting the young woman who would later become his wife (their marriage will be discussed in the following chapter) and his European trip for the purpose of visiting some neurosurgical clinics. Halsted's influence and, perhaps, a letter in the summer of 1923 from his friend, Edwards A. Park, a Yale pediatrician who 4 years later became professor of pediatrics at Hopkins, urging him to come to Europe, sparked Dandy's desire to see what was currently being done abroad in the field. Having visited France and Switzerland as well as planning to go to Vienna, Denmark, and England, Park wrote from Berlin: "This glimpse of Pediatric Europe has been one of the best things I ever did. Why don't you, with your wealth and your international reputation (this last is true) come abroad too and follow in the steps of your master. The cultivation of the ideas gained by European travel was one of the greatest of Dr. Halsted's assets and gave him new viewpoints and kept him open minded and able to see some good in an old devil like you" (87). In keeping with this advice and having meanwhile received a grant from the General Education Board, Dandy left for a 4-month sojourn in Europe shortly before Christmas (88).

He thoroughly enjoyed his stay in Vienna, for "the music here is the finest in the world and," as he wrote to his mother and father, "I have been taking it in every night" (89). He was able to do this by avoiding dinner invitations from "many of the foremost men," thus allowing himself ". . . to go to the operas" (89, 90).

In addition to these pleasures, Dandy met "a wonderful group of young men. One particularly [Rudolf Kutill]," he told his parents, "has been very useful in solving a very difficult problem in which I have been working for a long time. He is a clever mechanical genius and has done many new things in thoracic surgery. His instruments I believe will be of great help in doing finer operations on the brain when working through a long tube at great depth" (91). Even though Dandy enjoyed his associations in Vienna, he found the surgery there to be "very poor" (91).

During his stay in Berlin Dandy quickly came to know many of the leading medical men. While there he developed an appreciation for the anesthetic properties of a particular kind of Novocain (solution B of Novocain adrenalin), which upon returning to Baltimore he used in removing "a great many tumors" and found perfectly wonderful (92). He also prized some "wonderful socks," which he had bought with his friend Doctor Klaue whom he later asked to send, along with Novocain tablets, six more pairs (92, 93).

While in Paris, Dandy ordered some surgical instruments, which together with those from Kutill in Vienna, were subsequently detained by the U.S. Customs Bureau in Baltimore until he wrote letters explaining that they were for his own use and would not be resold (94).

Upon his return from Europe in April 1924, Dandy settled back into his busy routine at Hopkins. He had found that his methods were more acceptable in Germany than they were in the United States (95). Moreover, he felt in retrospect that he had not really learned very much about neurological surgery while away (96). This trip, as it turned out, was the only time Dandy ever visited Europe.

END NOTES

1. Mrs. Walter E. Dandy, Baltimore, to the author, letter, June 16, 1977. W.E.D. to Ralph Greene, M.D., Jacksonville, FL, letter, March 22, 1935, Dandy MSS. W. M. Firor, M.D., Baltimore, to the author, letter, Feb 7, 1980. In his letter to Greene, Dandy wrote that he had been laid up a few years before "for a period of fifteen months . . . ." A few years after his confinement in 1919–1920 he told Dr. Firor that he had been laid up for 3 months with a bad knee. There is no indication that he was ill between 1920 and 1935 for as long as 3 or 15 months.
2. Fulton JF: *Harvey Cushing: A Biography.* Springfield, IL, Charles C Thomas, 1946, p 320.
3. Hugo V. Rizzoli, M. D., Washington, DC, interview with the author, Jan 18, 1978.
4. W.E.D., Jekyll Island, Brunswick, GA, to Mr. and Mrs. John Dandy, Baltimore, letter, n.d. [1921], Dandy MSS.
5. W.E.D. to Dr. Frederick L. Reichert, Jekyll Island Club, Brunswick, GA, letter, Jan 18, 1926, Dandy MSS. Some years later, following a misunderstanding, Dandy wrote to Grob as follows: "You helped me when I was down and out, and no matter what you think of me, nothing could ever change my feeling for you. It is all very well for people to like you when you are on top, but when they do something for you at the bottom you can never forget it. Your picture is always in my library so that tells you what I think of you." W.E.D. to E. G. Grob, Bloomfield, NJ, letter, Dec 21, 1934, Dandy MSS.
6. W.E.D., Jekyll Island, Brunswick, GA, to Mr. and Mrs. John Dandy, Baltimore, letter, Feb 26, 1921, Dandy MSS.
7. W.E.D., Jekyll Island Club, Brunswick, GA, to Mr. and Mrs. John Dandy, Baltimore, letter, n.d. [1921], Dandy MSS.
8. Mrs. Walter E. Dandy, Baltimore, interview with the author, Jan 29, 1966.
9. W. S. Halsted, Baltimore, to W.E.D., letter, May 21, 1921, Dandy MSS. W.E.D. to W. S. Halsted, letter, June 2, 1921, Dandy MSS.
10. W. S. Halsted, High Hampton, Cashiers, NC, to W.E.D., letter, Aug 22, 1921, Dandy MSS.
11. W. S. Halsted, High Hampton, Cashiers, NC, to W.E.D., letter, June 25, 1922, Dandy

MSS. Caroline H. Halsted, High Hampton, Cashiers, NC, to W.E.D., letter, May 17, 1922, Dandy MSS.

12. Dandy was elected to honorary membership of The State Medical Society of Wisconsin at the 1922 meeting.

13. W.E.D., Baltimore, to Mrs. William S. Halsted, letter, Nov 11, 1922, Dandy MSS.

14. Abraham Flexner, New York City, to Mrs. Walter E. Dandy, letter, April 22, 1946, Dandy MSS. Turner TB: *Heritage of Excellence: The Johns Hopkins Medical Institutions, 1914–1947.* Baltimore, Johns Hopkins University Press, 1974, p 412.

15. Heuer GJ: Dr. Halsted. *Bull Johns Hopkins Hosp* 90, No. 2, Feb. 1952, Supplement, 105 pp. George J. Heuer, New York City, to W.E.D., letter, Jan 31, 1944, Dandy MSS.

16. W. M. Firor, M.D., Baltimore, to the author, letter, March 15, 1976.

17. Firor WM: Comment about the Surgical Chief at The Johns Hopkins Hospital between 1918 and 1928, unpublished ms, National Library of Medicine, p 1.

18. W.E.D., Baltimore, to J. Chalmers Da Costa, M.D., Professor of Surgery, Jefferson Medical College, Philadelphia, letter, Feb 1, 1921, Dandy MSS. J. Chalmers Da Costa, Philadelphia, to W.E.D., letter, Feb 5, 1921, Dandy MSS. As a token of his affection for Da Costa, Dandy sent him during his final illness a book prop. Meanwhile, in 1932, Dandy was invited to give the third annual Da Costa Foundation Oration of the Philadelphia County Medical Society on the subject "The diagnosis and treatment of tumors of the brain."

19. W.E.D. to Dr. Charles F. Nassau, Philadelphia, letter, May 18, 1933, Dandy MSS.

20. W.E.D. to Dr. Alexis Carrel, New York City, letter, Dec 14, 1922, Dandy MSS.

21. W.E.D. to George W. Crile, M.D., Cleveland, letter, March 6, 1923, Dandy MSS.

22. Franklin H. Martin, Chicago, to W.E.D., letter, Sept 2, 1925, Dandy MSS.

23. Frank Padberg, M.D., Assistant Director, American College of Surgeons, Chicago, to the author, letter, Aug 21, 1975. The late Dr. Harvey B. Stone, a colleague and friend of Dandy's, thought that Dandy was invited to join the ACS, as was he, before the requirement of submitting write-ups of operations was instituted. While this may have been true when Dandy was first asked to become a member, it was obviously not so when Franklin Martin wrote to him in 1925, nor in 1930 when he became a member. Harvey B. Stone, M.D., Baltimore, interview with the author, May 25, 1967.

   Eight years after he had joined the ACS, Dandy vented his feelings about the College's publication, *Surgery, Gynecology and Obstetrics* and the organization itself in a letter to Dr. A. D. Ballou of the publication: "I withdrew my subscription to *Surgery, Gynecology and Obstetrics* because of a personal pique and not because of any lack of merit of the journal. Several years ago I offered the journal what I thought was one of my best publications, and it was turned down with the statement that they did not want any more material of this kind. I realize perfectly well that this was a personal response on the part of the neurological editor, who was no friend of mine, but nevertheless the incident has rankled in my breast since that time and has soured me both on the journal and the American College of Surgeons." W.E.D. to Dr. A. D. Ballou, General Manager, *Surgery, Gynecology and Obstetrics*, Chicago, letter, Sept 22, 1938, Dandy MSS. The "neurological editor" may have been Loyal Davis who was assistant, later associate, editor in the early 1930s.

24. W.E.D. to Dr. A. W. Martin Marino, Brooklyn, NY, letter, Sept 22, 1938, Dandy MSS.

25. W.E.D. to Harvey Cushing, Boston, letter, June 30, 1921, Dandy MSS.

26. Sachs E: *Fifty Years of Neurosurgery: A Story.* New York, Vantage Press, 1958, p 70.

27. Harvey Cushing, Boston, to W.E.D., letter, Dec 15, 1921, Dandy MSS.

28. W.E.D. to Harvey Cushing, Boston, letter, Jan 11, 1922, Dandy MSS.

29. Dandy WE: *Bull Johns Hopkins Hosp* 33:344–345, 1922.

30. Cushing H: *Tumors of the Nervus Acusticus and the Syndrome of the Cerebellopontine Angle.* Philadelphia, WB Saunders, 1917, p 265.

31. Harvey Cushing, Boston, to Winford H. Smith, Baltimore, letter, Sept. 25, 1922, Cushing MSS, Yale Medical Library.

32. W.E.D. to Harvey Cushing, Boston, letter, Sept 29, 1922, Cushing MSS.

33. W.E.D. to Board of Editors, *Bull Johns Hopkins Hosp*, letter, Oct 4, 1922, Cushing MSS.

34. Harvey Cushing, Boston, to W.E.D., letter (unmailed), Sept 13, 1922, Cushng MSS. This letter, it should be noted, was written a little less than 2 weeks before Cushing

drafted the letter to Dr. Winford Smith which he sent to Dandy. About a month after he had received the Smith-Dandy letter from Cushing, Dandy wrote to his former teacher as follows:

My dear Dr. Cushing:

I have received your letter and have thought over it a good deal. I am sorry that you feel so strongly, as you apparently do, and that you consider that my publications are open to criticism and my statements unwarranted. Perhaps the best thing for me to do, under the circumstances, would be to publish so rapidly as I can the information that I have regarding the cerebellopontine tumors and the results that have been obtained in extenso. This I propose to [do] at the earliest possible moment.

W.E.D. to Harvey Cushing, Boston, letter, Oct 20, 1922, Cushing MSS.

35. Fulton JF: *Harvey Cushing: A Biography.* Springfield, IL, Charles C Thomas, 1946, p 490.
36. W.E.D., Baltimore, to Harvey Cushing, Boston, letter, Sept 22, 1924, Cushing MSS.
37. Harvey Cushing, Boston, to W.E.D., letter, Dec 14, 1923, Dandy MSS.
38. W.E.D. to Harvey Cushing, Boston, letter, Dec 7, 1927, Cushing MSS.
39. Harvey Cushing, Boston, to W.E.D., letter, Dec 10, 1927, Cushing MSS.
40. Harvey Cushing to W.E.D., letter, July 30, [1926], Dandy MSS.
41. Harvey B. Stone, M.D., Baltimore, interview with the author, May 25, 1967.
42. Madeline E. Stanton, New Haven, CT, interview with the author at the Yale Medical Library, Aug 17, 1966. Miss Stanton was Cushing's secretary from 1920 until his death in October 1939.
43. W.E.D. to John F. Fulton, New Haven, CT, letter, Nov 26, 1945, Cushing MSS.
44. John F. Fulton, New Haven, CT, to George J. Heuer, letter, Nov 16, 1945, Cushing MSS.
45. Fulton JF: *Harvey Cushing: A Biography.* Springfield, IL, Charles C Thomas, 1946, p 494.
46. Mrs. Carville D. Benson, Arlington, VA, interview by telephone with the author, Nov 25, 1967. Mrs. Benson was Dandy's secretary at the time Cushing was offered the chair of surgery.
    Cushing was not the only neurosurgeon whom Dandy did not particularly like; actually he did not have much use for most of his contemporaries in the field. Mrs. Walter E. Dandy, Baltimore, interview with the author, Dec 21, 1977.
    In the spring of 1939 the editor of *The Johns Hopkins Alumni Magazine* invited Dandy to give "a brief appreciation" of Cushing who had recently celebrated his seventieth birthday. The editor thought it appropriate to have one of Cushing's "lineal academic descendants, so to speak" prepare such a tribute. Dandy did not do so. Norma S. Heaney, Baltimore, to W.E.D., letter, May 2, 1939, Dandy MSS.
47. W.E.D. to Dr. Marvin T. Sudler, Kansas City, KS, letter, July 8, 1924, Dandy MSS.
48. The late Dr. Owen H. Wangensteen, the distinguished University of Minnesota surgeon, made the following interesting assessment of Cushing and Dandy as well as of their quarrel:
    Both Cushing and Dandy made significant contributions to American surgery. Cushing, of course, developed a world-wide school of neurosurgeons. He lived, of course, a decade longer than Dandy, though I believe he retired from the Brigham at age 63. Cushing was, of course, a very imperious person, the flavor of whose personality you can catch in Loyal Davis' *A Surgeon's Odyssey*, published in the late 1960's.
    Cushing was a Great Scholar and a Bibliophile which Dandy was not, but Dandy was, however, in my view the more original of these two great neurosurgeons. As a young professor here (at the University of Minnesota) in the early 30s, I said as much one day to Dr. C. M. Jackson, distinguished professor of anatomy, who expressed great surprise over my statement.
    It was very tragic that these two great figures in surgery could not have composed their difficulties. It was essentially, I presume, a conflict in temperament; only those who were actually on the scene and witnessed the nature of their disagreements could really have understood or fully appreciated how their differences came about. A sense of humor, with less irritation and anger, in my view, was the needed catalyst

in those disagreements.

Owen H. Wangensteen, M.D., Minneapolis, MN, to the author, letter, June 30, 1975.

49. Roland CG: *William Osler's The Master-Word in Medicine: A Study in Rhetoric.* Springfield, IL, Charles C Thomas, 1972, p 31.

50. W.E.D. to Dr. William B. Peck, Freeport, IL, letter, Dec 10, 1926, Dandy MSS.

51. George W. Crile, M.D., Cleveland, to W.E.D., letter, Nov 19, 1926, Dandy MSS.

52. Mrs. Walter E. Dandy, Falmouth, MA, to the author, letter, July 28, 1975. Nearly 10 years after he had left his service, Dr. Frederick L. Reichert wrote to Dandy that he was following ". . . your advice to talk my papers rather than read them. It takes me longer to prepare but I have more fun." Frederick L. Reichert, M.D., San Francisco, to W.E.D., letter, Sept 18, 1932, Dandy MSS.

53. W.E.D. to Dr. R. Eustace Semmes, Memphis, TN, letter, Aug 29, 1931, Dandy MSS.

54. W.E.D. to Dr. Owen H. Wangensteen, Minneapolis, letter, Nov. 24, 1930, Dandy MSS.

55. Turner TB: *Heritage of Excellence: The Johns Hopkins Medical Institutions, 1914–1947.* Baltimore, Johns Hopkins University Press, 1974, p 413.

56. Warfield M. Firor, M.D., Baltimore, telephone interview with the author, June 6, 1980.

57. W.E.D. to Frederick L. Reichert, M.D., Lane Hospital, San Francisco, letter, Feb 23, 1928, Dandy MSS.

58. W.E.D. to John Simon Guggenheim National Foundation, New York City, letter, n.d., Dandy MSS.

59. W.E.D. to Frederick L. Reichert, M.D., San Francisco, letter, June 23, 1933, Dandy MSS.

60. Frederick L. Reichert, M.D., Lancaster, PA, to W.E.D., letter, May 25, 1933, Dandy MSS.

61. Frederick L. Reichert, M.D., San Francisco, to W.E.D., letter, Nov 7, 1933, Dandy MSS. In a postscript to this letter, Reichert stated: "I am proposing your name for a certain prize and must have some of your reprints . . . ." Dandy complied with the request, adding that "I cannot imagine what prize you have in mind, but it is nice of you just the same." Dandy had perhaps deduced what the prize in question was. W.E.D. to Frederick L. Reichert, San Francisco, letter, Nov. 10, 1933, Dandy MSS.

62. Dandy WE, Reichert FL: Studies on experimental hypophysectomy. I. Effect on the maintenance of life. *Bull Johns Hopkins Hosp* 37: 13, 1925.

63. Reichert FL, Dandy WE: Polyuria and polydipsia (diabetes insipidus) and glycosuria resulting from animal experiments on the hypophysis and its environs. *Bull Johns Hopkins Hosp* 58:418, 1936.

64. Reichert FL, Dandy WE: Polyuria and polydipsia (diabetes insipidus) and glycosuria resulting from animal experiments on the hypophysis and its environs. *Bull Johns Hopkins Hosp* 58:423, 1936.

65. Dandy WE, Reichert FL: Studies on experimental hypophysectomy in dogs. III. Somatic, mental and glandular effects. *Bull Johns Hopkins Hosp* 62:122–155, 1938.

66. Dandy WE, Reichert FL: Studies on experimental hypophysectomy in dogs. III. Somatic, mental and glandular effects. *Bull Johns Hopkins Hosp* 62:153, 1938.

67. Dandy WE, Reichert FL: Studies on experimental hypophysectomy in dogs. III. Somatic, mental and glandular effects. *Bull Johns Hopkins Hosp* 62:154–155, 1938.

68. W.E.D. to Dr. Oscar Riddle, Dept. of Genetics, Carnegie Institution of Washington, Washington, DC, letter, Jan 18, 1939, Dandy MSS. Walker AE (ed): *A History of Neurological Surgery.* Baltimore, Williams & Wilkins, 1951, p 154. Chapter VII, Surgery of the Hypophysis, by Herbert C. Johnson, provides a good review of the subject.

69. W.E.D. to Frederick L. Reichert, San Francisco, letter, May 14, 1928, Dandy MSS.

70. Dandy gave Reichert for Christmas, 1936, a copy of *The Life and Convictions of William Sydney Thayer*, which Reichert, having been a student of Thayer's at Hopkins, much appreciated. For that same Christmas Reichert presented Dandy with a fine Paré print. The last Christmas before Dandy died Reichert sent him a gift of pears, which happened to be Dandy's "favorite fruit." Frederick L. Reichert, San Francisco, to W.E.D., letter, Dec 30, 1936; W.E.D. to Frederick L. Reichert, letter, Jan 25, 1937; W.E.D. to Frederick L. Reichert, letter, Dec 17, 1945, Dandy MSS.

71. Rear Admiral Alfred H. Richards, U.S.N. (retired), Berkeley, CA, to the author, letter,

spring (n.d.), 1966.

72. Joseph Addison, *Cato*, Act V, scene 4 (1713).

73. Warfield M. Firor, M.D., Baltimore, interview by telephone with the author, June 6, 1980.

74. Hilberman M: The evolution of intensive care units. *Crit Care Med* 3:159, 1975.

75. Warfield M. Firor, M.D., Baltimore, to the author, letter, March 15, 1976. Harvey AM: *Adventures in Medical Research: A Century of Discovery at Johns Hopkins*. Baltimore, Johns Hopkins University Press, 1974, p 65.

76. Harvey AM: *Adventures in Medical Research: A Century of Discovery at Johns Hopkins*. Baltimore, Johns Hopkins University Press, 1974, p 65. During the same year that Dandy introduced the postoperative recovery room, he was appointed to the Committee on Operation Nomenclature of the American College of Surgeons. There is no indication of the degree of his involvement with the work of this committee. Frederick W. Slobe, M.D., Chairman, Committee on Operation Nomenclature, American College of Surgeons, Chicago, to W.E.D., letter, July 26, 1923, Dandy MSS.

77. Warfield M. Firor, Baltimore, interview with the author, Jan 29, 1966.

78. W.E.D. to Barney Brooks, M.D., Nashville, TN, letter, June 25, 1926, Dandy MSS.

79. Harvey B. Stone, M.D., Baltimore, interview with the author, May 25, 1967; Warde Allan, M.D., Baltimore, interview with the author, Feb 11, 1967. In a comment made to his friend Dr. Ralph Greene in 1933 about the Cord, an early front-wheel drive car, Dandy thought it was ". . . a better car than the Packard [which he then was driving]; it is more solid, sits lower[,] has the protection in front where one needs it most in case of an accident." W.E.D. to Ralph Greene, M.D., Jacksonville, FL, May 17, 1933, Dandy MSS.

80. W.E.D. to Roy D. McClure, M.D., Detroit, letter, March 17, 1923, Dandy MSS.

81. W.E.D. to Franklin Automobile Co., Syracuse, NY, letter, Feb 6, 1934, Dandy MSS.

82. L. R. Hedge, Syracuse, NY, to W.E.D., letter, Feb 21, 1934; W.E.D. to L.R. Hedge, letter, March 29, 1934, Dandy MSS.

83. W.E.D. to Judge Edward M. Staylor, Justice of the Peace of the Traffic Court, Baltimore, letter, April 18, 1923, Dandy MSS.

84. Edwin N. Broyles, M.D., Baltimore, interview with the author, April 7, 1967. Dandy was skeptical about the effect that education of the public would have in reducing traffic accidents. "I still think the solution lies in force and fear rather than education, but that is an old fashioned idea." W.E.D. to Dr. Ralph Greene, Jacksonville, FL, letter, Nov 7, 1932, Dandy MSS.

85. Hugo V. Rizzoli, M.D., Washington, DC, interview with the author, Jan 20, 1978.

86. Mrs. Mary Ellen D. Marmaduke, Baltimore, interview with the author at her mother's home, July 21, 1976. In the course of the interview she made the paradoxically interesting but probably quite accurate observation of her father that "he wanted to be folks and he didn't want to be folks."

87. Dr. Edwards A. Park, Berlin, to W.E.D., summer (n.d.), 1923, Dandy MSS.

88. In view of his feelings towards Cushing, Dandy's advice to a Milwaukee physician regarding a young patient is interesting, though not especially surprising: "In case anything should happen while I am away, of course, consult Dr. Cushing; there is no one else whom you could consider." W.E.D. to Dr. S. H. Wetzler, Milwaukee, letter, Dec 6, 1923, Dandy MSS.

89. W.E.D., Vienna, to Mr. and Mrs. John Dandy, Baltimore, letter, Feb 2, 1924, Dandy MSS.

90. Dandy became interested in the opera during this trip to Europe. As a consequence he was for many years a patron of the Metropolitan Opera Company's Baltimore season and always had season tickets. Dandy also liked to go occasionally to symphony concerts. Mrs. Walter E. Dandy, Baltimore, to the author, letter, June 16, 1977.

91. W.E.D., Vienna, to Mr. and Mrs. John Dandy, Baltimore, letter, Feb 2, 1924, Dandy MSS.

92. W.E.D. to Dr. W. Klaue, Berlin, letter, July 25, 1924, Dandy MSS.

93. W.E.D. to Dr. W. Klaue, Berlin, letter, June 2, 1924, Dandy MSS.

94. W.E.D., Baltimore, to McKenzie Moss, US Treasury Dept, Washington, DC, letters, Jan 26 and May 21, 1925, Dandy MSS.
95. Mrs. Miriam C. Benson, Arlington, VA, interview with the author, Nov 25, 1967. She was Dandy's secretary at the time he returned from Europe.
96. Mrs. Walter E. Dandy, Baltimore, interview with the author, April 13, 1976.

Figure 1. John and Rachel Dandy with son, Walter, 1888.

Figure 2. Dandy's boyhood home, 1323 East 5th Street, Sedalia, Missouri.

Figure 3. John and Rachel Dandy with their son at the time of his graduation from high school. He was valedictorian of the Class of 1903 of Sedalia High School.

Figure 4. The Columns at the University of Missouri.

Figure 5. Dandy, second from right, with other undergraduates at the University of Missouri.

Figure 6.   The young Doctor Dandy.

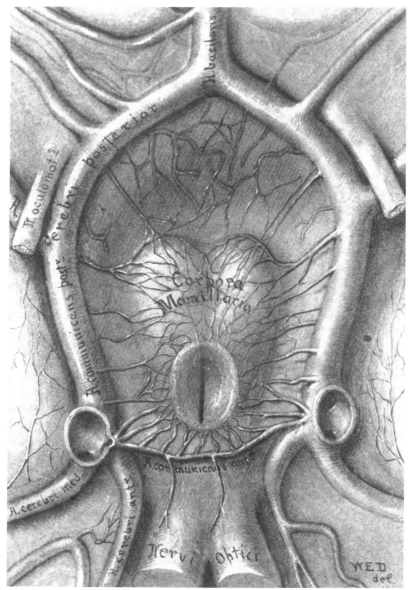

Figure 7. Dr. Dandy's own illustration for his paper on the blood supply of the pituitary body.

Figure 8. The Halsted house staff. Richard H. Follis, seated in the second row between the nurses, became an associate professor of clinical surgery; Dandy with his coat on is in the third row center.

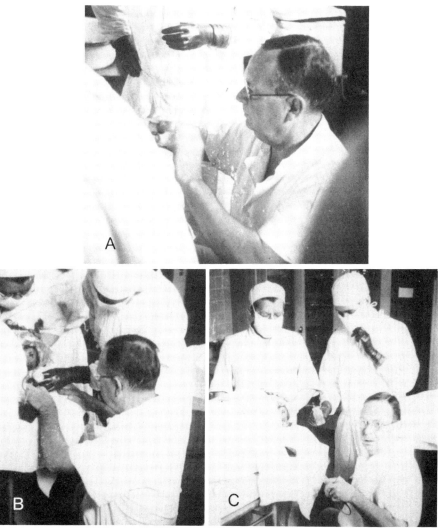

Figure 9. *A* to *C*, Rare scenes of Dandy later in his career performing a ventriculogram.

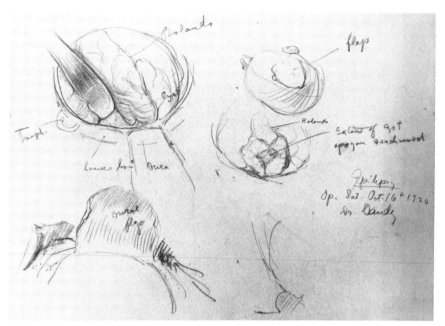

Figure 10. Max Broedel, the renowned Johns Hopkins medical illustrator, did this rough drawing of an epilepsy case of Dr. Dandy's, Saturday, October 16, 1920.

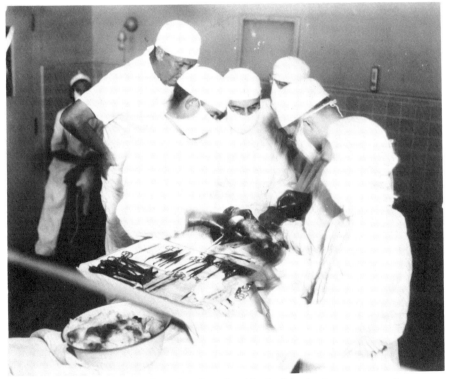

Figure 11. Dandy watching his friend, Alfred Blalock, doing a procedure.

Figure 12. Dandy caught by a candid photographer in a thoughtful moment at Johns Hopkins Hospital.

Figure 13. Dandy and Dr. Frank Ford, the distinguished neurologist, in Dandy's office.

Figure 14. Dandy, at right, with a patient, members of brain team, and nurses.

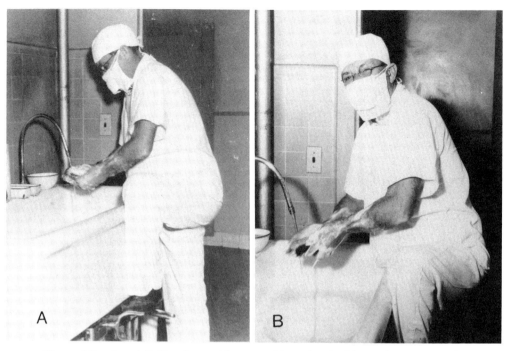

Figure 15. *A* and *B*, Dandy scrubbing up. Note the double mask to prevent his glasses from fogging up.

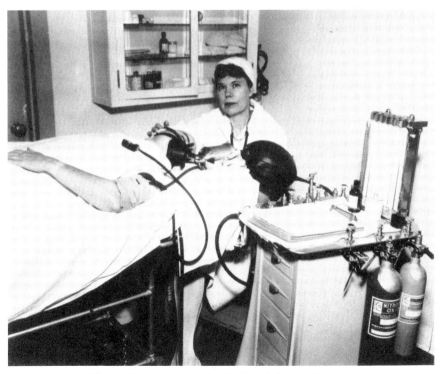

Figure 16. Grace L. Smith, Dandy's anesthetist.

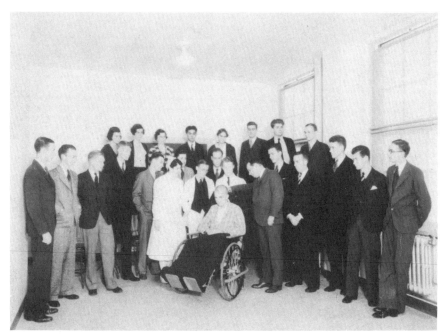

Figure 17. Neurosurgery rounds with the Medical School Class of 1933. Dandy pointing out the incision made on the patient to the group. Henry G. Schwartz is second from the right. Richard C. Tilghman is third from the left; Barnes Woodhall is immediately to the right of the nurse; and Fred Geib is standing between Woodhall and Dandy.

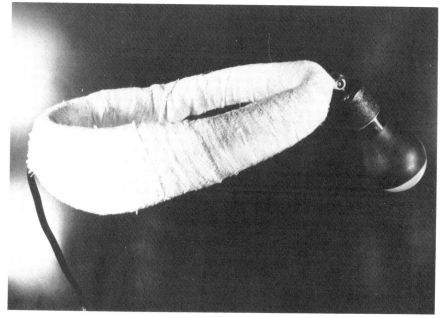

Figure 18. The headlight which Dandy designed and wore while operating.

106

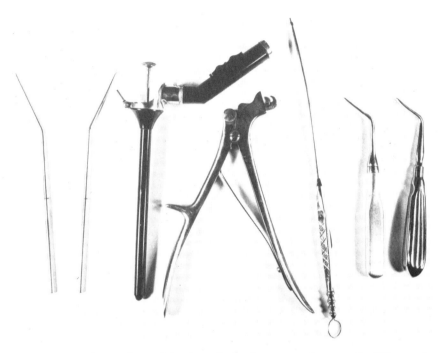

Figure 19. *Left* to *right*: Left hook, right hook, ventriculoscope, DeVilbis sucker and joker. Dandy developed the first, second, third, and fifth instruments.

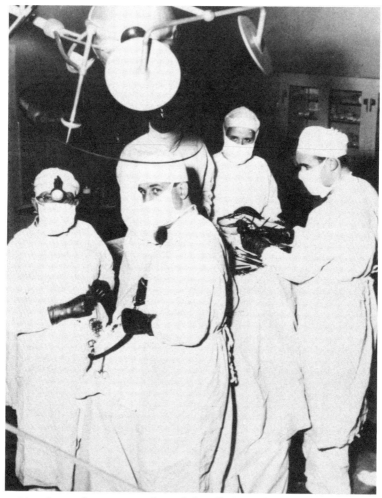

Figure 20. Surgical scene: Dandy with headlight and Fermin J. Barcala opposite him.

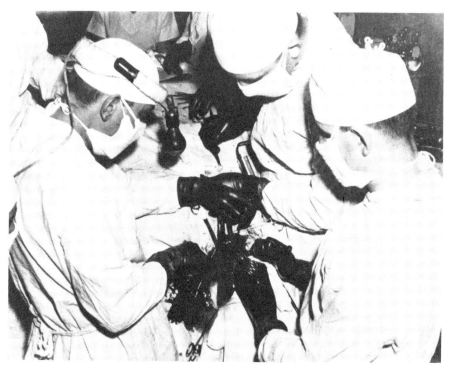

Figure 21. Frank J. Otenasek, who became Dandy's associate, wearing the headlight.

Figure 22. In the library of Halsted Clinic, Johns Hopkins Hospital, standing (*left* to *right*): John Chambers, Charles Burkland, Frank J. Otenasek, Fermin J. Barcala, and Hugo V. Rizzoli; seated (*left* to *right*): Mrs. Bertha Shauck, Miss Grace Smith, anesthetist, Walter E. Dandy, Miss Sarah ("Susie") Lambert, scrub nurse.

Figure 23. In the library of Halsted Clinic, Johns Hopkins Hospital, standing (*left* to *right*): Charles Burklund, John Chambers, Fermin J. Barcala, and Hugo V. Rizzoli; seated (*left* to *right*): Frank J. Otenasek and Walter E. Dandy.

Figure 24.   Profile of Walter E. Dandy.

Figure 25. Dandy, left, and Harvey Cushing at Jekyll Island, Georgia, 1921. This well known picture was taken by Mrs. Harry R. Slack, Jr.

Figure 26. Bookplate designed for Dandy by his illustrator, Dorcas Hager Padget.

114

CHAPTER 7

From Bachelor to Benedict

In the fall of 1923 Dandy was 37 years old. Somewhat short in stature, with stubby hands and small feet (shoe size: 7½E), Dandy, though not a man of commanding appearance, was fine-looking, his deep blue, penetrating eyes, which ". . . had a nice twinkle . . ." (1), being perhaps his most distinctive feature. His voice, according to those who knew him, was rather high pitched, more like "a whine" (2). Sartorially, he wore tailor-made suits "after he was able to afford them, partly because he was hard to fit" (3). While always well dressed, like his model and mentor Dr. Halsted, Dandy, with his figure and habit of stuffing his pockets with papers, had at times a rumpled appearance. As he did not want his mother to have to look after his clothes, he kept some of his suits at Opitz, a tailor and dry cleaner near the Hospital, so that he could conveniently change garments, a practice he continued after he was married (4).

At age 37 he had achieved wide professional recognition. Yet, he still remained a bachelor, not so much by choice as by the absence of the "right" woman becoming known to him. To be sure, he had been attracted to one or two women, including Marian Lewis. One of them, however, had shown no interest. For a certainty Dandy knew that he would never marry a nurse because nurses were such gossips (5)! His friend, Mont R. Reid, who had followed him as a surgical resident at Hopkins and who was then at the Cincinnati General Hospital, joshed him about his single state: "[Emile] Holman reported that you were doing well but he knew nothing of your love affairs. Hope you get married soon. I propose to bring a French girl back with me, but *shall not let you lay eyes on her* [italics Reid's]" (6).

A little over a year after Reid had expressed his hope that his friend would marry soon, he was the best man at Dandy's wedding!

Meanwhile, having taken notice of Sadie Estelle Martin, a young, attractive dietitian at the Hospital, Dandy called her one evening from the old Baltimore Club on Mount Vernon Place, where he frequently had dinner before checking on his hospitalized patients, to invite her to a football game in Annapolis. It was October 1923, the beginning of a romance which a year later led to marriage.

The youngest of three children of Howard W. Martin, a strict Presbyterian who was in the wholesale grocery business, Sadie had grown up in Baltimore, had graduated from Western High School for Girls, where she ranked in about the top 10% of her class, and had gone on to Goucher College, from which she graduated in 1921 with a bachelor of arts degree in nutrition and social science (7). Upon her graduation from Goucher, she spent a year at the University of Iowa, Iowa City, in graduate study and working at the University Hospital. In retrospect she felt that it was a good experience as it helped her later to understand Dr. Dandy as a Midwesterner—his directness and forthrightness (8). Following her return from Iowa, she accepted a position in the Dietary Department of The Johns Hopkins Hospital, where she looked after the diabetic patients in the dispensary (9).

Although their courtship was interrupted by his trip to Europe, they made plans to be married in her family's home, 3804 Sequoia Avenue, on Wednesday, October 1, 1924. This was just a little more than a month before President Calvin Coolidge won a lop-sided victory over John W. Davis and Senator Robert M. La Follette, the Democratic and Progressive candidates, respectively. After the wedding Dandy, who was now 38 years old, and his bride of 23, spent their honeymoon of several weeks at Lake Clear in the Adirondack Mountains of New York, canoeing and hiking (10).

Upon their return to Baltimore, the Dandys moved into Apartment 24 in the Temple Court Apartments behind Union Memorial Hospital, whose garage today stands on the site of those apartments. It was a good location, as it was not very far from The Johns Hopkins Hospital and had, moreover, a garage in the basement. The Dandys lived there just a little over 2 years.

The bride and bridgegroom were quite a compatible couple. Both had been raised in rather strict fashion, one of the factors which she later felt, upon reflection, had drawn them together (11). While he respected his parents' fundamentalist beliefs, he could never accept them. "Both of us," recalled Mrs. Dandy, "were reacting to our strict upbringing and we were a little vague about what we believed but we wanted the church & what it stands for to have a place in our lives and that of our children. We always had 'grace' at meals" (12). But whereas she faithfully attended church, he did so irregularly, often preferring to devote his Sunday mornings to playing golf (13).

While visiting Yellowstone National Park some years later, Dandy briefly summarized his religious feelings in a letter to his father: "I have always wished that you and mother could have seen some of the wonders of this world but I know you thought little of them and considered only the higher things. But such wonders only impress one the more with the greatness of the creator. These things don't just happen or evolve. Some great—overwhelmingly great—mind has created them together with ourselves. We have different ways of expressing our religion but it is fundamentally the same" (14).

Besides their concern about religion, the Dandys shared other interests. During the first year of their marriage they took an art history course together at Goucher College, which they both enjoyed. Dandy realized that he had missed some of the cultural pleasures and refinements associated with Osler and Cushing (15).

There was a ready rapport between the Dandys. Often at dinner he would discuss with her his professional problems, especially those related to hospital personnel. She obviously could be of no help to him on technical matters related to neurological surgery, but she could offer good counsel concerning problems he occasionally had with some of the hospital staff (16). Besides operatic and symphonic performances, the Dandys enjoyed attending once in awhile a football game or watching the old Baltimore Orioles baseball club. Sometimes they would take the train to Washington, D.C., in order to see a major league baseball game involving the Washington Senators.

Long used to his mother's cooking, Dandy wanted his food prepared the way she prepared it, including chicken which his wife found much too salty and meat which he liked sliced thin and fried. Fortunately—at least for him—they later had a cook whose cooking was like that of his mother. Fond of fresh fruits, he would frequently stop at Baltimore's North Avenue Market on his way home from the hospital for the purpose of buying what was in season. His young wife was delighted, as it saved her from having to do so (17).

Exactly a year from the day of their marriage—October 1, 1925—a son, the first of the Dandy's four children, was born. Named for his father, he was as a little boy, a "handful" according to his mother. But Walter Jr.'s mischievous behavior often brought from his father the understanding response, "Oh, he's just a boy." The young mother appreciated this assurance, as she had not played or associated with boys after she was 8 years old (18). When Walter Jr. was 16 months old, Dandy humorously referred to his son's progress in a note to his old friend Ernest Grob: "Our little protegé is developing rapidly. His disposition has really changed for the better. I believe the christening must have had the needed effect" (19).

Dandy's strong love for children was reflected in his correspondence with family and friends. When Walter Jr. was a little more than 2 years old, Dandy wrote to Fred Reichert that his namesake ". . . is scampering all around the house and keeps his mother constantly on edge. He is just beginning to talk. It is a lot of fun watching his little mind develop" (20).

Family relations were for Dandy ". . . the finest thing in life" (21). Yet, he also believed that ". . . those who cannot get along together are better apart . . ." (22). Writing to his mother and father some months before the birth of Walter Jr., he expressed with great feeling what he regarded as his good fortune:

Dearest Mother and Father:

It's such a wonderful thing—the most wonderful of this world's possessions to know that wherever you may be there is someone always thinking about you and of some way to help you. That has always been my fortune, far more than falls to the lot of most people. And somehow I seem to realize and appreciate it more with each passing year. How much you have both done for me and how much you have sacrificed to do it and never once looked at the sacrifices but always as a farther and higher goal. Long ago I realized that greatness was not frills and superficialities but the real true blue of unselfish devotion.

How fortunate I have also been in selecting my little girl. Few men have so much to be thankful for. She has been so sweet and unselfish and so eager to help. She seems so forgetful of herself. In so many ways she makes me always reminiscent of my other little girl—who happens to be father's too (23).

Dandy's devotion to his parents and his concern for their welfare was reflected in visiting them every Sunday afternoon and often once during the week (24). He made these regular visits to their home on Arunah Avenue through the remainder of their lives.

With one child and the prospect of others to follow, the Dandys felt that they must give up their quarters at the Temple Court Apartments for a home of their own. Despite the gift of $50,000 to his mother prior to their marriage, which amounted to a substantial depletion of the newlyweds' capital (25), they made plans to build a home according to their specifications. They chose the Guilford section of Baltimore—3904 Juniper Road—as "it was a very convenient place to live and," as Mrs. Dandy later recalled, "among our neighbors were many doctors who worked at J.H.H. & Union Memorial [Hospital]" (25). A large, comfortable home of colonial brick design, it became the only house the Dandys ever owned. In December 1926 they moved into it when Walter Jr. was 15 months old. The Dandys loved this house. There he could relax after long hours in the operating room, often lying "in a horizontal position" (26).

Although he had bought a fine desk for his study in the new home, Dandy seldom used it. Rather, he would set up quite unpretentiously a card table in the living room whenever he wished to work on a paper (27).

Shortly after moving into the new home, Dandy developed a middle ear infection—"a child's disease," as he called it—which incapacitated him for more than a month and which left him somewhat deaf (28). And about 2 years later he was disabled by a carbuncle for 4 days (29). These were the only illnesses he experienced during this period of his life.

With his recovery from the ear infection the Dandys were able to welcome in April 1927 as their first house guest Mont Reid, the best man at their wedding. A week before his arrival from Cincinnati, Reid had written to his old friend and former Hopkins colleague:

Please tell Sadie to clean the cob webbs [sic] out of that spare room and to lay in a good stock of sauerkraut, for I am coming to Baltimore next week.

I am coming to attend the meeting of the Society of Clinical Surgeons, April 22nd and 23rd. I will sit on the back seat and cheer like hell when you operate, and will afterwards become your bitterest enemy in a golf game, if we get a chance.

Am looking forward with great pleasure to seeing you. My love to both of you—most of it to Sadie (30).

Three months after Reid's visit—on July 22—the Dandys again became parents with the birth of Mary Ellen. With a large home, a small boy, and now a new baby, Mrs. Dandy needed help. Helen Davis (after her marriage 2 years later, Dorsey), a young Negro woman who loved children, answered the young mother's needs. In time, she came to be called by the children, first, "Haha," later amended to "Aha," as they could not correctly pronounce her name

(31). Over 50 years in Mrs. Dandy's employment, she has been "Aha" to all four of the Dandy children ever since.

Thirteen months after Mary Ellen's birth—on August 29, 1928—Kathleen Louise ("Kitty") arrived. And a third daughter, Margaret Martin, the "baby" of the family, was born nearly 6½ years later on January 21, 1935. In a later chapter the children's development and Dandy's role as a parent will be discussed.

Meanwhile, about 6 weeks before Kitty was born, Dandy, while on a train trip to El Paso, Texas, jokingly asked in a letter to his wife: "Who watched over Mary Ellen in the tub to prevent her demise at the hands of a villain [Walter Jr.]?" In a more serious vein he indicated that he had been writing on tic douloureux and that while he had gone to bed at 8 o'clock the previous night his ". . . mind kept whirling about a new instrument and was still going along that line when we reached Pittsburgh at midnight" (32). This passage revealed both his love for writing on trains and the great power of concentration he could give to a particular problem.

During these early years of his marriage Dandy served as a consultant in brain surgery and neuropsychiatry to the United States Veterans Bureau in Washington, D.C. In December 1924, he learned that the Bureau was establishing at the Monte Alto Hospital in Washington a clinic for veterans who were patients. He was ". . . most eager to be of any help . . . ." There was ". . . no project which I should consider more so than assisting in any way I can the Veterans, if I could be assured of considerable latitude in my arrangements of days to visit the Hospital, so that it would not conflict too greatly with plans here [at Hopkins]" (33). Dandy came to have, however, a low opinion of the Veterans Bureau. "I know of no place," he opined to his friend Ralph Green, "where people who are more deserving get poorer treatment than at the Veterans Bureau. It is a disgraceful state of affairs" (34). Only a few months before, Colonel Charles R. Forbes, the former chief of the Veterans Bureau, it may be recalled, was found guilty of charges of bribery, fraud, and conspiracy and was sentenced to 2 years in a federal penitentiary and a fine of $10,000.

On personal grounds Dandy also had reason to complain about the Bureau's considerable delay in payment for services he rendered to five veterans in the respective amounts of $850.00, $550.00, $550.00, $550.00, and $500.00 (35). Delays in the payment of bills owed to him, other than for reasons of genuine hardship, were always a source of annoyance to Dandy, whether they stemmed from bureaucratic red tape or from indifference or chicanery of a patient or his family.

Dandy's marriage in 1924 in no way interfered with his clinical work, research, or publication of papers. In the December issue of *Surgery, Gynecology and Obstetrics* for that year he published an important paper, "The Treatment of Staphylococcus and Strepto-coccus Meningitis by Continuous Drainage of the Cisterna Magna," and in the following year published no fewer than seven papers (36)! Noting that "the treatment of meningitis as a distinct clinical entity probably begins with the great Victor Horsley in 1890," Dandy, in his introduction of the 1924 paper, pointed out:

There is a very general impression that all forms of septic meningitis are almost universally fatal. If this were true, the reported cures, even though scattered, might be considered the result of the procedure advanced. But, although the mortality is extremely high, spontaneous cures do occur, a fact which makes it open to doubt whether many recoveries—including my own—have really not occurred in spite of, rather than because, treatment. Indeed, some forms of therapy are so vigorous and many so devoid of surgical and physiological reasoning, that one is forced to the conviction that actual damage has been added to very sensitive tissues which need all their strength to combat the infection (37).

He in turn discussed the types of treatment of meningitis (inflammation of the meninges, the membranes that envelop the brain and spinal cord) arising from staphylococcal or streptococcal infection that had been tried. No method had been shown to have any particular advantage over nature (38). The method he developed called for opening the cisterna magna, which is a space situated between the cerebellum and the medulla oblongata, and then suturing the funnel end of a drainage tube to the dura mater. Dandy thus found that continuous drainage through the tube for several days was "remarkably effective" (39). But he emphasized the meningitis could not be cured by drainage alone. "In the final analysis," he cautioned, "the body must be able to combat the infection, and if this is impossible, drainage will be unavailing. Drainage can only help nature fight this battle by removing the intracranial pressure and by eliminating much of the infection. It is, therefore, not to be expected that any method is going to do more than reduce the high mortality rate which exists at the present time" (40).

Of the four cases of suboccipital drainage which he reported in this paper, three survived, an impressive record. Dandy warned, however, that this method should not be used in other forms of meningitis because, although not verified, ". . . the character of the inflammatory [fibrinous or thick] exudate would probably make drainage impossible" (40).

A few months before Dandy's wedding, Dr. Evarts A. Graham of the Department of Surgery, Washington University School of Medicine, who was editing a volume on surgical diagnosis, invited Hopkins' neurosurgeon to prepare the section on diagnosis of various surgical lesions of the skull, brain, and its membranes. Dandy responded that he was interested in doing so but that his schedule precluded writing up the section then. He wondered if he could have 3 months longer. Three years later Dandy wrote to Graham, expressing regret for the delay and asking him to indicate how many pages he wanted (41)!

Dandy was not by nature a procrastinator. Rather, as sometimes happens with very busy people, he occasionally made a commitment that he really could not at the moment discharge. Ultimately he sent to Graham a manuscript, which may not have been the only one to have arrived late. Graham had hoped to have published the work on surgical diagnosis in 1925; instead, it did not come off the press until 1930 (42).

Meanwhile, during this 5-year period Dandy published more than 2 dozen papers on a variety of neurosurgical topics, including glossopharyngeal neuralgia, trigeminal neuralgia (tic douloureux), Ménière's disease, and protrusion of intervertebral disks. It is no wonder that there that there was a lengthy delay in submitting the manuscript to Evarts Graham.

END NOTES

1. Kathleen Louise D. Gladstone, Wellesley Hills, MA, to the author, letter, March 31, 1976. With age, Dandy became somewhat paunchy. He had trouble with this right ankle turning, a condition which he said "the orthopedic surgeons here call ' . . . the reverse Thomas heel,'" and which he thought could be corrected in his golf shoes by building up "the upper side of the right heal." W.E.D. to Frank Brothers Footwear, Inc., New York City, letter, June 30, 1938, Dandy MSS.
2. Raymond E. Lenhard, M.D., and C. William Schneidereith, Sr., Baltimore, interview with the author, Nov 8, 1975.
3. Mrs. Walter E. Dandy, Baltimore, to the author, letter, June 12, 1975.
4. Mrs. Walter E. Dandy, Baltimore, inteview with the author, April 6, 1978.
5. Mrs. Harriet Rossiter Lewis, Naugatuck, CT, to W.E.D., letter, Nov 12, 1925, Dandy MSS. Mrs. Walter E. Dandy, Baltimore, interview with the author, Oct 13, 1975.
6. Mont R. Reid, M.D., Cincinnati, to W.E.D., letter, July 7, 1923, Dandy MSS.

7. Mrs. Walter E. Dandy, Baltimore, interviews with the author, May 25, 1967, Oct. 13, 1975, and April 13, 1976. The Martins had a son, who later became a research engineer with the American Telephone and Telegraph Co., as well as two daughters. At Goucher College the future Mrs. Dandy was a member of the Delta Gamma sorority.
8. Mrs. Walter E. Dandy, Baltimore, interview with the author, April 6, 1978.
9. Mrs. Walter E. Dandy, Baltimore, interview with the author, Oct 13, 1975.
10. Mrs. Walter E. Dandy, Baltimore, to the author, letter, June 16, 1977.
11. Mrs. Walter E. Dandy, Baltimore, interview with the author, Oct 13, 1975.
12. Mrs. Walter E. Dandy, Baltimore, to the author, letter, June 12, 1975.
13. Dandy never joined the Brown Memorial Presbyterian Church, Baltimore, where Mrs. Dandy has been a member for many years.
14. W.E.D., Yellowstone National Park, Wyoming, to Mr. and Mrs. John Dandy, Baltimore. (He included his mother as " . . . she was always eager to hear from her boy when he was making his frequent trips," even though she was no longer living.), letter, July 24, 1937, Dandy MSS.
15. Mrs. Walter E. Dandy, Baltimore, interview with the author, April 6, 1978.
16. Mrs. Walter E. Dandy, Baltimore, interview with the author, Oct 13, 1975. Mrs. Dandy never watched him perform a craniotomy, as she thought it might be too much for her. On one occasion, however, she did see him do an air injection for a ventriculogram.
17. Mrs. Walter E. Dandy, Baltimore, interview with the author, June 3, 1975.
18. Mrs. Walter E. Dandy, Baltimore, interview with the author, Oct 13, 1975.
19. W.E.D. to Ernest G. Grob, Brunswick, GA, letter, Jan 18, 1926, Dandy MSS.
20. W.E.D. to Dr. Frederick L. Reichert, San Francisco, letter, Feb 9, 1927, Dandy MSS.
21. W.E.D. to Dr. James M. Mason, Birmingham, AL, letter, Nov 7, 1938, Dandy MSS.
22. W.E.D. to Mr. DeForrest W. Golden, Altoona, PA, letter, June 1, 1934, Dandy MSS.
23. W.E.D. to Mr. and Mrs. John Dandy, letter, May 13, 1925, Dandy MSS. "Little Girl" was Dandy's term of endearment for his wife.
24. Mrs. Helen D. Dorsey, Baltimore, interview with the author, July 30, 1965.
25. Mrs. Walter E. Dandy, Baltimore, interview with the author, April 6, 1978.
26. Mrs. Mary Ellen D. Marmaduke at the home of her mother, Mrs. Walter E. Dandy, Baltimore, interview with the author, July 21, 1976.
27. Mrs. Walter E. Dandy, Baltimore, interview with the author, June 10, 1976.
28. W.E.D. to Dr. Ralph Greene, Jacksonville, FL, letter, Feb 17, 1927, Dandy MSS.
29. F. T. Weaver, G. C. Swope & Co., Inc., Baltimore, to Dr. J. W. Pierson, Baltimore, letter, Dec 4, 1928, Dandy MSS.
30. Mont R. Reid, M. D., Cincinnati, to W.E.D., letter, April 13, 1927, Dandy MSS.
31. Mrs. Helen D. Dorsey, Baltimore, interview with the author, Sept 12, 1977.
32. W.E.D., Pennsylvania R.R., "Spirit of St. Louis," approaching St. Louis, to Mrs. Walter E. Dandy, Baltimore, letter, July 18, 1928, Dandy MSS.
33. W.E.D. to Lewellys Barker, M.D., Baltimore, letter, Dec 22, 1924, Dandy MSS.
34. W.E.D. to Dr. Ralph Greene, Jacksonville, FL, letter, June 8, 1925, Dandy MSS.
35. W.E.D. to Dr. Henry A. Smith, U.S. Veterans Bureau, Fort McHenry, Baltimore, letter, July 15, 1925, Dandy MSS.
36. See bibliography: *The Complete Writings of Walter E. Dandy.*.
37. Dandy WE: The treatment of *Staphylococcus* and *Streptococcus* meningitis by continuous drainage of the cisterna magna. *Surg Gynecol Obstet* 39:760–762, 1924.
38. Dandy WE: The treatment of *Staphylococcus* and *Streptococcus* meningitis by continuous drainage of the cisterna magna. *Surg Gynecol Obstet* 39:761–762, 1924.
39. Dandy WE: The treatment of *Staphylococcus* and *Streptococcus* meningitis by continuous drainage of the cisterna magna. *Surg Gynecol Obstet* 39:769, 1924.
40. Dandy WE: The treatment of *Staphylococcus* and *Streptococcus* meningitis by continuous drainage of the cisterna magna. *Surg Gynecol Obstet* 39:773, 1924.
41. Dr. Evarts A. Graham, St. Louis, to W.E.D., letter, June 23, 1924; W.E.D. to Evarts A. Graham, St. Louis, letter, July 8, 1924; W.E.D. to Evarts A. Graham, St. Louis, letter, June 14, 1927, Dandy MSS.
42. Dandy WE: Skull, brain and its membranes. In Graham EA (ed): *Surgical Diagnosis: By American Authors*, vol 3. Philadelphia, WB Saunders, 1930, pp 846–898.

CHAPTER 8

In Full Stride

Among Dandy's medical friends there was none for whom he had a greater professional regard and affection than Ralph Nelson Greene (1883–1941) of Jacksonville, FL. Toward the end of his life Dandy referred to Greene, who had meanwhile died, as " . . . one of my best friends and one of the most talented neurologists in the United States" (1). Sometime before 1925 they had met and were on the way to becoming close friends. To the surprise of both Dandy's widow and this writer, a large correspondence between the two men turned up in the Dandy Papers. Not only did they write to each other frequently about professional matters, especially cases which Green had referred to Dandy, but about their families, sports, trips together, and politics. In one reference to the last mentioned, Dandy drolly suggested to his friend: "Why don't you send your dumb politicians to Baltimore for a brain operation? That usually cures them" (2).

Between 1923 and 1926 Greene, a former State Health Officer of Florida (1919 to 1921), served as the director of St. Luke's Hospital in Jacksonville, after which he returned to the full-time practice of neurology. Not only was he an able neurologist—Dandy once referred to his having "a brilliant piece of diagnostic acumen" (3)—he was also a licensed pilot who enjoyed flying his own airplane, somewhat to the concern of his Baltimore friend: "I hope these numerous airplane accidents will have some influence in toning your enthusiasm down a little and restricting your travel to the train" (4).

A lighter side of the friendship between the two men was reflected in the enjoyment they derived from kidding each other from time to time, such as when Greene sent Dandy a clipping from *The Pathfinder* which quoted the latter about a method he had allegedly developed for reducing hypertension:

The 'disease of the business man,' says Dr. M. E. [*sic*] Dandy of Johns Hopkins university [*sic*], can be cured by an operation. This disease is caused by over-work, tension and loss of sleep, which results in high blood pressure. The opera-tion consists of removing certain glands at the base of the brain and nerves adjoining arteries. Experiments, he says, proved that such an operation is largely successful (5).

Greene (6), in a covering note to Dandy, indicated that " . . . the enclosed clipping would seem to indicate that you have not given your country doctor friends all the fine points yet. Does the oper-ation hurt and do you offer discounts to doctors? How many feet below the base are the glands to be found?" Such banter was common between the two friends.

During the early months of 1926, Dandy and Greene had an interesting exchange of correspondence about a recently published book entitled *Headache: Its Causes and Treatment* by Dr. Thomas F. Reilly (7). Dandy was angry that this book, some of the contents of which read like folk medicine, had ever been published. His remarks to Greene clearly showed how incensed he was: "I have looked over Reilly's book on headache. I think your remarks were most modest. It is really criminal to perpetrate such a thing on unsuspecting doctors" (8). Dandy found not only the English "atro-cious," but also the author was " . . . writing about something of which he knows only a smattering; also that he is trying to pad up to the stature of the book. Not only are the most simple features of brain tumor entirely unknown to him, but the jumble of words and sentences—so often one sentence follows another and completely contradicts it and so often the reader is left in entire uncertainty as to the meaning which the writer wishes to convey because he is not clear in his own mind" (9).

Later that year Dandy urged Greene to come up for the Demp-sey-Tunney fight and to bring along a patient for an excuse. He added that he had no desire to see it, as he had seen "real fights" and "second-rate fights" had no appeal for him. "Tunney," he declared, "will be knocked out about the fifth round" (10). Tunney, it may be recalled, won that fight and the rematch with Jack Dempsey a year later.

In the spring of 1927 Dandy became a member of the prestigious American Neurological Association which, as he told Greene sev-eral years later, he was " . . . held out of . . . for fifteen years and, finally, I was not enough interested in it to make an application or to state my publications" (11). Yet, he wanted his friend to become a member of this "organization of standing," which in his judgment "presumably, though not actually, contains the elite" (12). With Beverly R. Tucker of Richmond, Virginia, Dandy proposed Greene for membership, even though it would put Greene, he believed " . . . in the hands of the Philistines . . . " for he was "not persona grata among the members, particularly those who dominate the society . . . " (13).

Dandy was quite annoyed to learn that Greene had been requested to prepare a thesis as a requirement of membership. Was Greene being singled out, he wondered, or was this a new, general requirement of admission? "If the latter I can make no objection, but if the former I should take it as an indignity. To me it sounds like high school methods" (14). Dandy subsequently told Greene that he would not himself write a thesis and that he was about to tender his resignation from the society because, he wrote, "I have had nothing but insults from them and I get nothing in return" (15).

Meanwhile, after his section in Lewis's *Practice of Surgery*, volume XII, was published (1932) (16), Dandy sent Greene an inscribed copy, which the latter very much appreciated, along with "the kind things" Dandy had written (17). In turn, Greene presented his Baltimore friend with a lovely pipe and tobacco as Dandy was a confirmed smoker, not only of pipes but cigars and cigarettes as well.

Their professional interests, aside from the cases which Greene had referred to his surgeon-friend, covered a variety of topics, one of which was the incidence of multiple sclerosis which Dandy noted in 1934. "Sometime I wish you would tell me," he wrote, "why multiple sclerosis was one of the uncommon conditions occurring among a series of spinal cord tumors; now a tumor is uncommon and a large series of cases of multiple sclerosis [appear]." Greene replied that he thought the reason why they were then seeing more cases of m.s. than earlier was because " . . . the whole human race has been infected and ill with that diagnostic condition which we have been prone to call 'Flu.' This is an infection that the human family battled against ever since the war. I wonder if this is not the principal factor in the production of so many cases of multiple sclerosis" (18).

Later that year Dandy expressed to Greene his views about the effectiveness of hypnotism and its use in a case involving a man from San Antonio, TX, to whom Greene had recommended an appointment with Dandy. The patient " . . . was paralyzed in both legs from a blow on the head. It is pure hysteria," noted Dandy. "We had him hypnotized and he could move his leg perfectly well. Have you even done hypnotism? I have the impression that the medical profession throws a cloud over it, but it certainly is a splendid diagnostic procedure" (19). This was but one example of Dandy's enthusiasm for a new idea, procedure, or instrument, once he was satisfied with its superiority and effectiveness.

In the meantime, Greene, who was involved with the case of Giuseppe Zangara, the would-be assassin of President-elect Franklin D. Roosevelt at Miami, FL, February 15, 1933 (20), had asked Dandy for his opinion with regard to a forensic medical question confronting the Jacksonville neurologist in a jury trial in which he was professionally involved. Dandy responded with the following interesting comments about the effect that one or more bullets would have upon penetrating the brain:

In regard to your troubles with the ballistic experts, it would be my impression that a man cannot fire two shots. The moment the first shot struck the head he would be unconscious, but I realize that it takes but a very short time for the second bullet to be fired. Certainly he would not do any moving about, nor would he have a convulsion immediately. If the shot went through the motor tracts he might have a tonic rigidity, but I do not think he would have a convulsion.

A chicken runs around the yard because its motor functions are not controlled by the brain; the same thing happens with a dog if we remove his cerebral hemispheres, he can still walk around perfectly well. Of course, that does not hold with the human being, except the Congressman you should have sent up here for an operation—I think his functions are still in the spinal cord.

In your trial I think your jury should know that amnesia is always hysterical or feigned. I know men who have gotten out of much by the latter.

Come up here in a very enlightened community, the eastern shore of Maryland, and work, and you won't need juries (21).

The next summer Dandy drove the family to Maine for a vacation. He left them there to return to Baltimore by train sometime later. Upon his arrival home, Dandy invited Greene to "run up" to see him: "We could keep bachelor quarters and the kiddies [Dandy's favorite term for his children] won't disturb you" (22). Apparently, Greene was unable to accept Dandy's invitation.

Two years later (1936) the Jacksonville neurologist became the medical director of Eastern Air Lines and was thus to establish " . . . the first civil aviation medical laboratory in this country," which was to be located in Coral Gables, FL (23). Within a year after he had become Eastern's medical director, Greene faced a difficult problem involving a pilot with possible epilepsy. He asked

Dandy, who later did an air injection study of the pilot and who backed Greene's handling of the case, for his opinion on how to deal with a convulsive pilot in the air. A most interesting question, Dandy carefully replied:

I have thought so many times about the horrible result that would have occurred had this poor boy had an attack in the air. I do not know that it would do any good but I should think one might insist upon each applicant swearing on the Bible that he has not had a spasm or convulsion or an unconscious attack at any time; this would include the period of infancy and early childhood; so many have attacks then and they pass off only to return in a later period. They are good jobs and a young man is not going to tell about past experiences voluntarily.

If a person were having a convulsion it would be difficult indeed to get him out of the seat, and before this was done I should think the steering wheel would probably be upset. It makes one shiver to think what would happen with such an episode.

Some day there may be a drug that will test the individual's response to a convulsive producing drug. This acts in animals, and I understand there is a drug now that produces attacks without doing harm. It may well be that such a drug would give an index of the person's response, and this would indicate whether or not there is a low susceptibility to such attacks. It is, of course, too soon to predict.

I do not know whether one could hit a man on the head hard enough to stop the attack once it is on, I doubt it very much, but it may be possible (24).

This case, which involved the grounding of the pilot in question, produced strained relations between Greene and the officials of Eastern Air Lines. Dandy, in trying to lift his friend's spirits, paid Greene what was his ultimate compliment of another person: "Above everything else I feel that you are the person that stands without hitching [a figure borrowed from the railroad tycoon James J. Hill, which Dandy was fond of quoting], and I only hope that you feel the same way about me, for you know perfectly well there is no one in the country for whom I have more admiration and for whose judgment I have more respect than yours" (25).

Dandy and Greene also shared an enthusiasm for railroad medicine and surgery. In March 1925 the Pennsylvania Railroad appointed Dandy as a medical examiner (consulting neurological surgeon) at Baltimore at a salary of $25.00 per month and receipt of a company pass which was good for travel "east of Pittsburg, Erie and Buffalo" (26). Years later the pass could be used over the entire Pennsylvania system (27).

Meanwhile, Greene recommended to the chief surgeon of the

Seaboard Air Line Railway the appointment of Dandy as that railroad's consulting neurosurgeon (28). Early in December 1926, Dandy was a guest with his wife (though her way was not paid) at the twenty-third annual meeting of the Association of Seaboard Air Line Railway Surgeons at Havana, Cuba. He thoroughly enjoyed this trip and the opportunity it afforded of being again with his friend Greene.

Several years later the Pennsylvania-Reading Seashore Lines asked Dandy to become a consulting medical examiner for a compensation of an annual pass for his wife and himself and $1.00 per year (29). He delighted in his association with railroad surgeons and spoke from time to time at their meetings. In the fall of 1928 at an assemblage of Pennsylvania Railroad surgeons at Virginia Beach, VA, Dandy spoke on the subject "The Treatment of Injuries to the Head" (30). And at a meeting of the surgeons of the Missouri Pacific Lines some 3 years later he talked about the "Diagnosis and Treatment of Various Lesions of the Cranial Nerves." To the Missouri Pacific's chief surgeon he enthusiastically wrote: "It is always a pleasure to return to my old stamping grounds" (31).

Besides enjoying the association with railroad surgeons and the economies that passes for himself and his family provided (32), Dandy liked the rhythm of train travel and the freedom from the distractions of the telephone and the interruptions at the hospital. He often prepared papers while riding on a train. "Traveling is a great boon to me," he once told his mother and father. "It is real economy from a financial standpoint and better a great opportunity from a construction point of view—also a good rest. Isn't it fortunate I didn't live 100 years ago or even 50 when there was no surgery and no railroads (Pullmans). Without the latter I wouldn't be able to think" (33).

In 1929 when the Pennsylvania Railroad introduced rail air service (a combination of rail and airplane travel over a given route), Dandy was on the maiden trip which he considered "a brilliant stroke" (34). His love of trains and the lore of railroading remained with him throughout his life: "Frankly I think I get more thrill out of seeing a big Pennsylvania locomotive and the railroad that runs perfectly. I have never forgotten the impression the big red engine gave me when it came rolling into the North Philadelphia station" (35). Further proof of his enthusiasm for railroads was evidenced when he arranged for his 11-year-old son and himself to ride in an electric locomotive one summer morning from Baltimore to New York (36). Moreover, in a drawer of his office desk he kept a variety of train schedules which he would readily produce to help a patient and his family arrange their transportation. Having grown up in a railroad town the son of a locomotive engineer Dandy, one might say, came by naturally his devotion to railroading.

An important concomitant of Dandy's work in neurological surgery following his introduction of ventriculography was his constant interest in the improvement of instruments and supportive equipment. "As the brain and spinal cord are encased in bone it was natural that instruments should be devised for peering inside the cavities. For direct vision of the ventricular system, Dandy in 1922 devised a ventriculoscope which he also used for removal or cauterization of the choroid plexus" (37). After experimenting for some time, he adapted Dr. Howard A. Kelly's cystoscope (an instrument for the diagnosis and treatment of the urinary bladder, ureter, and kidney) "with the reflected light" which was considerably better than anything else he had tried in ventriculoscopy (38).

In 1924 Dandy's attention was drawn to the radio knife as it had a dual purpose of cautery and surgical dissection. Dr. Nelson H. Lowry of Chicago wrote in response to a letter of inquiry Dandy had written to the Acme International X-Ray Company, manufacturer of the knife: "It separates tissue rapidly like a knife and it seals tissue very much as a cautery. The microscopical sections, however, show no carbonization or vascular changes such as thrombosis and embolism" (39). Dandy, after experimenting with the radio knife and inquiring of others like Howard Kelly (40), ultimately concluded that it was "a wonderful aid in brain surgery, but only as a hemostatic agent. I see no advantage over the knife when all the vessels on the surface of the brain are thrombosed" (41).

By the summer of 1925 Dandy had become quite interested in the potential application of quartz light for illumination, cauterization of blood vessels on the surface of the brain, and a possible measured heat which could be applied to animals' brains, for example, in the study of sunstroke. He had visited the West Lynn plant of the General Electric Company "and was amazed at the wonderful possibilities which . . . it holds in surgery . . . " particularly for cautery. He wondered if G.E. could be induced to make this quartz cautery and light available to surgery (42). The following year Cushing's attention " . . . was drawn to the possibilities of using high-frequency currents to assist with the more vascular tumors and in July he consulted the physicist attached to the Harvard Cancer Commission, Dr. W.T. Bovie, who had developed two separate high-frequency circuits to aid in removing cancerous growths, one designed to cut tissue without bleeding, and the other to coagulate, for example, a vein that had to be severed or a vessel already open and bleeding" (43). While Cushing was quite pleased with the results from electrosurgery in the removal of brain tumors, Dandy, as indicated above, saw no advantage in its use over the knife (44).

Another problem, pertaining to equipment, which Dandy called upon General Electric's Nela Park Lamp Development Laboratory, Cleveland, Ohio, to help him resolve, concerned an improved headlight which he wore during surgery. The problem, which extended over a period of several years, involved not only the best light (wattage) but also the need to blacken a part of the bulb to avoid diffusion of the light. To Dandy's satisfaction the problem by the fall of 1932 had been met, as the headlight got very close to the wound and yet was completely out of the way. In expressing his gratitude, he noted: "It is such a pleasure to work with the new lights and, of course, it means more lives are saved in this difficult branch of surgery" (45).

Besides resolving the problem of the headlight, Dandy, who in time wore glasses during surgery, found a solution to their slipping and fogging up while operating after he had been "fiddling with masks for a long time" (46). It was to wear two masks, a larger one over the mouth and a smaller one over the nose which was " . . . left rather loose at the botton"; he thus overcame the twin difficulties associated with wearing glasses while operating (47).

New and improved instruments were of course a primary concern of Dandy's. In 1927 he asked the Bard-Parker Company of New York if it could manufacture " . . . a special type of knife with a long slender handle and a tiny blade at the end for cutting nerves in deep places in the brain." He added that the blades would have to be changeable just as those of regular surgical knives. The president replied that the company would be glad to work with him in meeting this need (48).

Five years later Dandy approached another American firm, Uneeda Blades Company, about the possibility of making " . . . a Gigli saw for use of brain surgeons in opening the skull. This is a long thin, round toothed saw which cuts through the skull by pulling back and forth. There is not a decent saw of this type made in this country or abroad, and, I am sure, solely because good steel is not used." While Dandy realized that the profits from the manufacture of this saw would not be large, as compared with those from razor blades, he believed that the company could earn enough to justify this endeavor; moreover, he added, " . . . it would be a great boon to surgery" (49). Apparently the Uneeda Blades Company was not interested. Meanwhile, Dandy had the Pennsylvania Railroad Research Department working on this problem, which a Swedish instrument manufacturer, the well-known Stille Forsaljnings A/B of Stockholm, finally met. Dandy regarded the products of this firm as far superior to those of others: "If I had my way there would not be an instrument used in the operating room except Stille made" (50).

In August 1925, nearly 3 years after Halsted's death, Dr. Dean DeWitt Lewis (1874–1941) of Chicago became chief of surgery at The Johns Hopkins Hospital and professor of surgery in the Hopkins School of Medicine, having meanwhile declined similar offers at the University of Chicago, Harvard, Yale, and Wisconsin. For the next 14 years he was associated with Hopkins until his retirement in 1939. An enthusiastic teacher whose attention was directed more to his teaching than to research and a colorful personality, he had devised an impressive method of nerve anastomosis by which two ends of a nerve were joined with a "cable" transplant (51). "His vitality, exceptional memory, clinical judgment and charm," as Firor recalled, "carried him a long way" (52). Dandy and Lewis got along so well together that Dandy was able to say of the chief of surgery 10 years later: "He is really a great Professor of Surgery, and his tower of strength, with his common horse sense, has appeared when every one is going off on a tangent. I should say he is the greatest stabilizer and the strongest man on the medical faculty" (53).

Shortly after Lewis's arrival at Hopkins an elective course in neurological surgery for 4th-year students was introduced, "but it was not until 1931 that Dandy's title was changed from professor of general surgery to clinical professor of neurosurgery . . . " (54). Yet, neurological surgery never became a formal division of the Department of Surgery, as was respectively true of gynecology, laryngology-otology, orthopedics, and urology, until 1947, a year after Dandy's death. It is worth recalling, as Turner has observed, that "in the 1920s neurosurgery was a new specialty with a few full members of the guild; fifty years later, partly as a result of catastrophies engendered by the motor car and two world wars, there is a neurosurgeon in almost every medical center" (55), if not a division or department of neurological surgery. Dandy was never handicapped in his direction of the brain team, as his service became known, by the lack of a formal division.

An instance of the rapport between Dandy and Lewis was shown shortly after the new chief of surgery arrived at Hopkins when they jointly worked on studies of taste (56). They found, contrary to earlier theory, " . . . the sensory part of the seventh nerve is the nerve of taste to the anterior two-thirds of the tongue" (57). Their findings resulted from the " . . . intracranial division of the isolated cranial nerves in patients" (58). Thus in contrast to a prevalent theory of a variable nerve supply conducting the sensations of taste, Lewis and Dandy concluded that only one nerve serves as the conductor of this sense from the anterior two-thirds of the tongue (59).

With the arrival of Dean Lewis as the new chief of surgery, the birth of Walter Jr., and his clinical and research advancements, 1925 was indeed a noteworthy year for Dandy. It was also the year that he presided as president of The Johns Hopkins Medical Society which met on the first Monday evening of the month in the medical amphitheater of the Hospital. This was the only instance in which Dandy ever served as an officer of a professional society.

During 1925 he published no less than seven papers, some of which have been referred to earlier, as the research involved a period of his career already discussed. In the February issue of the *Bulletin of The Johns Hopkins Hospital*, he gave a preliminary report of an operative procedure for the treatment of trigeminal neuralgia (tic douloureux) which involves the fifth cranial nerve and is one of the most painful diseases known to man. Surgical relief, prior to Dandy's approach, generally called for sectioning the nerve through the temporal route, slightly in front of and above the ear. Dandy felt that the advantages of his approach through the occipital region (back part of the head) on the side affected were twofold: "(1) the ease of the approach to the sensory root [of the fifth nerve], due largely to the bloodless intracranial course . . . ; (2) the seemingly easier preservation of the motor root" (60). In a definitive paper which he published 4 years later, Dandy advocated the partial rather than complete sectioning of the sensory root because several advantages followed, among them the preservation of the motor root, the retention of sensation, "approaching the normal," over the entire fifth nerve (trigeminus), regardless of the branch wherein the pain was situated, and an operation "much easier and quicker to perform" (61). Dandy's approach in treating trigeminal neuralgia via the cerebellar route was not without its critics. Charles H. Frazier of Philadelphia, with whom Dandy was often at odds, thought that "the temporal route in the hands of the majority of surgeons will be the safer of the two routes, and if it guarantees permanent relief with a hazard of 0.2 percent, this route should be given preference" (62).

For years trigeminal neuralgia had been regarded as idiopathic; but Dandy, a decade and a half after the publication of his first paper on the subject, showed on the basis of 500 cases that there is almost always a cause for it. "In 5 percent the cases, a tumor or aneurysm will be in the cerebellopontine angle pressing upon the fifth nerve and causing this pain. In nearly all of the remaining cases an artery will be found on either the under surface of the outer surface of the sensory root" (63). Today, some 40 years later, according to Hugo V. Rizzoli, chairman of the Department of Neurological Surgery, The George Washington University Medical Center, " . . . Peter Jannetta [of Pittsburgh] and several other neurosurgeons are using Dr. Dandy's approach to an even greater degree at this time because they feel that there is an abnormal vessel compressing the [fifth] nerve" (64).

The other form of tic douloureux, glossopharyngeal neuralgia, affecting the ninth cranial nerve and potentially as painful as trigeminal neuralgia, Dandy first successfully cured early in April 1927 when, as he told his friend Ralph Greene, " . . . we cut the ninth nerve at the medulla and got a beautiful result. The patient's attacks have entirely stopped. To my knowledge this is the first time this procedure has been done" (65). Until this time the surgery involved in the treatment of glossopharyngeal neuralgia, which affects the posterior third of the tongue, pharynx, middle ear, and mastoid air cells, was peripheral in nature and difficult to perform. "The first accurate knowledge of the function of the glossopharyngeal nerve was obtained by Dandy when he divided the nerve intracranially" in the spring of 1927 (66).

Dandy's treatment of glossopharyngeal neuralgia brought him into conflict with Temple Fay, a Philadelphia neurosurgeon, who was told that his Baltimore colleague had stated that Fay "knew little or nothing" about this painful condition. In a fiery note Fay charged Dandy had " . . . made a deliberate attempt to discredit my findings so as to establish your own" (67). Three weeks later Dandy answered Fay's blast with what can best be described as a masterful response:

> I had intended not to answer your letter for I always feel that if one is willing to accept such malicious slander without verification it is needless to try to convince them [sic] and furthermore a friendship so obtained is not really worth the effort. I could not, however, fail to recall the pleasant evening with you on the train and to make the mental reservation that the meeting and the letter seemed so strangely paradoxical. I am therefore, writing you that there is not the slightest basis for the malice which has been so gratuitously offered you. Never have I said a word which in any way could be interpreted as being derogatory to you or to your work. I have only words of praise for your article and for the new trail which you were making an effort to blaze. How you could have drawn such inference of tremendous import from my brief reference to your work is more than I can understand except on the assumption of an obsession which is fanned along by green-eyed monsters, but again I can only say that if you cannot see your mistake I have not the slightest desire to make the effort to correct it (68).

Fay promptly replied that he was glad to know that the statement attributed to Dandy had "no foundation in fact" (69). But Dandy's respect for Fay and his work never improved, even though this misunderstanding was cleared up (70).

There were other neurosurgeons with whom Dandy battled on occasion. Following the 1932 meeting of the American Neurological Association he reported to his friend and first resident, Frederick Reichert, that he had been the object of a concerted attack at that meeting:

> You should have been to the American Neurological meeting. There was a well planned attack by [Charles H.] Frazier, Loyal Davis, [Byron] Stookey and [William G.] Spiller and I got nothing but very hard words from all of them. Frazier feels most bitter, as you might suspect, but I do not think you could ever suspect the actual degree of his feeling; he is quite rabid on the subject, which, of course, is encouraging for its shows that his back is against the wall. I had one of his recurrences recently. The tic was due to an acoustic tumor (71).

It is not surprising that Dandy, who was often in advance of other neurosurgeons, ran into opposition. In addition the well-developed egos of more than a few in the specialty may have contributed to the situation as Dandy described it at the meeting of the American Neurological Association in 1932.

While Dandy was perfecting his procedures for treating trigeminal neuralgia and glossopharyngeal neuralgia, he also had developed an operation for Ménière's disease which he announced in a preliminary report in the *Archives of Surgery* for June 1928 (72). Named for Prosper Ménière (1799–1862), a French otologist who described it in 1861, this disease or, as Dandy preferred to call it, syndrome, which had beset such figures as Martin Luther and Jonathan Swift, has a clearly defined set of symptoms. "The patient," noted Dandy, "is suddenly seized with a violent attack of dizziness, at once associated with nausea, vomiting and unilateral tinnitus referred to an ear which is progressively growing deafer. These attacks are repeated from time to time, usually with increasing frequency. The patients are well between the attacks, though eventually they may recur so frequently as to be almost continuous. At such time . . . the patient for weeks may not be able to take food or to retain it when it is taken. The attacks are of such violence and come on with such suddenness that the patient lives in terror of their reappearance. They last from a few hours to several weeks. The symptoms have been known and described for more than a century, but it was Ménière who first suspected their aural origin. Whether or not his impression proves to be correct, he at least rescued a clinical entity from a hopeless confusion of symptoms which had not implied any pathologic significance" (73).

In making a differential diagnosis of Ménière's disease, Dandy noted that two conditions might be confused with this disease or syndrome, one of these being pseudo-Ménière's disease, in which the attacks are like those of Ménière's disease but with an absence of unilateral deafness and tinnitus (74). Frequently, pseudo-Ménière's disease is but the initial stage of Ménière's disease. "The other condition is a cerebellopontine [acoustic] tumor" (75). While there is also a loss of hearing with this tumor, there are never the terrible attacks of dizziness that are symptomatic of Ménière's disease. In the course of his work with this syndrome, Dandy found that in about 10% of the cases partial deafness occurred in both ears at the outset or later (bilateral Ménière's disease) (76).

The cure which he was the first to devise was the sectioning of the eighth cranial (auditory) nerve. On January 11, 1927, Dandy first performed this operation under local anesthesia. While the attacks ceased, permanent deafness resulted. "After the cure of Ménière's disease had been established, there naturally suggested itself the possibility of a further refinement by which the remaining hearing on the defective side would be preserved" (77). As the disturbing symptoms of the attacks stemmed from the vestibular branch of the auditory nerve, Dandy in 1933 divided, as had K. G.

McKenzie of Toronto the year before, the vestibular branch. "Approximately the anterior ⅝ of the nerve in cross section was divided; the posterior ⅜ of the nerve (the auditory part) was preserved" (78). Thus hearing, or what remained of it prior to surgery, was preserved. By 1945 Dandy had performed no fewer than 682 operations for Ménière's disease with but one death and that was due to meningitis. This was a remarkable record, for there are few procedures in which there are not some fatalities. Following his 700th operation for Ménière's disease, Mrs. Dandy and he celebrated with a dinner party (79).

Almost none of the neurosurgeons today use Dandy's approach for Ménière's disease, " . . . primarily because the ENT [ear-nose-throat] men felt that they had found [the] etiology for Ménière's disease in the inner ear and insist that it is due to hydrops of the semicircular canal" (80). Jannetta, whose work on tic douloureux was mentioned earlier, thinks however that " . . . the etiology is the same as that for tic douloureux and is recommending the exploration of the eighth nerve and the posterior fossa as Dr. Dandy did even though he [Dandy] recommended partial section of the nerve" (80). In Jannetta's view an abnormal vessel is the source of irritation of the eighth cranial nerve. To alleviate this problem, "he dissects the blood vessel free and displaces it from the nerve with a little fragment of plastic which he uses to pull the vessel away from the nerve" (80).

Forty years ago Dandy indicated that Ménière's disease is almost always "a disease of middle or more advanced age. This favors its production from thickening of the arteries along the nerves" (81), an interesting observation in the light of Jannetta's findings.

In 1926, while he was doing surgery for trigeminal neuralgia and moving towards the introduction of procedures for the treatment of glossopharyngeal neuralgia and Ménière's disease, Dandy was concerned with serious infection in two different respects. Late in October he published an article in *The Journal of the American Medical Association* concerning "Treatment of Chronic Abscess of the Brain by Tapping" (82). He had found that brain abscesses on more than a few occasions were spontaneously cured and that in other instances needed only a little help. Thus he hit upon a procedure of inserting a ventricular needle into the abscess and leaving it there until the pus stopped its discharge. Both aspiration and irrigation were to be avoided so as to prevent "stirring up the infection." This procedure, Dandy stressed, could only be used for chronic abscesses and not for those acute in nature, many of which were "so virulent and fulminating" that a cure was hopeless (83).

About a month after the publication of the article on the treatment of chronic brain abscess, an outbreak of infection occurred on Dandy's service as well as on the general surgical service at the Hospital. Dandy, who was most upset by what he believed was an inexcusable situation, gave vent to his feelings in the following note to his mother and father: "It's a long time since I felt so keenly the desire to get away from work. The terrible and—I think— inexcusable infections have made the work a nightmare. It's like an engineer driving a fast limited train and all the switches left in the hands of anyone who chances to come along—and unlocked. No matter how careful his work he is helpless. But I do believe this thing is going to come to a head." And a line or two later he added that "it's difficult to think that in a modern age human beings in such responsible positions can be so callused and heartless as to put a few measly dollars ahead of these preventable horrors. The hospital should be the first to use every effort to obliterate reflections of this character on its good name" (84).

In an unusually long letter to Dean Lewis, the chief of surgery, Dandy began by noting that during the past week he had had two deaths at surgery from infection, one of whom had died "in forty-eight hours of a virulent streptococcus hemolyticus infection"; and he added that he had another patient who was dying from a staphylococcus aureus infection. He strongly believed that the hospital's sterilization was inadequate—18 months before, the sterilization time had been increased from 30 to 45 minutes with a corresponding cessation of infection—and that it "should be in the hands of an expert" (85). Dandy reported that the hospital's sterilization was then being handled by two Negro employees, "whereas until recently the sterilization was performed by a man who was quite competent. I believe," he continued, "there is no more important post in the hospital for a well trained, intelligent man than this particular one. I also believe that sterilization should not be under the control of a nurse; there is such a rapid turn over in nurses and they do not understand the principles of sterilization. It is my firm conviction that until sterilization is in the hands of the Chief of Surgery, defective sterilization is going to continue" (85).

Dandy's deep concern with sterilization led him to publish a little over 5 years later, in the *American College of Surgeons Bulletin*, an article entitled "The Importance of More Adequate Sterilization Processes in Hospitals" (86). He cited two reasons why defective sterilization existed: (a) the time of sterilization as he had noted in his letter to Dean Lewis mentioned above, was inadequate and (b) the sterilization procedure was not adequately controlled. These deficiencies, Dandy felt, were " . . . easy to correct" by a minimum of 1 hour for sterilization of hospital dressings and linen under a constant pressure of 20 lbs and by a fixed, well-trained personnel adequately compensated. Although in the smaller hospitals it might not be possible to avoid assigning this responsibility to the head nurse in the operating room, "certainly in the larger institutions it is far better and safer to institute a separate 'department of sterilization' and to place in charge a capable individual who has been trained in bacteriology" and who should be directly responsible to the chief of the department of surgery (87). This had been done at Hopkins with the result that not only was the problem of sterilization completely resolved but the hospital had made "a financial saving" as well (87).

Besides his involvement in 1926 with serious hospital and brain infections as well as the usual heavy operating schedule, Dandy reported the first successful treatment of rhinorrhea, a condition involving the discharge of cerebrospinal fluid from the nose (88). With otorrhea the discharge is from the ear. "Both conditions are due to a fistula connecting the cerebrospinal spaces—either the subarachnoid spaces or the ventricular system—with the exterior. Pneumocephalus (air in the cranial chamber) is frequently but not necessarily in association" (89). Fractures of the skull and openings made by surgery are the major causes while erosions by tumors or infections and congenital abnormalities are less frequently the source of these problems. Often the cerebrospinal fistulas heal themselves but with those that do not, there is the danger of meningitis or cerebral abscess "and," as Dandy observed towards the end of his career, "if the draining fluid persists long enough several attacks of meningitis may occur, and eventually one will be fatal" (89).

In successfully treating rhinorrhea, Dandy sutured autogenous grafts of fascia lata (deep fibrous tissues enclosing the muscle of the thigh) " . . . over the dural opening behind a depressed fracture of the orbit and the frontal sinus" (90). He developed three other methods for closing the fistula through which the cerebrospinal fluid might escape, including the direct suturing of the dural opening and covering the opening of the petrous bone with bone wax. Over a period of nearly 20 years, he treated 11 cases of rhinorrhea and otorrhea, 8 of the 11 patients having been permanently cured (91).

It is common knowledge that brain surgery lends itself on occasion to dramatization and awe-inspiring accounts in the press. Such was the case of an 18-year-old student at the City College of New York from whom Dandy in the late winter of 1926 successfully removed a brain tumor "the size of a baseball," as reported in *The Baltimore Sun*, which noted that "the success of the operation is considered a triumph in brain surgery by New York surgeons . . .. The operation necessitated the removal and replacing a large section of the skull above the right temple. A six-inch triangular piece of the skull was removed in order to take out the tumor" (92).

A year and half later the *Philadelphia Public Ledger* reported that Dandy had " . . . removed a tumor and part of the brain from a patient and replaced the brain part with flesh from the leg" (93). These stories and others similarly dramatic involving Hopkins neurosurgeon were, of course, "good copy."

But brain surgery for Dandy did not always end with a brilliant success. As the result of an air injection (ventriculography), he lost, in February 1927, a patient with an inoperable diffuse glioma (a tumor consisting of neuroglia which makes up the supporting tissue of the central nervous system). It was for Dandy "the first air death or untoward result of any kind since 1919" (94), certainly an impressive record, especially for that period.

By 1928 Dandy had become a model for more than a few aspiring young surgeons. One of these was Alfred Blalock (1899–1964), a Hopkins graduate who had come to know Dandy well through the Hopkins residency program and had gone on to Vanderbilt. Blalock, who would later achieve world renown for his "blue baby" operation and who would become the chief of surgery at Hopkins in 1941, expressed his deep regard for Dandy in a touching letter he wrote after Christmas 1927, from the Trudeau Sanitarium, Saranac Lake, New York, where he was recovering from pulmonary tuberculosis:

Dear Doctor Dandy,

    I realize at the beginning of this letter that I shall be entirely unable to convey to you even the faintest idea as to the amount of happiness which you have caused me at this Christmas time. It had not been my pleasure to read "Lord Lister" and I am sure that I shall enjoy it, but I am even more sure that I shall never forget the letter which I received from you and which I value very highly. I am very proud to be one of a number of young men who have been extremely fascinated by you, who holds you up as a model to be followed, and whose lives you are playing a large part in their shaping. I have always been a "Hero worshiper," and now that a great many things in life are denied me, I am more extreme than ever in this respect.

You are very charitable to say that I have received my troubles without complaining for I frequently think that I am a very poor sport, for I see so many people who have been so much more unfortunate than I it makes me feel very lucky at times.

I think that I will leave Trudeau in a month or two but it will probably be quite a few months before I can work again. It is my sole ambition in life now to be able to become active in Surgery again for I would like so much to try to justify the confidence which you and Doctor [Samuel] Crowe and others have placed in me.

It has been pleasing to me to learn of your beautiful home and the happy life in it.

Please remember me to Mrs. Dandy and I want to thank you again for your thoughtfulness of one who is very fond of you.

Sincerely,
Alfred Blalock (95)

By the time Dandy turned 42 in the spring of 1928, his contributions to the field of neurological surgery were so impressive that they called for some special recognition. It appropriately came from the University of Missouri whose president, Dr. Stratton D. Brooks, informed him that at the forthcoming commencement the University wished to confer upon him an honorary degree. Dandy was naturally delighted with this recognition, as he indicated in his reply to Brooks: "That the Honorary Degree of Doctor of Laws should first come from my Alma Mater will always be a source of even greater pride and satisfaction" (96). Staying in Columbia at the home of his old friend and classmate, Stanley "Bat" Battersby, who had become a pediatrician, he had a wonderful time during commencement week "in renewing acquaintanceship" with his old teachers, as he told Dr. Winterton C. Curtis, who had been largely responsible for his receiving the honorary degree. Curtis's absence that week was the "one regret" his former student in zoology had (97).

"I was delighted to see the Biological Building," he wrote to Curtis, "and especially to see that it was named for our beloved Doctor [George] Lefevre; this also I understand is another example of your unselfish devotion to your friends. Surely I have never seen a more beautiful relationship between the head of the department and his associate than between Doctor Lefevre and yourself. It is an inspiration which I shall always carry through life" (97).

A devoted alumnus of the University, Dandy readily acceded to requests for advice about the medical school and contributions to its scholarship funds. About a year and a half after acquiring the honorary degree, he received an inquiry from C. W. Greene, a former teacher of his in the department of physiology, concerning the location of the medical school's clinical department. Dandy's response revealed some of his thoughts about medical education and what he considered to be the best course for the University to follow:

> In reply to your query concerning the clinical department, I should feel very strongly that the last two years should be kept in Columbia and not taken to Kansas City. Above everything you want a university atmosphere for a medical school; otherwise it will fall into the usual pitfalls of becoming merely a mechanical institution, of which there are plenty. I am far more anxious to see a university which will develop research and make clinical progress, than to see one of the great mass of clinical material. If the state will support the institution properly, you can get all the material in Columbia that is needed. The success or failure of the clinical department, of course, is entirely dependent upon the character of the men who are selected to lead it, and the selection is by no means an easy one. I hope the mistake will not be made of getting men who are purely practitioners of medicine and surgery (98).

Dandy's devotion to the University of Missouri was also shown in other ways such as his willingness to serve on the board of trustees of the Medical School Foundation and, for a term of 2 years, on an advisory council of 21 members which the Board of Curators (trustees) established in 1932 "to aid the University in realizing some of its legitimate purposes through a sympathetic and understanding presentation of its problems to the public" (99). Moreover, during the 1920s and 1930s he would frequently send Curtis a check in order to help out students whom his former teacher had taken with him for the summer to the Marine Biological Laboratory at Woods Hole, MA (100).

Dandy also demonstrated concern for his alma mater and the principles of academic freedom when he learned of the dismissal of Harmon O. DeGraff, an untenured assistant professor of sociology, and the suspension for 1 year of Max F. Meyer, a professor of psychology who had been a member of the faculty for nearly 30 years. The cause for this disciplinary action in 1929 originated in "a printed questionnaire . . . relating to the changing economic status of women, the sexual code, and the moral ideas on which the family as a social institution is based [which] was circulated among the students at the University of Missouri. This questionnaire was part of regular undergraduate student work in a course in Sociology, called 'The Family,' given by Professor DeGraff. The testimony shows that it was the first three questions [relating to sexual conduct] that particularly offended some people outside the University, the President, and the Board of Curators" (101). After he had read the report on Meyer's lectures and tabulation on sex in his course on social psychology and the report of the investigating committee of the American Association of University Professors, Dandy observed in a letter to Curtis: "I hope the time will come when freedom of speech will not be a criminal offense in the University and particularly its faculty" (102). Later he made inquiry at Hopkins on Meyer's behalf, but no opening was available (103).

Besides his professional activities and the acquisition of an honorary degree in 1928, Dandy found the time to join a whist club, which revealed his continued enjoyment of the game that dated back to college days, and the Maryland Club, an exclusive men's club in Baltimore, famous for its superb cuisine and excellent bar. He remained a member of the Maryland Club for about a decade (104).

In the fall of 1928, Herbert Hoover, the Republican candidate, won a decisive victory in the presidential election over Governor Alfred E. Smith of New York, the Democratic nominee. Interestingly enough, it was not until after he was married that Dandy became a registered Democrat and voter, as his wife felt strongly about the responsibilities of citizenship.

A little over 6 months following Hoover's inauguration (March 4, 1929) the crash of the New York stock market occurred, generally regarded as the beginning of the Great Depression of the 1930s. Dandy, along with several other members of the Hopkins medical staff, suffered a substantial loss, amounting to several thousands of dollars. As a consequence he was reluctant thereafter to invest in stocks, preferring instead municipal and county bonds (105).

In October 1929, the same month in which the stock market plummeted, Dandy published an historically important paper—truly a first—in the A.M.A.'s *Archives of Surgery* on the subject "Loose Cartilage from Intervertebral Disk Simulating Tumor of the Spinal Cord" (106). He reported in this paper on two cases of loose cartilage whose " . . . signs and symptoms were so progressive and the pain in the spinal column so severe that presumptive diagnoses of carcinoma of the vertebra were made. The fact that the two cases appeared only a few months apart," he continued, "leads me to believe that the lesion may not be so infrequent, although a review of the literature has failed to disclose other cases of their kind. The lesion is a completely detached fragment of cartilage from an intervertebral (lumbar) disk and is surrounded by serum. It bulges dorsally into the spinal canal as a tumor, and by compressing the roots of the cauda equina [the nerve roots serving the legs and bladder] causes motor and sensory paralysis, loss of reflexes, and loss of rectal and vesical control. The lesion is undoubtedly of traumatic origin" (107). Although Dandy concluded in his summary that "the lesion is cured by removal of the cartilage," he did not seemingly act on this advice until after the publication 5 years later—in 1934— of W. J. Mixter and J. S. Barr's article "Rupture of Intervertebral Disc with Involvement of the Spinal Canal" (108). The late Frank Otenasek, one of Dandy's residents, noted years later that "Dandy had a tremendous willingness and determination to learn, but was very hard to convince, and stubborn until shown." In 1940 Barnes Woodhall of Duke University, also a former resident of Dandy's, spoke to the Johns Hopkins Medical Society about the frequency of lumbar disks. Dandy could not accept their frequency as Woodhall had reported. But "shortly thereafter . . . ," Otenasek recalled, "he made a pilgrimage to the Mayo Clinic, where he watched [J. Grafton] Love, who was then doing a good many disks. He developed a great respect for Love, recognized the frequency of the condition, learned to do the operation as it had been evolved, and brought back to Baltimore [Alfred W.] Adson's clamp and rongeurs for use in disk operations" (109). And, in time, Dandy did many such operations; yet before he did so, he first had to be convinced that surgery was warranted. Dandy was indeed from Missouri!

END NOTES

1. W.E.D. to To Whom It May Concern (for Major Ralph N. Greene, Jr.), letter, Jan 19, 1946, Dandy MSS. Dandy's regard for Greene is reflected in the following lines: "I am enclosing copy of the operative note on Miss ——, whom you saw with the spinal cord tumor. If these poor things could just contact high class men like yourself instead of the trash that abounds in your region how much better off they would be." W.E.D. to Dr. Ralph N. Greene, Coral Gables, FL, letter, Jan 17, 1939, Dandy MSS.
2. W.E.D. to Ralph N. Greene, Jacksonville, FL, letter, Feb 3, 1934, Dandy MSS.
3. W.E.D. to Ralph N. Greene, Jacksonville, FL, letter, June 15, 1928, Dandy MSS.
4. W.E.D. to Ralph N. Greene, Jacksonville, FL, letter, March 4, 1930, Dandy MSS.
5. The Pathfinder, Aug 29, 1925, 30.
6. Ralph N. Greene, Jacksonville, FL, to W.E.D., letter, Aug 29, 1925, Dandy MSS.
7. Reilly TF: Headache: Its Causes and Treatment. P. Blakiston's Sons 1926, p. vii. The

author listed his name: "Sometime Professor of Medicine, Fordham University, Attending Physician, Bellevue and Allied Hospitals, Fordham Division, and at St. Vincent's Hospital."

8. W.E.D. to Ralph Greene, Jacksonville, FL, letter, Feb 23, 1926, Dandy MSS.
9. W.E.D. to Ralph Greene, Jacksonville, FL, letter, March 19, 1926, Dandy MSS.
10. W.E.D. to Ralph Greene, Jacksonville, FL, letter, Sept 18, 1926, Dandy MSS. Nine years later, Dandy kidded Greene for picking Max Baer in a heavyweight fight (Jimmy Braddock vs. Max Baer, a 15-round fight; the decision went to Braddock): "All I can say is that you had better stick to your last as a neurologist, for you certainly missed it on Max Baer: he just didn't have anything." W.E.D. to Ralph Greene, Jacksonville, FL, letter, Sept 26, 1935, Dandy MSS.
11. W.E.D. to Ralph Greene, Jacksonville, FL, letter, April 30, 1934, Dandy MSS.
12. W.E.D. to Ralph Greene, Jacksonville, FL, letter, April 10, 1934, Dandy MSS.
13. W.E.D. to Ralph Greene, Jacksonville, FL, letter, April 10 and 30, 1934, Dandy MSS.
14. W.E.D. to Dr. Israel Strauss, New York City, letter, Aug 18, 1934, Dandy MSS.
15. W.E.D. to Ralph Greene, Jacksonville, FL, letter, Aug 31, 1934, Dandy MSS. In response to the author's inquiry concerning the memberships of Dandy and Greene, a secretary (Dee Dee) in the office of James F. Toole, Bowman Gray School of Medicine, Winston-Salem, N.C., reported that all of the A.N.A.'s files had been checked and that the files for the two men could not be found. Dee Dee in the office of James F. Toole, Winston-Salem, N.C., to the author, note to a letter he had written to the former secretary-treasurer of the A.N.A. on Nov 12, 1980, Nov 27, 1980. Greene's obituary does not include a reference to membership in the A.N.A. (*J Fla Med Assoc* 28(4):185–186, 1941). Whether Dandy ever dropped his membership in the A.N.A. is conjectural.
16. W.E.D., *Surgery of the Brain*. In Lewis D: *Practice of Surgery, Clinical, Diagnostic, Operative, Postoperative*. Hagerstown, MD, W.F. Prior 1932, Vol 12.
17. Ralph Greene, Jacksonville, FL, to W.E.D., letter, Sept 16, 1932, Dandy MSS.
18. W.E.D. to Ralph Greene, Jacksonville, FL, letter, March 15, 1934; Ralph Greene, Jacksonville, FL, to W.E.D., letter, March 19, 1934, Dandy MSS.
19. W.E.D. to Ralph Greene, Jacksonville, FL, letter, Oct 18, 1934, Dandy MSS.
20. Zangara's brain, following his execution, was sent to Hopkins for examination. Regarding this action, Dandy wrote to Greene: "I will let you know about Zangara's brain around the first of October—when Dr. [Adolf] Meyer returns." Meyer was then director of the Phipps Psychiatric Clinic of The Johns Hopkins Hospital. W.E.D. to Ralph Greene, Jacksonville, FL, letter, Sept 16, 1933, Dandy MSS.
21. W.E.D. to Ralph Greene, Jacksonville, FL, letter, Feb 3, 1934, Dandy MSS. Dandy's reference in the last paragraph was to an Eastern Shore lynching of December 1931, and a subsequent lack of indictment and trial of the accused. See Walsh R, Fox WL (eds): *Maryland: A History 1632–1974*. Baltimore, Maryland Historical Society, 1974, pp 719–720.
22. W.E.D. to Ralph Greene, Jacksonville, FL, letter, Aug 16, 1934, Dandy MSS.
23. Ralph Greene, Jacksonville, FL, to W.E.D., letter, June 13, 1936, Dandy MSS.
24. W.E.D. to Ralph Greene, Coral Gables, FL, letter, Feb 4, 1938, Dandy MSS.
25. W.E.D. to Ralph Greene, Newark, NJ, letter, Aug 10, 1938, Dandy MSS. In a letter to his friend C.W. Sheaffer, vice president of the Pennsylvania Railroad, some 5 years later, Dandy referred to James J. Hill's expression when he wrote in part: "You have been one of my real friends. Did you ever hear the remark of James J. Hill when someone told him that Lord Strathcona had some Northern Pacific stock and that he might sell it to Harriman's group. Mr. Hill said 'My friends stand without hitching'— that is the way I always think of you." W.E.D. to C.W. Sheaffer, Wayne, PA, letter, Sept 17, 1938, Dandy MSS.
26. E.B. Hunt, superintendent, Pennsylvania Railroad System Voluntary Relief Dept, Philadelphia, to W.E.D., letter, March 16, 1925, Dandy MSS.
27. The Pennsylvania Railroad Pass, 1946, BA 856, Dandy MSS.
28. Ralph Greene to Dr. Joseph M. Burke, Norfolk, VA, letter, Dec 20, 1926, Dandy MSS.
29. J.O. Hackenberg, general manager & traffic manager, Pennsylvania-Reading Seashore Lines, Camden, NJ, to W.E.D., letter, Jan 13, 1934, Dandy MSS.

30. See Dandy's bibliography for papers dealing with this topic.
31. W.E.D. to Dr. O.B. Zeinert, chief surgeon, Missouri Pacific Hospital Association, St. Louis, MO, letter, Dec 15, 1931, Dandy MSS.
32. In response to a request from Dandy in the summer of 1937, E.B. Hunt, superintendent of the Pennsylvania Railroad Voluntary Relief Department, sent him a trip pass for his two older daughters from Baltimore to Chicago and return. E.B. Hunt, Philadelphia, to W.E.D., letter, July 6, 1937, Dandy MSS.
33. W.E.D., on board a train, to Mr. and Mrs. John Dandy, Baltimore, letter, July 21, 1928, Dandy MSS.
34. W.E.D. to Daniel M. Sheaffer, Philadelphia, letter, July 18, 1929, Dandy MSS.
35. W.E.D. to Daniel M. Sheaffer, Philadelphia, letter, Dec 27, 1934, Dandy MSS.
36. W.E.D. to J. Gilbert Nettleton, general agent, Pennsylvania Railroad, Washington, DC, letter, June 25, 1937, Dandy MSS.
37. Walker AE: *A History of Neurological Surgery*, pp 25–26. Dandy WE: Cerebral ventriculoscopy. *Bull Johns Hopkins Hosp* 33:189, 1922.
38. W.E.D. to Dr. Howard A. Kelly, Baltimore, letter, May 22, 1923, Dandy MSS. Six months later Dandy requested Mr. A. Wassing of the Wappler Electric Co. to forward to him " . . . the Wappler battery handle to be applied to the cystoscope which you made me for use in brain work. When I come to New York I will bring the obdurator [sic] to show you how it should be made." W.E.D. to A. Wassing, Long Island City, NY, letter, Nov 2, 1923, Dandy MSS.
39. Nelson H. Lowry, Chicago, IL, to W.E.D., letter, Oct 2, 1924, Dandy MSS.
40. W.E.D. to Howard A. Kelly, Baltimore, letter, Dec 15, 1924; Howard A. Kelly, Baltimore, to W.E.D., letter, Dec 18, 1924, Dandy MSS.
41. W.E.D. to Ralph Greene, Coral Gables, FL, letter, June 2, 1939, Dandy MSS. In an interesting postscript to this letter, Dandy told Greene that he had forgotten " . . . to mention that there is a little trick also that is very important in coagulating big sinuses in the dura. If a piece of muscle is applied to the bleeding point, this can be coagulated with the cautery and it closes the opening in the sinus and makes the hemostasis permanent. Without this method it would be very difficult to control the bleeding."
42. W.E.D. to H.H. Adams, General Electric Co., letter, Aug 19, 1925, Dandy MSS.
43. Fulton JF: *Harvey Cushing*. Springfield, IL, Charles C Thomas, 1946, p 537.
44. Fulton JF: *Harvey Cushing*. Springfield, IL, Charles C Thomas, 1946, pp 538, 548–549.
45. W.E.D. to Carl E. Egeler, Cleveland, Ohio, letter, Oct 14, 1932, Dandy MSS.
46. W.E.D. to Dr. Cayetano Panettiere, Miami Beach, FL, letter, Aug 9, 1937, Dandy MSS.
47. W.E.D. to Ralph Greene, Coral Gables, FL, letter, Dec 4, 1940, Dandy MSS.
48. W.E.D. to Bard-Parker Co., New York City, letter, March 31, 1927; Morgan Parker, New York City, to W.E.D, letter, April 8, 1927, Dandy MSS.
49. W.E.D. to King C. Gillette Factory, Uneeda Blades Co., New York City, letter, Oct 19, 1932, Dandy MSS.
50. W.E.D. to Dr. Herbert Olivecrona, Stockholm, Sweden, letter, Feb 17, 1933, Dandy MSS.
51. Turner TB: *Heritage of Excellence*. Baltimore, Johns Hopkins University Press, 1974, p 114.
52. Firor WM: Comments about the Surgical Chiefs at The Johns Hopkins Hospital between 1918 and 1938, unpublished ms., National Library of Medicine, p 8.
53. W.E.D. to Dr. Frederick L. Reichert, Lane Hospital, Stanford University, San Francisco, letter, Jan 7, 1935, Dandy MSS.
54. Turner TB: *Heritage of Excellence*. Baltimore, Johns Hopkins University Press, 1974, p 158.
55. Turner TB: *Heritage of Excellence*. Baltimore, Johns Hopkins University Press, 1974, p 411.
56. Lewis D, Dandy WE: The course of the nerve fibers transmitting sensation of taste. *Arch Surg* 21:249–288, 1930.
57. W.E.D. to Dr. M.H. Winters, Galesburg, IL, letter, Feb 20, 1928, Dandy MSS.

58. Lewis D, Dandy WE: The course of the nerve fibers transmitting sensation of taste. *Arch Surg* 21:249–288, 1930.
59. Lewis D, Dandy WE: The course of nerve fibers transmitting sensation of taste. *Arch Surg* 249:82, 85, 1930.
60. Dandy WE: Section of the sensory root of the trigeminal nerve at the pons: preliminary report of the operative procedure. *Johns Hopkins Hosp Bull* 36:106, 1925.
61. Dandy WE: An operation for the cure of tic douloureux: partial section of the sensory root at the pons. *Arch Surg* 18:687–734, 1929.
62. Dandy WE: The treatment of trigeminal neuralgia by the cerebellar route. *Ann Surg* 96:794, 1932.
63. Fairman D: Evolution of neurosurgery through Walter E. Dandy's work. *Surgery* 19:587, 1946.
64. Hugo V. Rizzoli, M.D., Washington, DC, to the author, letter, Dec 19, 1977.
65. W.E.D. to Ralph Greene, Jacksonville, FL, letter, April 9, 1927, Dandy MSS.
66. Fairman D: Evolution of neurosurgery through Walter E. Dandy's work. *Surgery* 19:587, 1946.
67. W.E.D. to Dr. Temple Fay, Philadelphia, letter, Jan 31, 1928, Dandy MSS.
68. W.E.D. to Temple Fay, Philadelphia, letter, Feb 20, 1928, Dandy MSS.
69. Temple Fay, Philadelphia, to W.E.D., letter, Feb 23, 1928, Dandy MSS.
70. W.E.D. to Ralph Greene, Jacksonville, FL, letter, March 30, 1932, Dandy MSS.
71. W.E.D. to Frederick L. Reichert, San Francisco, letter, Sept 23, 1932, Dandy MSS. In an earlier letter to Reichert, Dandy warned of what other neurosurgeons would do to him: "Doctor [Dean] Lewis brought in the Journal [of the A.M.A.] with your report on the glossopharyngeal case. You have a wonderful opportunity because you are doing a much more progressive type of work than the other brain surgeons, although they surely will knife you to the limit. You will have to make your appeal directly to the physicians, particularly in the west." W.E.D. to Frederick L. Reichert, San Francisco, letter, June 12, 1931, Dandy MSS.
72. Dandy WE: Ménière's disease: its diagnosis and a method of treatment. *Arch Surg* 16:1127–1152, 1928.
73. Dandy WE: Ménière's disease: its diagnosis and a method of treatment. *Arch Surg* 16:1127–1152, 1928.
74. Dandy WE: The diagnosis and treatment of Ménière's disease. *Trans Am Ther Soc* 32:128, 1932.
75. Dandy WE: The diagnosis and treatment of Ménière's disease. *Trans Am Ther Soc* 32:128, 1932.
76. Dandy WE: The surgical treatment of Ménière's disease. *Surg Gynecol Obstet* 72:422, 1941.
77. Dandy WE: Treatment of Ménière's disease by section of only the vestibular portion of the acoustic nerve. *Johns Hopkins Hosp Bull* 53:52, 1933.
78. Dandy WE: Treatment of Ménière's disease by section of only the vestibular portion of the acoustic nerve. *Johns Hopkins Hosp Bull* 53:54, 1933.
79. Mrs. Walter E. Dandy, Baltimore, interview with the author, Nov 23, 1976.
80. Hugo V. Rizzoli, M.D., Washington, DC, to the author, letter, Dec 19, 1977.
81. Dandy WE: The surgical treatment of Ménière's disease. *Surg Gynecol Obstet* 72:423, 1941.
82. Dandy WE: Treatment of chronic abscess of the brain by tapping. *JAMA* 87:1477–1478, 1926.
83. Dandy WE: Treatment of chronic abscess of the brain by tapping. *JAMA* 87:1478, 1926.
84. W.E.D. to Mr. and Mrs. John Dandy, letter, Dec 1, 1926, Dandy MSS.
85. W.E.D. to Dean Lewis, M.D., Baltimore, letter, Dec 1, 1926, Dandy MSS.
86. Dandy WE: The importance of more adequate sterilization processes in hospitals. *Am Coll Surgeons Bull* 16:11–12, 1932.
87. Dandy WE: The importance of more adequate sterilization processes in hospitals. *Am Coll Surgeons Bull* 16:11–12, 1932.
88. Dandy WE: Pneumocephalus (intracranial pneumatocele or aerocele). *Arch Surg* 12:949–982, 1926.

89. Dandy WE: Treatment of rhinorrhea and otorrhea. *Arch Surg* 69:75, 1944.
90. Dandy WE: Treatment of rhinorrhea and otorrhea. *Arch Surg* 69:76, 1944.
91. Dandy WE: Treatment of rhinorrhea and otorrhea. *Arch Surg* 69:84, 1944.
92. *Baltimore Sun* (Morning), March 11, 1926, p 3. In an interesting observation to a colleague, Dandy noted the paradoxical condition that some brain tumors present in their final stage: "It is amazing how well one can be and still have a tumor which is approaching the last stages of pressure." W.E.D. to Dr. Lewellys Barker, Baltimore, letter, Feb 24, 1927, Dandy MSS.
93. *Philadelphia Public Ledger*, Sept 15, 1927, p 1.
94. W.E.D. to Lewellys F. Barker, M.D., Baltimore, letter, Feb 24, 1927, Dandy MSS.
95. Alfred Blalock, M.D., Trudeau, NY, to W.E.D., letter, Dec 28, 1927, Dandy MSS.
96. W.E.D. to Stratton D. Brooks, Columbia, MO, letter, April 10, 1928, Dandy MSS. The LL.D. which the University of Missouri conferred upon Dandy was the only honorary degree he ever received.
97. W.E.D. to Dr. Winterton C. Curtis, Marine Biological Laboratory, Woods Hole, MA, letter, July 16, 1928, Dandy MSS.
98. W.E.D. to C.W. Greene, Columbia, MO, letter, Dec 24, 1930, Dandy MSS.
99. Walter Williams, president, University of Missouri, Columbia, to W.E.D., letter, Sept 8, 1932; W.E.D. to Walter Williams, letter, Sept 14, 1932, Dandy MSS.
100. Winterton C. Curtis, Columbia, MO, interview with the author, Aug 25, 1965.
101. Academic Freedom at the University of Missouri: Report on the Dismissal of Professor DeGraff and the Suspension of Professor Meyer. *AAUP Bull* 16(2):145, Feb. 1930.
102. W.E.D. to Winterton C. Curtis, National Research Council, Washington, DC, letter, Oct 31, 1930, Dandy MSS.
103. W.E.D. to Winterton C. Curtis, Columbia, MO, letter, Jan 23, 1932, Dandy MSS.
104. W.E.D. to H. Kent McCay, Baltimore, letter, Feb 17, 1928, Dandy MSS; L.G. Shreve, president, Maryland Club, Baltimore, to the author, letter, Aug 30, 1977.
105. Mrs. Walter E. Dandy, Baltimore, telephone interview with the author, March 31, 1981.
106. Dandy WE: Loose cartilage from intervertebral disk simulating tumor of the spinal cord. *Arch Surg* 19:660–672, 1929.
107. Dandy WE: Loose cartilage from intervertebral disk simulating tumor of the spinal cord. *Arch Surg* 19:660, 1929.
108. Mixter WJ, Barr JS: Rupture of intervertebral disc with involvement of the spinal canal. *N Engl J Med* 211:210–215, 1934.
109. Frank J. Otenasek, M.D., Ruminations about Walter E. Dandy, unpublished ms, delivered informally at the Annual Meeting of the Florida Association of Neurosurgeons, Hollywood-By-The-Sea, May 19, 1963, p 12.

CHAPTER 9

The Thirties

One of the most difficult problems confronting the operator in brain surgery during the early decades was the use of general anesthesia, particularly ether. Anesthesiology had not as yet become a specialty. Thus the type of anesthetic agent and its administration by inhalation or rectum, which a nurse-anesthetist handled, were decisions that the neurosurgeon had to make. Like other surgeons Dandy found that "ether, administered by inhalation, has three serious liabilities in intracranial surgery. It causes (a) swelling of the brain; (b) postoperative vomiting; and (c) pneumonia. Together, these three effects," he noted, "are alone responsible for quite a high percentage of the mortality associated with operations on the brain" (1). Consequently, he eagerly sought an alternative to ether, which he found in Avertin, a German product (tribromethanol), and which he began using in 1929, 2 years after it had first been tried as a complete anesthetic.

To avoid the dangers from the swelling of the brain, postoperative vomiting (the straining from which could produce venous stasis and a reopening of vessels "that otherwise would remain sealed," with a resulting cerebral hemorrhage) (2), and postoperative pneumonia, neurosurgeons were employing two substitutes for ether by inhalation—local anesthesia and rectal ether—by the late 1920s. But Dandy was looking for a superior agent. After testing Avertin for a year, he informed The Winthrop Chemical Company of New York, which had made it available to him, that it was "the best anesthesia that can be used," and that it was now possible to achieve "results in brain surgery which heretofore were not possible by ether, whether administered by inhalation or by rectum" (3). Moreover, he used Avertin in some "250 major cranial operations of every type" and had had no fatalities from the anesthetic, "no instance of

postoperative pneumonia, and no deleterious effect either immediate or remote" (3a).

Dandy was fortunate to have as his nurse-anesthetist, Grace L.
Smith, who had joined him a year or two before he begun using
Avertin and who would remain with him for the rest of his career.
Shortly after she started working for him, however, she thought
that she could not take it, as he was such a "disciplinarian," involved
not only with a busy practice but with research as well (4). To
accommodate the anesthetist Dandy arranged for a high operating
table and platforms 14 to 16 inches high placed around the table.
". . . This made it possible for the Anesthetist to sit under the drape
with the patient" (5).

With an excellent anesthetist and the use of Avertin as a basal
anesthetic (with a small admixture of ether), Dandy's problems with
anesthesia including, in some cases between 1927 and 1929 the
unwitting use of an inferior grade of ether (6), were satisfactorily
resolved.

Besides Grace Smith, Dandy's permanent operating room staff
comprised two or three others, including Agnes Doetsch, a surgical
nurse, whom he was happy to recommend ". . . for a position on
the State Board of Nursing Examiners" in 1938 (7). Dorcas Hager
(later Mrs. Paul Padget), a medical illustrator who, having attended
Vassar College, came to Hopkins in 1926 for a 2-year course with
Max Broedel, the leading medical illustrator of the day and a friend
of Dandy's. Her expenses for this program were borne by Dandy,
who promptly hired her when she completed it (8).

During an operation she would position herself behind Dandy
and with sketch pad in hand would deftly draw whatever he wanted.
She was more than a medical artist; she was an anatomist as well.
Dandy thought so well of her that he later invited her to do a study
of the "Circle of Willis: Its Embryology and Anatomy," which
appeared as Chapter 3 in his book *Intracranial Arterial Aneurysms*
(9). Thus Mrs. Padget, "through the courtesy of Dr. George W.
Corner, undertook a study of the incomparable material of the
Carnegie Embryological Collection" (10).

Her drawings which appeared in Dandy's articles and books were
beautifully done, the work of a master. Max Broedel, it is worth
noting, considered Dorcas Padget to have been his best student
(11).

Some years after she became Dandy's illustrator—he continued
to call her "Miss Hager" after her marriage to Dr. Paul Padget—

she cleverly designed a bookplate for him in the form of a humorous coat of arms containing, besides the Hopkins' seal, a brain, a pair of rongeurs, a neurosurgeon's headlamp, and crossed golf clubs with balls, a delightful gift. Despite occasional clashes of temperament between two gifted people, she remained with Dandy until his death.

Another permanent member of Dandy's operating room staff by the early 1930s was Lawrence, the orderly, sometimes called Barney, who performed a variety of tasks for Dandy and the brain team. One afternoon Lawrence, whose full name is unfortunately lost to memory, was involved in an incident which drew Dandy's wrath but which had a very funny ending. He tripped over the cord of Dandy's headlamp which threw the operating room into total darkness as the only light Dandy permitted was from his headlamp. Dandy yelled "Put the light on!" Lawrence promptly plugged in the cord but then proceeded to trip over it again and even a third time that afternoon. Finally, Dandy screamed at him "Get out of here and stay out; don't come back." With nothing to do for the remainder of the day, Lawrence went upstairs to the gallery of the operating room, quietly sat down and watched the operation. A member of the brain team, seeing a head in the gallery, thought that it was a visiting surgeon and nudged Dandy. "With this prompting, Dandy dutifully explained the entire operation, step by step, and said, 'We are glad to have you with us, Doctor.'" Following this cheery welcome, Lawrence wasted no time in stealing out the door (12). His boss never knew who the real visitor was!

Lawrence was devoted to Dandy and was always on hand in the operating room to do whatever was necessary, including sometimes pulling up his boss's pants when asked to do so. Dandy was obviously fond of Lawrence, for he paid for his modest house when Lawrence's mother was about to be evicted (13).

There was probably no one at Hopkins whose knowledge and judgment Dandy valued more greatly than Frank Rodolph Ford (1892–1970). His "emergence as a brilliant clinical neurologist was rapid indeed and was rewarded by his appointment as head of neurology" (14). A graduate of The Johns Hopkins Medical School in 1920, Ford served a year in psychiatry under Adolf Meyer, studied clinical neurology at Bellevue Hospital in New York City under Foster Kennedy, and then returned to Hopkins as a house officer in neurology on the medical service. Aside from his adult cases, he became particularly interested in pediatric neurology and published in 1937 a definitive work, *Diseases of the Nervous System in Infancy, Childhood and Adolescence*, which went through six editions (15).

By the early 1930s Ford and Dandy had developed a mutual esteem and ". . . saw eye to eye on most clinical problems," as Curt P. Richter, the distinguished Hopkins psychobiologist, who knew them both well, has recalled. "They had a high regard and affection for one another. That Frank Ford thought well of Dandy, actually worshipped him, removed any doubt that I might have had about Dandy" (16). Though Ford considered Dandy a genius who was blessed with "great powers of observation" and extraordinary surgical skills, particularly "in the posterior fossa," he was also well aware of his friend's other virtues—"He was an extremely kindly man"—and his shortcomings, such as his "violent temper"—"He never did learn to control it" (17).

In a letter to his old friend Ralph Greene, the Jacksonville neurologist, Dandy affectionately referred to Ford, whose ever-present cigar became a trademark, as "a queer bird," adding that "he does not like to talk, and he won't join any associations, not even the American Medical Association. It is not that he has any feeling against them: it is just that he thinks he is not doing anybody any good, and he is a poor mixer. It is too bad because he is such a great fellow" (18). Here was another example of Dandy's loyalty to and regard for an esteemed colleague and friend, feelings which he also extended to Ford's colleague, Frank B. Walsh, a neuro-ophthalmologist who ". . . became perhaps the most prominent representative of his subspecialty" (19).

There are countless stores about Dandy's ability as a diagnostician which, as Charles E. Troland, a former resident, stated in an unpublished paper ". . . came through alert observations of patients" (20). One which Troland recounted concerned a patient who had been checked by several physicians, including Frank R. Ford, without a resulting diagnosis. ". . . Dandy stood at the foot of the bed and talked to the patient for a few minutes, and then stated that he would take out the tumor the following day. The family and other physicians were quite upset and finally Dr. Dandy did state that the patient had an acoustic tumor." This was the only time that Troland ever asked Dandy about his method of arriving at a diagnosis, to which Dandy replied: "Didn't you notice that he didn't blink with his left eye?" At surgery the following morning his diagnosis was borne out (21). Such a diagnosis was indeed dramatic, especially because the surgery verified its correctness. One might question such a "short-cut" diagnosis; but it was made, after all, in the presence of other physicians, not before medical students who are taught the importance of a step-by-step procedure in reaching a conclusion about a patient's disease. It was an example of Dandy's great powers of perception and profound clinical knowledge.

For Dandy to do as many operations as he did on the days he was in surgery (Tuesdays, Wednesdays, Fridays and Saturdays, with the operating room closed at noon on Wednesdays and Fridays), he had to develop a strict and efficient schedule—he might have five brain tumor operations in one day or his daily schedule might involve two craniotomies and two disc operations, once he began doing the latter (22). Saturdays were especially heavy operating days during which the residents would handle cases in the afternoons so that Dandy could play golf (23).

When a prospective patient or his physician telephoned for an appointment, the resident and Mrs. Bertha B. Schauck, Dandy's secretary, were instructed to give the patient a 12 o'clock noon appointment (24)—all patients, regardless of the number, on a particular day were given appointments at that hour! If Dandy were in surgery at this time, he would slip out to examine the patient(s) in his small, unimposing office. The residents were expected to do the work-ups on patients, as he considered this a part of their training. Probably his residents once in awhile saved him from a mistake or a wrong diagnosis; no clinician or surgeon, after all, is infallible. On one occasion, Dandy was about to operate on a patient with a pituitary tumor; at least that was the report he had received from the attending physician. But Charles Troland, who was then the neurosurgical resident, thought differently and insisted that an air study (ventriculogram) be done, as he suspected that the seat of the patient's problem was an eroding hydrocephalus (25). Dandy reluctantly agreed to the study; and as it turned out, Troland was right!

On a typical operating day the schedule would begin at 6:00 a.m., with the resident checking the patients. At 7:00 a.m. the resident would have breakfast, and at 8:00 o'clock would head for the operating room. "However, no patient could enter the operating room until 8 a.m. because of a long-standing feud with the operating room supervisor (Miss Sherwood). Therefore, it was common practice for the patient to be balanced on the shoulders of the assistant resident and Lawrence the orderly. At the stroke of 8 a.m., the patient was rushed onto the operating table; the resident began shaving and cleansing the operative area" (26). In the meantime, burr holes were placed for patients awaiting ventriculography. At about 9:00 o'clock Dandy would arrive at the operating room, having parked his big car by the fire plug in front of the emergency room. The resident would then give the "Old Man," who was standing in the doorway, a report on the patients. After this briefing Dandy would change his clothes in the locker room and scrub up while the first case was under way, "which was frequently a posterior approach for a tic or Ménière's syndrome" (27). He would come into the operating room wearing two masks, one over his nose and the other over his mouth, so as to prevent his glasses from fogging over. A nurse would put on his head light; Dandy complained that the nurses "always" burned his nose in doing this (28). Usually, the schedule included a brain tumor, a Vth nerve section, an VIIIth nerve section, or a herniated lumbar disk after he began to do this procedure.

"With regard to time for lunch, this was never taken by the members of the brain team. Doctor Dandy would drop out between operations and go to lunch in the regular [dining] hall on many occasions. The resident staff, however, kept the operating room moving. There was a small room above the operating room where lunch was obtainable" (29). When Dandy dropped out, the resident would proceed with the closing of the case while the assistant resident would go upstairs for a quick lunch of soup or a sandwich. The assistant resident, upon returning to the operating room, would finish the closing of the operation or put on a dressing while the resident would go upstairs for his light lunch, which never took more than 10 to 15 minutes. "The same system was carried out with the nurses. The operating room itself never stopped working" (29). By 3:00 p.m. or shortly thereafter the surgery was generally finished. There followed the necessary cleaning up of the operating room, which everyone dreaded because, as a perfectionist, Dandy was quite demanding (30).

An hour and half later he would begin rounds on Halsted 7, the neurosurgical floor, with his resident, assistant resident and, often, an intern bringing up the rear. Between 5:30 and 6:00 o'clock he would leave the hospital for home, having gotten four cigarettes from the resident and, earlier, a similar number from Lawrence.

This act of bumming salved his conscience about buying (giving up) cigarettes. Meanwhile, the resident would go to the wards to work up the cases for the next scheduled day for surgery and to do whatever else was necessary. Promptly at 7:00 p.m. the resident on duty would call Dandy at his home to report on patients and the operating schedule for the following day, if it were a day when he did surgery. But on Sunday nights the resident was expected to call instead at 7:30 because the "Old Man" wanted to listen to Jack Benny's radio program and would not take calls then. It was not uncommon for Dandy to call the resident at 2:00 a.m. for the temperature readings at that hour and at midnight. Thus the residents frequently made night rounds among the patients.

In the operating room Dandy, who never used the sitting position for a patient who was undergoing a craniotomy (31), was an indefatigable worker. He had a power of intense concentration and a constant curiosity about the nervous system which was often revealed at surgery by the questions he asked himself aloud, beginning with how, what, or why. He possessed, as one of his early residents aptly observed, "an exquisite surgical technique" which embodied no wasted effort and no deliberation (32). And he never regretted his small hands; in fact, he thought that they were an advantage in difficult situations.

Dandy's behavior in the operating room fluctuated. ". . . He was easy to work with if everything went well. When he became upset, he certainly was a holy terror! This included screeming and throwing instruments" (33). He would not hesitate to blame a resident for whatever had gone wrong, "and he would continue to whine throughout the case if things were not going well" (33). Although he was generally not a profane man, Dandy would occasionally in surgery explode with a "goddamn" (34). A former resident, in assessing Dandy's behavior in the operating room, thinks that "it is difficult to tell if he needed to blame somebody else for his problems or whether he bawled us out to keep us on our toes to make a teaching point. Often I think it was a little bit of both" (35).

A comical instance (36) of Dandy's display of temper in surgery occurred one day when a fly was buzzing around him. He became so exasperated that he threw a clamp at the fly!

Following surgery Dandy would succinctly dictate his operative notes, which frequently began with "This is an interesting case" (37). His notes were precise and to the point, as the following example reveals:

Halsted 7

Herman————————   240198
OPERATION: September 12, 1941
          Dr. Dandy
          Avertin 5 (70 mgm)—Ether 8—Miss Smith
          SUBTOTAL SECTION EIGHTH NERVE RIGHT FOR
          MÉNIÈRE's DISEASE
   The usual unilateral cerebellar approach was made. The mastoid cells were
not seen. There was ample room. There was an unusual topography in that the
petrosal vein ran along-side the dura and the eighth nerve. However, it could be
avoided and was not disturbed. The anterior nine-tenths of the nerve was divided. There was a tiny filament remaining. The dura, galea and skin were closed
with interrupted sutures of silk.
   This is the 455th case of Ménière's disease.
cp   (Dr. Dandy) (38)

   Service on the brain team was demanding and exhausting. If
Dandy selected one as an intern, assistant resident, or resident, it
meant for the appointee unremitting duty and dedication to the
work of the neurosurgical service, above all to the care and needs
of the patient. It was not uncommon for the resident who bore the
day-to-day responsibility of the service to be confined to the hospital for months at a time. And the assistant resident, who was
obviously next in line, never could directly approach Dandy, a
stickler for protocol; his communication with the"Old Man" was
always through the resident.
   Dandy never called a resident by his first name but invariably by
his last name. Moreover, he had trouble with the names of some of
the residents. Consequently, Charles Troland was always called
"Tolson" and William Watson, "Watkins" (39).
   "In making rounds [with Dandy] the Resident would be practically at his side, and the Assistant Resident would be just about one
pace behind the Resident" (40). And in view of the fact that Dandy
was hard of hearing, especially in his right ear, the resident had to
walk to his left, being careful not to touch him. Under such circumstances Dandy would speak in a low voice and would not repeat
himself. "It made the resident walk somewhat like a crab," recalled
a former member of the brain team, "and after a year or more of
walking like this it became a habit" (41).
   Dandy's stress on protocol had a humorous twist in an incident
(42) that has regaled neurosurgeons over the years. Charles Troland
was then resident, Frank Otenasek was assistant resident, Collin
MacCarty was the intern who was about to leave the brain team,
and Herbert Sloan was the intern who was replacing MacCarty.

Dandy invited them to join him for a baseball game at the old Orioles' park. When they arrived at the park, Dandy carefully arranged the seating with himself at one end, Troland next to him, then Otenasek, MacCarty next to Otenasek, and finally Sloan. Shortly, he realized that the men had had no lunch; so he bought beer for Troland and Otenasek, cokes for MacCarty and Sloan, two hamburgers apiece for Troland and Otenasek, and one hot dog apiece for the interns!

Actually Dandy was much more generous than this incident of largesse based on rank showed. On occasion, he would help a medical student who needed financial aid and would pay the hospital expenses of indigent ward patients (43). And his gifts to residents came to include luggage and cash amounting to several hundred dollars at Christmas and vacation time. Just before one resident left to join the Army during World War II, Dandy gave him a check for $500.00 to have a brief vacation (44).

Fifty years ago, it was the custom at Hopkins as well as at other hospitals for the senior staff "to beat on" the interns and residents, thus making their lives often quite uncomfortable; and Dandy, in his relations with the brain team, was no exception to this practice (45). Yet he took a personal interest in the residents and followed their professional careers after they left Hopkins. In a rare instance, Dandy gave a party for Bill Watson, a resident, at the Baltimore Country Club, when Watson was married. "He felt a great responsibility to his students and of course Halsted's dignified manner was the pattern he tried to emulate. Also the meticulousness of his (Halsted's) dress. Any one on his staff had to have his shoes polished, his hair combed & his buttons fastened while on duty. He would have hated the modern slovenliness" (46).

Aware that the residents called him the "Old Man," Dandy once asked Bill Watson, who was then resident, about this. Caught off guard, Watson did not quite know what to say. Finally, he replied that it was a term of affection. With a twinkle of the eye Dandy said, "Yes, I know" (47).

Dandy's regard for his residents was reflected by the end of the 1930s in his collecting photographs of them to hang on the wall of his waiting room—what he affectionately called the "rougues' gallery." Eldridge Campbell, a former resident, was involved with this in a humorous way when he innocently failed to cite a publication of Dandy's in an article on the removal of foreign bodies from the brain. His "punishment" was to have his picture turned towards the wall. Each night the cleaning woman would turn it around, only to have Dandy the next day reverse it until Campbell, upon learning what was happening, made amends (48).

Another resident of the 1930s, Barnes Woodhall, also experienced Dandy's displeasure, but in another way. He had written a paper on pseudotumor and had failed to ask his former mentor to review it. "Dandy was highly offended and didn't speak to him for 18 months. Finally, one day, with a warm smile, he stopped . . . Woodhall in the corridor at Hopkins and said, 'The Yellow Cab Company is suing me again. Yesterday, Fagin [a bulldog that Woodhall and his wife had given the Dandys] chewed up all four tires on a cab stopped at our house'" (49). Some years later Woodhall expressed his affection and regard for the "Old Man" when he wrote: "Next to my father, Dr. Dandy did more for me and meant more to me than any other man" (50).

Dandy was fond of all his residents; otherwise, he would not have kept them. But he especially liked James M. Mason, III, the son of one of his good medical friends, James Mason of Birmingham, AL. Those who came after Mason, remembered Mrs. Walter E. Dandy, called him "angel child" (51). Bill Watson, who became a general surgeon, and later Frank Otenasek also enjoyed Dandy's special regard. In recommending the latter for membership in the Cushing Society to his old friend and classmate, R. Eustace Semmes of Memphis, TN, Dandy noted that "he is the best man I have ever had and is a very nice boy" (52).

In the 1930s, as in earlier years, Dandy trained only Hopkins graduates who were rotated through his service. Yet, Americans from other universities and foreign physicians who were interested in a career in neurological surgery were invited to spend time with him but only as visitors and observers. Hopkins regulations did not permit them to have appointments as interns or residents, and so they could not serve on the brain team. They could attend, however, Dandy's operations, make ward rounds, study x-ray film, take ventriculograms, and study postmortem material (53). Among the substantial number of visitors to the neurosurgical service were Emile Seletz of Los Angeles, California, who as an amateur sculptor, it will be recalled, did a bust of Dandy that is now in The Johns Hopkins Hospital, and Ferdinand Verbeek of Groningen, The Netherlands. Proud of their association with Dandy, the visitors were as devoted to him as were members of the brain team.

From time to time Dandy received inquiries about the training required for neurosurgery. This was a subject on which he had decided views. In the spring of 1935 Kenneth D. Blackfan, with whom he had done the studies on hydrocephalus 20 years before, wrote to Dandy about a young man who was serving an internship in pediatrics with him at Children's Hospital in Boston and was hoping to become a neurosurgeon. In his usual, forthright way Dandy replied:

My very strong advice to a young man wishing to do brain surgery is to get a thorough training in general surgery first. I know this is unorthodox advice, for most brain surgeons are trained first in physiology, anatomy and pathology and the patient received no consideration, but I am old-fashion[ed] enough to believe that the time will come when what is best for the patient is best for the surgeon too. There would not be anything like the mortality in brain surgery in this country if the brain surgeons were properly trained (54).

A few days later, in response to a similar inquiry from Joseph C. Bloodgood, a prominent Hopkins surgeon, on behalf of a Baltimore boy, Dandy stated that prospective neurosurgeons should devote while in school their electives ". . . to lines of activity related to neurology and neurosurgery. But above all, one should have a thorough training in general surgery before undertaking neurosurgery. The trouble today is that too many men are trained in anatomy and pathology and then diverted without proper training to surgery of the brain. It will be a good ten years after graduation before he will be competent to do neuro-surgery" (55). Many men who wished to become neurosurgeons, Dandy felt, were unwilling to devote the time necesary for a thorough preparation (56).

A young medical student of the 1930s who wanted to become a neurosurgeon and to receive his training at Hopkins had a traumatic experience upon meeting Dandy. Many years later, as a well-established neurosurgeon, he vividly recalled in a letter to the author that encounter:

My one encounter with Dr. Dandy was not a particularly happy one for me. I was a senior medical student at Ohio State University and wanted very much to intern at Johns Hopkins since my family lived in Baltimore. My record at Ohio State was not brilliant, but was above average and I carried with me a letter of recommendation from Dr. Harry LeFever, a neurosurgeon in Columbus. I arrived at Dr. Dandy's office at an appointed time and introduced myself. I had my letter of recommendation in my hand and he held out his hand and I gave it to him. He read it and said, 'You have no chance.' That ended by interview with Dr. Dandy. Fortunately I was able to obtain internship at the University of Michigan and I then completed by neurosurgical residency there, so all was not lost. It was, however, an experience I will never forget (57).

Dandy's snap judgment here was wide of the mark just as it was in some other instances. Perceptive and intuitive as he was, Dandy was not always "right" in his evaluation of other people or in his clinical assessment.

Another instance of his expressing himself in an abrupt fashion occurred when Frank Otenasek, then a resident in the early 1940s, asked him, while making rounds, to meet his father, who was a patient in the Hospital. After the introduction Dandy remarked, "Your son is a fine man and a good surgeon. There is only one thing wrong with him. He got married too soon." Years later Otenasek, in recalling this moment, noted that he had been married at the age of 25 following his graduation from medical school. At the time Dandy met his father, Otenasek had been married about 6 years. "You can imagine," he mused, "the consternation with which my father received this statement" (58).

In the training of people on his service Dandy avoided direct teaching, which he of course did when he appeared before a class of medical students. Rather, with his residents he more or less assumed that they ". . . would learn by working with him and observing his management of cases and his operative technique." In time he would allow them to perform ". . . significant portions of various operative procedures although he did not usually remain in the operative room when. . ." they were operating (59).

Towards the end of his life, Dandy reflected "that perhaps he should have trained more people. . ." than he did (60). Actually he did train a respectable number, although not equal to that of Cushing. Moreover, it may have been that Dandy, as one of the "old school" of neurosurgeons, did not want too many around, as one former resident has suggested; in other words, he may not have desired to see too many trained in neurological surgery (61). Too much competition!

In the preparation for this specialty Dandy would probably have not accepted Wilder Penfield's contention that "the specialties of *clinical neurology* and *psychiatry* and *neurosurgery* [italics his] should always be considered parts of a functional whole, at least for the purposes of medical education and medical therapy" (62). Dandy found that neurosurgeons had very little interest in or understanding of psychiatry (63), which probably reflected his own disinterest in that field and the not uncommon disdain for psychiatrists among medical people. But the linkage of clinical neurology and neurosurgery in medical training and therapy, Dandy of course readily supported; and he wanted his residents to have a sound preparation in both.

The system of residency at Johns Hopkins until 1941 when Alfred Blalock became professor and chairman of the Department of Surgery underscored Dandy's views on the preparation for neurosurgery. Before Blalock's appointment the neurosurgical service was a part of general surgery; consequently, so-called residents in neurosurgery went on to general surgery after they had completed 2 years with Dandy. For those in the approximately 8-year residency program, "the rotation," according to Otenasek, "was something like this: First Year, Surgical Intern; Second Year, Fellow in Experimental Surgery; Third Year, Fellow in Surgical Pathology; Fourth Year, Fractures, Trauma, Plastic Surgery, Perineal Surgery; Fifth Year, Assistant Resident, Neurological Surgery; Sixth Year, Resident in Neurological Surgery; Seventh Year, First Assistant in General Surgery; Eighth Year, Chief Resident in General Surgery. As a result, the most accomplished surgeon generally and neurosurgically on the hospital resident staff was the Resident in General Surgery. Since Dandy was the only practicing Neurological Surgeon in the Hospital, when he was away any emergencies were taken care of by the Resident in General Surgery with the assistance of the Neurosurgical [brain] Team" (64). Such a program (65) gave emphasis to Dandy's belief that his men should think and act like surgeons, even to the point of using a straight razor when they shaved!

After Blalock became chief of surgery, neurological surgery was made a division of general surgery and thus had its own house staff, except for the intern who came from surgery. A discussion of this change and its implication for Dandy will follow in the next chapter.

In 1932 when Franklin D. Roosevelt, the Democratic governor of New York, was elected president the country was deep in the worst depression it had ever experienced. With large unemployment and many banks having closed their doors, desperation was in the air. Following this inauguration, Roosevelt quickly undertook to push legislation through Congress that would ameliorate, if not rectify, these conditions. This was the first so-called New Deal.

The Depression had little effect on Dandy, other than suffering a substantial loss in investments when the stock market crashed in the fall of 1929. His case load of patients did not seem to decline during the 1930s. And while his tastes were simple and his style of living unpretentious, his income was such that the family could afford two maids, the children could attend private schools and summer camp, he could go to Florida in the winter for a couple of weeks, and the family could enjoy summer vacations.

As Roosevelt extended his New Deal program of relief and reform, Dandy, though a registered Democrat, developed an intense antipathy towards the president and what he was doing that amounted to hatred. Moreover, he had a strong dislike for liberals in general and was "terribly afraid of socialism," towards which Roosevelt, he may have felt, was moving the country (66).

During these years he continued to exact of himself and the brain team the highest standards of patient care. ". . . I have always instructed my men to bear in mind that they must treat patients with the utmost consideration because they need sympathy as well as medical examinations, and this I insist upon. I know that some people are very much more difficult to handle than others, but this is a test of their ability just as much as a professional test" (67).

A significant aspect of Dandy's concern for patient care was his insistence that with a positive ventriculogram (confirming the presence of a lesion), an operation should immediately follow. To wait a day or so after obtaining this information was unfair as well as dangerous to the patient (68).

A further evidence of Dandy's concern for his patients was his refusal to use bottled blood during surgery, as he believed that in the process of taking it the blood hemolyzed and thereby made possible adverse reactions. Furthermore, he had no use for citrated blood; only fresh blood was permissible. A humourous instance in this regard, relates DeWitt Fox, occurred when a house officer who was to be a blood donor for one of Dandy's cases was scheduled to assist in another operating room. He told the intern to take his blood before 7:00 a.m. and to have it ready in a bottle for Dandy's surgery.

> When Dandy saw that bottle, he screamed, "No bottled blood for my patient! Stop it immediately; go get that house officer and bring him in here."
> The young doctor had to break scrub, come into the theatre with Dandy's patient, and lie down beside him, while they took another pint of blood. When he stood up, he promptly fainted.
> Dandy said, "Give him that pint of blood from the bottle," (which, of course, was his own blood). "He can have bottled bood, but not my patient" (72).

As noted earlier, the establishment of a postoperative recovery room with trained staff was an important part of Dandy's dedication to giving the best care possible to his patients. Despite his difficulty in remembering patients' names—he referred to Mrs. Castleberry, the mother of movie actress Dorothy Lamour, as Mrs. Cranberry (70)—he was very good about following up through correspondence the recovery of patients after they left the hospital. He often told patients to avoid dwelling on their condition as when he wrote to one: "You are fine. Just keep busy working and playing and keep your mind off yourself." To another patient who had expressed concern about her facial appearance, he advised: "You must get your mind off yourself and forget the past. You are free of the worst pain in the world [tic douloureux], but you can get one just as bad if you let your mind linger on yourself." And to a patient who had been operated on for Ménière's disease, he wrote: "It always makes me very happy to hear from one who is so enthusiastic and appreciative as you. If you will just dismiss the noise in the head I am sure it will gradually calm down and you won't notice it eventually. Just keep on working hard and pay no attention to it" (71).

For the hopelessly ill Dandy favored euthanasia, as he indicated in a letter to a Venezuelan physician: "I have just seen your little patient with hydrocephalus. It was blind and deaf, and these in addition to a hairlip [sic], just made it appear cruel to try to prolong its life. Moreover, it had a bad heart with cyanosis with the least exertion, and it certainly would not stand very much. I thought it was much the kindest thing to let nature take its course" (72).

In billing patients for his professional services Dandy usually took into consideration their ability to pay, and he made it a policy not to charge clergymen or teachers. For people of very limited means or without savings, he did not expect a fee. Interestingly, he had several patients with brain tumors from the little town of Welch, West Virginia, which knew the poverty brought on by the Depression. Dandy, it is believed, not only gave his services to them but paid their hospital expenses as well (73).

Upon learning that one of his patients on whom he was to operate was a high school teacher (74), Dandy told the woman that he was not going to charge her anything since he had been encouraged to study medicine by a high school teacher. The woman replied that she would like to pay something; Dandy said "no," that would not be necessary. But she persisted; finally Dandy, who was not one to debate such matters, abruptly said "all right, a thousand dollars." The woman, according to one who was present, almost keeled over on hearing that!

To a man who in the fall of 1938 complained of a charge of $1500.00 for an operation, Dandy responded: "I thought I was making you a very small charge for the operation, particularly as I charge up to $5000.00. I doubtless did operate for $500.00 on a similar case, but that probably was all he could afford. The charge is more than fair" (75). Such an adjustment of fees, based on the patients' ability to pay, had been a longstanding practice among American physicians and surgeons.

In one instance—during the early 1940s—Dandy charged a wealthy Argentinian woman $10,000.00 for an operation. The woman would not be operated on during the summer since The Johns Hopkins Hospital did not then have air conditioning; consequently, she went to New York, where she stayed at the Waldorf-Astoria until September, and then returned to Baltimore for surgery (76).

Barnes Woodhall recalls that "Dr. Dandy was not amenable to flattery" and that he would become irritated with people who tried to deceive him (77). Unfortunately he experienced with some Jewish patients deception concerning their ability to meet his fee, which lead him to insist on payment from them in advance. To his old friend Ralph Greene, who had had similar experiences, Dandy once wrote:

> I am naturally prejudiced against Jews and when _____ came here he told me he had nothing, and then he very promptly send [sic] me an insurance blank to make out in which he stated he had an income of $300.00 a month, and naturally I joined the two up together. I am so sick of being beaten by Jews. I am, of course, eager to do all I can to help any one, but when I find they are playing a dirty game against me I have no sympathy for them (78).

Despite Dandy's feelings about Jewish patients, which were not unique among his contemporaries in medicine, it should be noted that he did number among his friends, professional and nonprofessional, several Jews for whom he had a high regard.

Occasionally, Hopkins' neurosurgeon received an acerbic letter from a patient or patient's relative about a charge or some other annoyance such as the one that he had from F.J.S. Grace of New York City in December 1938:

> Dear Sir:
> Mrs. Grace and I saw a good many doctors in Baltimore with her visit to Dr. [Lewellys F.] Barker's Clinic, and I am sure you will be very happy to know that you were the only one who showed us the slightest discourtesy.
>
> Yours truly,
> F.J.S. Grace

To which Dandy promptly replied:

I just cannot understand how you could have thought that I was discourteous to you. Certainly there was no reason for it, certainly it is not my habit to be discourteous to anybody, especially without reason. I can assure you you are very much mistaken.

Yours very truly,
W.E. Dandy (79)

Perhaps in this instance Dandy was brusk, as he sometimes could be, without realizing it. But he was not one to show discourtesy towards his patients or members of the hospital staff. His abruptness of speech at times caused others, however, to think that he was discourteous. Yet, Ervan F. Kushner remembered some years later that whenever he visited Dandy at his office, he " . . . was always accorded the courtesy and understanding which only a great man can give" (80).

In the course of treating patients at Hopkins, Dandy from time to time had to deal with Winford H. Smith (1877–1961), the hospital's estimable director, who years before had given Dandy a room at the hospital after Cushing had abruptly reversed himself about taking the younger man with him to Boston. "Smith was a man of candor and spoke forthrightly on issues affecting the Medical Institutions (81). Dandy and he, while they had a great respect for each other, did not always see eye to eye on matters of hospital policy, such as out-of-state patients' ability to pay their expenses. Dandy felt "that it was unfair to patients and harmful to the hospital to ask patients in straitened circumstances to bring $150.00 when half of that will cover their expenses. I am quite sure," he added in a letter in May 1933 to Smith, "if you will look up the records of the past few years there will be very few patients who have been brought here through correspondence with me who have not come prepared to pay all of their expenses. I know the one patient whose delinquency you remember, who was taken into the hospital purely by Miss [Edith A.] Howland's [director of admissions] kindness and distinctly against my advice. I do not think it is fair to hold up unduly all other patients because of this exception (82). Smith, in his candid reply, was equally emphatic:

During these times I do not think that people from out of the State should be encouraged to come here unless they are able to pay. I realize that there are few men competent to do the sort of work which you are doing; but, on the other hand, if the work can not be done at home, there is usually some way of raising money or having responsible authorities provide for the expenses of patients who cannot pay. This will not be done if their way is made easy.

So far as I am concerned, if the bill is paid, I can have no complaint. I shall therefore accept your proposition; namely, "if at any time patients come to the hospital through correspondence with me that I will guarantee their hospital expenses so that the hospital may not lose." I am disinclined to waive the operating room charge entirely in the event you are forced to pay, but I will make it as near cost as possible (83).

The following year Dandy expressed to Smith his objections to a new, though experimental, policy concerning a maximum fee for patients on the semiprivate wards and the hospital's collecting personal accounts of the medical and surgical staffs. He thought that the hospital expenses for patients who earned between $2000.00 and $5000.00 per year were "too great"; consequently he had "shifted many of these patients to the semi-private ward" (originally intended for those with incomes of about $2000.00).

Believing that the hospital's collection of professional fees was "an unfair obligation" to both the institution and the physician, Dandy argued that Hopkins was in no position to force payment of medical and surgical accounts that "are notoriously delinquent. This charge should in all fairness be carried out by the one who has rendered the service" (84). His thinking here reflected the strong feelings he had long had about the relationship between the patient and the physician and the latter's fee for the service provided.

During the 1930s Dandy published nearly 60 articles, a few of which, to be sure, were on the same subject, and three books, if Chapter 1 in Volume XII—"Surgery of the Brain"—in *Practice of Surgery: Clinical, Diagnostic, Operative, Postoperative*, edited by Dean Lewis, is included. This monograph of more than 600 pages was republished some years later as an independent book (85). Dandy's impressive list of publications for this decade stemmed from numerous cases, selective research, and much thought.

In *Archives of Surgery* for June 1930, Hopkins' master of neurological surgery presented "An Operation for the Treatment of Spasmodic Torticollis." An intermittent or continuous spasm of the neck muscles which, beginning in early or middle life affects women more than men, characterizes this condition. Torticollis, or wryneck, could be cured, Dandy stated, "by removing the nerve supply from the major muscles of rotation. The remaining muscles will overcome in time and by training the lost motor function and in most instances any remaining traces of the condition" (86). Dandy's procedure, involving the intradural sectioning of the first, second, and third sensory and motor roots and dividing peripherally the spinal roots, was done on eight patients, five of whom appeared cured, two of whom were much improved, and one of whom died of pneumonia, not contracted during surgery, 3 weeks later.

Meanwhile, Dandy was much pleased to receive a copy of a letter that John M. T. Finney, acting chief of surgery at Hopkins following Halsted's death, had written to a patient about the younger surgeon's treatment of torticollis as compared with his own operation:

> I am delighted to learn from your letter and Dr. Dandy's report that as a result of Dr. Dandy's operation, you have entirely recovered from your former trouble. Spasmodic torticollis, from which you were suffering when I first saw you, is a condition that is permanently relieved only by putting out of commission the nerve supply of the muscles involved. This can be done either by division or excision of the muscles themselves, including their nerve supply, or, as suggested and performed by Dr. Dandy, a division of the nerve supply high up. Dr. Dandy's operation is less mutilating than mine. I, therefore, advised you to have him do the operation, rather than myself (87).

A year after the publication of the article on the treatment of spasmodic torticollis, Dandy reported on a procedure for curing migraine, based on just two cases, in which the results, he found, were "striking"; but he readily admitted that time and more patients were needed before a definitive conclusion could be reached (88). He never did arrive at a final conclusion about the desirability of removing the stellate ganglion (ganglion refers to a group of nerve cells, usually found outside the central nervous system) as a remedy for migraine. Today " . . . it has been well established that stellate ganglion surgery never effected a cure for migraine" (89).

Shortly after Dandy's article on the treatment of migraine appeared, he removed "a hickory nut sized tumor" from the interior of the brain stem of a woman patient. This was the first time a tumor, which proved to be an encapsulated hematoma (a circumscribed, extravenous collection of blood, generally clotted, forming a mass) was successfully excised from within the brain stem (90).

In the meantime, Dandy was invited in the spring of 1931 to present a paper at a joint meeting of the New York Academy of Medicine's Section of Neurology and Psychiatry and the New York Neurological Society on the "Effects of Total Removal of Left Temporal Lobe in A Right-Handed Person: Localization of Areas of Brain Concerned with Speech." He reported that there is no auditory center in either the left or right temporal lobes of the brain and that "unquestionably, there is a relationship between the tracts for hearing and the auditory center, but, the connection must be in the parietal lobe" (91). He extended these remarks during the discussion period following his presentation to make the general observation that while other parts of the brain, including the opposite side, it has been widely believed, have assumed the loss of speech, motor powers, etc., "I think positively that there can be no restoration of function by education of the opposite side of the brain. For example, after the total removal of a right hemisphere there will never be restoration of motor function in the left side of the body. Moreover, after resection of the left occipital lobe with hemianopia [blindness in one half of the visual field], there is no restoration of visual speech or of the hemianopia" (91).

About a year and a half later, Dandy quietly made a dramatic report on the physiological effects of removal of the entire right cerebral hemisphere from three patients—apparently he was the first surgeon to undertake this procedure—one of whom lived for 2 years and 2 months following surgery, a second 6 months, and a third, who died from meningitis 10 days after the operation (92). The first of these operations he had performed 10 years before (1923), and the other two in 1927. "From accurately defined and well performed removals of this type," Dandy observed, "the functional results, if positive, must be regarded as specific, and, if negative, must exclude the part of the brain concerned from participation in the function tested. Nor can [Sir William] Broadbent's old theory that the corresponding part of the opposite hemisphere assumes these functions be given even remote consideration. The arm, leg and visual areas receive no relief, and losses of function due to injuries of the left hemisphere are not aided in the least by any participation of the right hemisphere" (93).

In his summation Dandy expressed disappointment that with the excision of such a large area of brain tissue, as reported in these three cases, there was no indication "of any resulting defect in mental functioniong." Yet, he was unwilling "to say that the mentality of the patients was normal; but rather that abnormalities have not been disclosed." Interestingly, Dandy found that the two patients who lived longer "were always perfectly oriented as to time, place and person. Their memory for immediate and remote events was unimpaired. They could read, write and compute without error." And the first patient (infection reduced the amount of activity with the second patient) who revealed quickness and keenness as reflected in his style of humor, "was also interested in serious conversation, in reading and in following the world's events" (94). Moreover, smell and hearing were not affected, though some loss of taste resulted. Hemianopsia (hemianopia) was complete, as would be expected.

Dandy must have enjoyed a letter with a light touch which he received some months after his extirpation of the right cerebral hemisphere in 1927 from W.W. Keen of Philadelphia, whom he considered to be "America's pioneer neurological surgeon." Keen, who was then 91 years old, wrote to his Baltimore friend thus:

My dear Dandy:
    As I have told you before, your are rightly named. Here you are removing half of a fellow's brains and letting him go around just as usual. Whenever you get to the point when you can take out all the brains,° I may consult you.

                                                    Sincerely yours,
                                                    W.W. Keen (95)
°for all those who have any

Certainly one of Dandy's most important contributions to the literature of neurological surgery was his chapter in Volume XII of Lewis' *Practice of Surgery* that was later republished, as previously noted, as a separate book, *Surgery of the Brain*, in 1945, again as *The Brain* in 1969, and is still in print under the last title. Dandy was encouraged to prepare this monograph not only by Dean Lewis, who was then professor and chairman of the department of surgery at Hopkins, but also perhaps from the inspiration he had derived from reading M. Allen Starr's little book, *Brain Surgery* (96), which he had read on a trip to Chicago early in 1923. Upon his return Dandy wrote a letter of appreciation to Starr indicating " . . . what a great stimulus it had been to read it because of its great intrinsic merits and particularly when realizing that it was written thirty years ago in the very dawn of brain surgery. Surprisingly little has been added and much forgotten. So many things I found there that I had considered information rather recently acquired. I have been reading a number of books on brain surgery by the European masters since the beginning on this subject, and in none has there been so much real information as is contained in your wonderful little book" (97).

In his usual, clear and readable prose, Dandy sought to present in his monograph on the subject, which was published almost 40 years after Starr's book, the most recent information about brain lesions, their symptoms, and the operative technique necessary for their correction or alleviation. Divided into twelve sections, beginning with an introduction and historical background, *Surgery of the Brain* included such topics as general considerations concerning intracranial surgery (anesthesia, routine operative exposures, control of hemorrhage and intracranial pressure, electro-cautery, immediate postoperative care, etc.), lesions of the cranial nerves, hydrocephalus, epilepsy, infections of the brain, meninges, and skull, and brain tumors—their general diagnosis and treatment.

Dandy, in dealing with examinations used in diagnosing and localizing lesions of the brain (Section II), was emphatic that "ventriculography should be used only when careful studies of intracranial tumors make additional information necessary." He cautioned that " . . . no exploratory operative attack should be made upon a tumor or a presumed tumor unless the diagnosis and localization are absolutely certain. Therein lies the tragedies of brain surgery" (98).

Later in the monograph Dandy pointed out that "brain tumors are among the most common tumors of the body" and that they occur at all ages and many are present during intrauterine life." Moreover, there is no essential difference in the incidence of these tumors between men and women. But after the age of 50, "there is a steady decline in the number of cases" (99).

In approaching the diagnosis of brain tumors, "not their localization," Dandy urged that heavy emphasis be placed upon "common sense." "Particularly is this true of tumors in the early stages, i.e., before the advent of absolute signs of intracranial pressure or localization." Brain tumors are among the most common lesions of the brain, and few other lesions produce between birth and 60 years of age headaches "which arise *de novo*, i.e., are not of congenital or hereditary origin." Furthermore, few other lesions induce a gradual development of such neurological signs as motor or sensory paralysis, loss of hearing, speech, or vision or, in youth, the enlargement of the head. "Diplopia [double vision], coming on without ascertainable cause, is an important early sign of brain tumor." But by far the most important of all signs or symptoms is headache (100).

By the time Dandy prepared this monograph on brain surgery, his thinking about the causes of brain tumors had undergone a change from what he had written to a patient in 1924: "The difficulty is that I am never able to say that a blow is the cause of a tumor. That is one of the things which medical science has never proven, though I must confess that there is a feeling on the part of a great many physicians, and I among them, that tumors are a product of blows" (101).

By contrast, in *Surgery of the Brain*, he felt "very strongly that there is no relationship whatever between trauma and the development of any intracranial tumors. To the lay mind trauma is always regarded as the starting point of the intracranial symptoms, but a careful history will usually disarm this explanation" (102). More recently Albert B. Butler and Martin G. Netsky, in a chapter of Youman's *Neurological Surgery*, state that "a traumatic cause can be accepted for a small number of meningiomas such as that in General [Leonard] Wood . . . . In most cases, however, trauma probably initiates or aggravates clinical symptoms of a tumor already within the cranial cavity" (103).

Elsewhere in the section devoted to brain tumors Dandy dealt with palliative operations or cerebral decompressions that involve the removal of a portion of the skull, with or without the dura mater, so as to relieve intracranial pressure. Decompressions became popular in the early days of brain surgery as a means of giving patients relief from either an inoperable tumor or until such time as the tumor's steady growth gave localizing signs. Cushing technically improved upon this longstanding procedure. Soon it became common practice to make the decompression in the right subtemporal region of right-handed patients, as this part of the brain was silent and the temporal muscle somewhat restrained the cerebral protrusion (104).

When all brain tumors could now be localized by ventriculography, Dandy argued that so-called primary decompressions could not be justified except, perhaps, in some instances of sinus thrombosis and in many cases of head injuries. "They are decidedly harmful because they postpone localization of a tumor until the local destructive effects are evident and, therefore, make many operable tumors inoperable. Beneath the operative area the brain is injured irreparably, and they make much more difficult a rational effort later to attack the tumor on the same side" (104). Inasmuch as decompression had become entrenched, Dandy felt that it would be years before "its pernicious influence" could be eliminated. He allowed, however, that as a *secondary* procedure decompression might be employed beneficially in two ways: "(1) after the tumor has been explored and found inoperable, and (2) as a temporary relief for cerebral edema resulting from partial or complete removal of a tumor" (104).

In the last section of *Surgery of the Brain*—"Special Tumors of the Brain–Diagnosis and Treatment"—Dandy revealed his thinking about treatment of terminally ill patients—those with metastatic lesions—by recommending that surgery be avoided unless the patient or his relatives desire a prolongation of life or that such prolongation would be for several months and free of serious physical defects. "It does not seem fair to the patient or to the patients' relatives, who must endure the physical and mental agonies of an incurable lesion and its progressive sequelae, to prolong a life unless very material benefits are probable" (105).

By the summer of 1931 Dandy had finally finished his magnum opus on brain surgery which, towards the end of his labors, he characterized as "a terrible undertaking" (106), but he shortly had that special satisfaction, enjoyed by authors, of seeing it in print. More than 20 years later, his successor at Johns Hopkins, A. Earl Walker, wrote that "this treatise on neurological surgery, beautifully illustrated as were all his papers, is still the best text available on the technique in brain surgery" (107). Meanwhile, its importance warranted translation into other languages, including German and Italian.

No sooner had Dandy finished *Surgery of the Brain* than he began preparing for publication *Benign Tumors in the Third Ventricle of the Brain: Diagnosis and Treatment*, which he read in abstract form on June 7, 1932, at the annual meeting of the American Neurological Society at Atlantic City, New Jersey (109). This study, which is still in print, dealt with 21 cases of benign, removable tumors found in the third ventricle (110). One group of these tumors were colloid cysts, which Dandy found " . . . unlike, so far as I know, any other tumors in the brain and perhaps in the body; nor have they been found in any other part of the brain" (111). A second group of tumors of the third ventricle included a heterogeneous collection of largely solid tumors "but with varying histological structure" (112). The author, while indicating that both groups were curable by surgery, cautioned that the possibility of their recurrence could not be "excluded—particularly in the group of ependymal gliomata [bulky, solid, vascularized tumors derived from ependymal cells]" (113).

He reported a mortality of 33.3% for the entire series but added that during the 2½ years preceding publication 14 of the 21 tumors had been removed, with a mortality rate of 14.3%. For the patients who recovered, practically all functions, "except for occasional minor effects," were restored (113).

Published in 1933, *Benign Tumors* drew a vitriolic review in the

Western Journal of Surgery, Obstetrics, and Gynecology from a Doctor A.J. McLean of Portland, OR, the brother of a man whom Dandy had earlier discharged from his service for unacceptable conduct. McLean concluded his review with the injunction that "no neurosurgeon can afford to be without this handbook of technic, both for its utility and as an example of the way not to write a book" (114). The review smacked of a desire to settle professional accounts and was, in Dandy's judgment, "perhaps the nastiest of all the book reviews" of his recent major publications that had come to his attention (115).

The same year in which *Benign Tumors* was published, Frederick Reichert of Stanford University Hospital, whom it will be recalled was Dandy's first resident, submitted, as noted in Chapter 6, his friend and former teacher's name as a candidate for the Nobel Prize for Physiology and Medicine in 1934. "This recommendation," wrote Reichert, "is made on Professor Dandy's basic researches in neurophysiology and neuropathology, in particular, his introduction of ventriculography and encephalography and his work on the circulation of the cerebrospinal fluid" (116). Six weeks after he had submitted Dandy's name to the Nobel Committee for Physiology and Medicine, he sent a copy of his statement of nomination to his old friend in Baltimore with a covering letter in which he asked that it be kept confidential. "I still don't see," Reichert wondered, "how they asked me to nominate but I was glad of the opportunity to tell them of you. Here's hoping you get it for you surely deserve it" (117).

Dandy did not receive the Nobel Prize in 1934, or anytime later. Undoubtedly he was disappointed but realized with the international competition what the odds were for such an award (118). Meanwhile, he was the recipient of other honors. In 1931 he was made an honorary member of the National Academy of Medicine of Mexico, and 2 years later he became one of 30 foreign members of the Society Radio-neuro-chirurgica Italiana. At its meeting on December 19, 1934, the Société Nationale de Chirurgie de Paris named him a corresponding member, as did the Gesellschaft der Chirurgen in Vienna in 1937 (119).

Busy as Johns Hopkins' neurosurgeon was in the early 1930s with his operating schedule and publications, he did find the time for vacationing with the family. In the summer of 1932 he and Sadie took a trip—they both loved to travel, although he never did as much as he would have liked—by automobile to Montreal,

Quebec, and around the Gaspé Peninsula. Upon their return they took the children to the ocean "and had a grand time with them." He later admitted to Fred Reichert: "I too have not had an opportunity to get acquainted with my little kiddies, as you have expressed it" (120).

In November of the following year Dandy published a short article in the *Annals of Surgery*, "Benign Encapsulated Tumors in the Lateral Ventricles of the Brain: Diagnosis and Treatment" (121), which was a harbinger of his next book, bearing the same title, which appeared in 1934. He experienced transient difficulty in finding a publisher for the book. Paul Hoeber of Paul B. Hoeber, Inc., Medical Publisher, indicated that the manuscript in question sounded like a second volume of *Benign Tumors in the Third Ventricle of the Brain* but that a decision could not be reached without seeing the manuscript. Perhaps, he added, they could chat about it at the forthcoming A.M.A. meeting in Cleveland. Dandy tartly replied that the manuscipt " . . . was essentially the same size and same character as 'Tumors in the Third Ventricle.' Of course, the contents are entirely different and in no way similar. I am sure sending the manuscript would be noncontributory." He added as a caveat that inasmuch as Hoeber was not interested in publishing his book (122), he would not be interested in considering him "for any future publications of any kind." Moreover, he would not be in Cleveland!

A series of 15 cases formed the basis for *Benign Encapsulated Tumors in the Lateral Ventricles* which, as it turned out, came from the press of The Williams & Wilkins Company of Baltimore, a reputable medical publishing house. Dandy reported that the 15 cases of primary benign encapsulated tumors were treated surgically "and all but one totally removed. Twelve patients recovered and three died" (123), with the fatalities occurring towards the beginning of this series of operations. As these tumors were encapsulated, they were curable, he emphasized, when totally excised. With the use of electrocautery, continuous suction, and Avertin anesthesia the risk entailed in removing such deep-seated tumors was much lessened (124). Some of these tumors were sufficiently hard so as to permit extirpation by the finger, a defensible practice under certain circumstances which Dandy did not originate (125).

Among the most common signs and symptoms of such tumors were "headache, vomiting, dizziness, papilledema, diplopia with or without extra-ocular palsies, focal or Jacksonian convulsions, hemiplegia and corresponding reflex changes, and hemianes-thesia . . . ." There was no clinical syndrome by which these tumors could be localized. Ventriculography, however, made possible accurate diagnosis and precise localization (126).

Just as the volume *Benign Tumors in the Third Ventricle of the Brain* had drawn a sharp criticism, so did Dandy's latest publication in a review in the *Journal of the American Medical Association* by Percival Bailey, for whom Dandy had no use. The feeling was mutual. Bailey was unsparing in his attack on Dandy's new book, as the following passage reveals:

> That the author, among the thousands of brain tumors recorded in the medical literature, was able to find only twenty-five similar tumors indicates that the book deals with a great rarity. One might ask why a monograph should be written on such a rare condition, which has no constant clinical or pathologic characteristics. The answer is given in the introduction—to point again to the value of ventriculography, now generally recognized. The book abounds in dogmatic statements. That "this precision in diagnosis (by ventriculography) is not only easy and certain but is attainable without risk to life or function" is not strictly true (127).

Dandy, who had in earlier writings warned of the dangers of ventriculography, especially from people with insufficient training in the procedure, left himself open here, it would seem; and Bailey took full advantage. He did close his review, however, on a positive note: "The author's cases are a welcome addition to the causistics of brain tumors" (127).

Shortly after the appearance of this review Dandy told Ralph Greene that he should have warned the editor not to give Bailey "an opportunity to give vent to his personal dislikes through its journal as a medium, but I neglected to do so. I have had many protests. I think one written in your inimitable style [and] sent to [Morris] Fishbein of the A.M.A. might do some good. Bailey is one of those individuals who could make a tremendous profit by buying himself for what he is actually worth and selling himself for what he thinks he is worth" (128).

Although Dandy's entire career was spent at Johns Hopkins, where he enjoyed the advantage of a trained staff and a complete surgical armamentarium, he did occasionally operate elsewhere. For several years he was a member of the active staff of Union Memorial Hospital, whose origins in Baltimore anteceded the Civil War. In 1934 he learned that, as he had not used the Hospital's facilities at least three times during the past year, he automatically became a member of the senior staff. This change was made, according to hospital regulations, so as to make it possible for younger men to gain access to the active staff (129). Dandy was upset by this alteration of status because, as he noted in his response, he had ". . . always wanted to keep an active interest in the Union Memorial. I realize that in the past year or two I have not sent many cases there, though I should be very glad to do so in the future. I cannot, of course, operate on tumors and tics, because I haven't the instruments there, but there are many other operations that I could do perfectly well." He added that he had had a "half dozen other patients there in conjunction with other doctors in the past year, and would have had other cases of fractures of the skull if the wishes of the relatives and parents had not been side-tracked by members of the hospital who told them I was not available. I have always felt that this was not a square deal, and I do not think it meets the spirit of most of the men connected with the hospital" (130). He continued his association with Union Memorial Hospital where his son, Walter Jr., who has been a full-time member of its staff for many years, now heads the intensive care unit.

When Dandy attended out-of-town meetings, he often took with him a small bag of instruments, including a favorite pair of rongeurs. Despite his disclaimer about the benefits of attendance at professional meetings, he did attend and participate in a good many. He especially enjoyed the annual meetings of the Southern Surgical Association, of which he became a fellow in 1930, and of the Surgical Research Society, from which he resigned with regret in 1936 because of increasing difficulty of attendance (131). Moreover, that same year he consented to serve as Regent in Neurological Surgery for the International College of Surgeons and a year later became a member of the Founders Group of Diplomates of The American Board of Surgery, which was established for the certification of properly qualified surgeons.

While it has been said that "in his intense preoccupation in his work, he seemed to stand aloof from the rank and file of the growing specialty of neurosurgery" (132), his involvement with such organizations as the International College of Surgeons and the Southern Surgical Association, his service on the editorial board of the *Archives of Surgery* in the 1940s, and his wide correspondence, both foreign and domestic, which reflected a professional interest in others and a willingness to be of help when called upon, indicated that his seeming aloofness "from the rank and file" was deceiving.

Following his attendance at the Pan-American Medical Congress in the summer of 1931 at Mexico City, Dandy wrote to Dr. J.C. Villagrana of the Hospital Juarez there as follows:

I have often thought of my pleasant morning with you and the inspection of the hospital which you are so skillfully transforming. It was a most delightful experience, in fact, one of the brightest spots in my visit to Mexico.

I am just in receipt of the *Revista De Cirugia* with the splended translation of my little talk before your group of Mexican physicians. It is very well done indeed.

Do permit me to extend my thanks and appreciation and my very best wishes for your continued success. I shall be most interested to watch your progress (133).

Two years later he congratulated José Iglesias Torres for "a beautiful diagnosis of glossopharyngeal tic douloureux . . . ," adding that "as a matter of fact you put one over on me, for despite your diagnosis I thought it was trigeminal neuralgia" (134).

The late Owen H. Wangensteen, a distinguished professor of surgery at the University of Minnesota, who first met Dandy in September 1928 while visiting Hopkins' department of surgery, recalled another meeting with him 3 years later at a convention of railroad surgeons in Glacier National Park at which Dandy was the featured speaker. Wangensteen gave a short talk, "Present Concepts of Traumatic Shock and Its Treatment." In the audience was Dandy, who afterwards told Wangensteen how much he had enjoyed his talk. Years later, Wangensteen recalled: "This was my first informal meeting with Walter Dandy on a cordial and personal basis. In fact, we had planned to take a trip together on July 4, on horseback through the mountains of Glacier Park. The day before, he got an emergency call from The Hopkins concerning one of his patients and returned to Baltimore at once" (135).

After Dandy's talk at this meeting, one of the senior railroad officials, Wangensten remembered, ". . . remarked that he was only sorry that he did not have a brain tumor so that he could have Dandy remove it for him—a reflection of the confidence that Dandy conveyed to his auditors" (135).

The 1930s were not only years of depression that was worldwide in scope but of dictatorship as well. On January 30, 1933, Adolf Hitler became the chancellor of Germany and thus ushered in the 12 years of Nazi authoritarianism, half of which were to involve Europe and most of the rest of the world in the conflagration of

World War II. Once the United States joined the Allied nations in the struggle against the Axis powers, Germany, Italy, and Japan, Dandy became involved in the American war effort, as will be discussed in a succeeding chapter.

Meanwhile, Hitler's rise to power was to effect Hopkins' professor of neurosurgery in another—and quietly dramatic—way. Since the mid-1920s Dandy had known Doctor Robert Wartenberg, a neurologist at the University of Freiburg whom he had helped to become a Rockefeller Foundation Fellow. During his year here Wartenberg, who was Jewish, visited Dandy's clinic for several months and, as a consequence, they struck up a friendship. Dandy came to regard him as "one of the best neurologists in Germany" (136).

Seven months after Hitler came to power, Dandy received from Wartenberg this imploring letter:

S.O.S.! Save me and help me! As a non-aryan man is my outlook in Germany very bad. I cannot find here any position, and to go abroad is for me the question of the mere existence. As a front-soldier and politically unsuspected man I retain my venia legendi and can remain for some months in the clinic, but I fear for long there is absolutely no place for me in Germany.

In this very serious condition of my life I dare to trouble you and to ask you for an advice [of] what to do, whom to apply to in order to get a neurological position abroad eventually for later on. I will content myself with a very modest one, at any part of the world whatever. U.S.A. or any English speaking country I would of course like the best (137).

In a letter several weeks later Dandy, while showing genuine concern for his friend's situation, failed to comprehend, like many others of that day, what actually was happening to the Jews in Nazi Germany and what in turn proved to be the harbinger of the Holocaust.

I am terribly distressed to hear of your situation in Germany as a non-aryan. I cannot believe for a moment that the situation will not blow over in time and that your former status will return. It would be my very strong feeling that you should bide your time and see if this will not develop. I have thought of the possibilities in this country, but we are in the midst of a depression, such as this country has scarcely known before, and it is almost impossible to find an opening anywhere. There is not one at Hopkins. I have been thinking of some of the other Universities of lesser standing, and as long as you can hold in Freiburg I should certainly think this was the best thing to do. If the situation becomes worse, do let me know, and you may depend upon it that I will do everything in my power to help you.

I think perhaps Cushing might be in a better position to help you than I for his influence is very much wider. Your work has been of such high standing that Germany most of all cannot afford to let you wander elsewhere (138).

The following spring Dandy informed Wartenberg that he hoped to be able to give him shortly "some definite information" and that he thought it might be possible to place him in a position here through the Committee in Aid of Displaced Foreign Physicians (139). Later that spring Dandy told his friend that he would likely have a position in Colorado with a Doctor Ebaugh, "a very fine man" (140), but that did not materialize. Another year passed, and still Wartenberg had not left Germany and had no prospect of a position in the United States. Dandy wrote that he was "greatly distressed to know that your efforts have been unavailing. You have no idea how difficult the situation for physicians is in this country; thousands are on the relief and many more thousands are not making a living. Have you thought of going to Buenos Aires or Rio de Janeiro?" (141).

Before the end of 1935 Wartenberg finally arrived in the United States but without a job. Within a few months he at last received an appointment at the University of California Medical School in San Francisco. To his friend in Baltimore he gratefully wrote: "For your touching interest in my behalf, for your so kind endeavors to place me, for what you have done for me, I am thanking you most profoundly. It is you to whom I owe my first and my second trip to America" (142).

When Dandy learned a little less than 3 years later that his friend Doctor Arthur Schüller of Vienna, whom he had met on his European trip of 1923–1924, was going to Australia, he was quite upset. It did not seem possible to him that a man of Schüller's stature "could be forced out," but he wondered if it might still be possible for him to come to the United States. Dandy asked if there was anything he could do to help. "I should be very happy to send you a check if you need and will let me do so" (143).

Thus, through these friends Dandy came to know something of the evils of Nazism. A little more than 6 months after his correspondence with Schüller, Germany invaded Poland and World War II began.

In January 1935 the Dandy's last child, Margaret Martin, was born. Her brother, Walter Jr., would be 10 years old on his next birthday, while her sisters, Mary Ellen and "Kitty," would turn 8 and 7, respectively, the following summer. As the baby of the family, "Maggy" was the apple of her father's eye. Many years later she remembered that "everytime there was roast chicken for dinner, we two were the ones who got the wishbone, and everytime the wish was the same—'for a little baby brother.' He would speak the wish, and then we would look over (he with a twinkle in his bright blue eyes) to poor harrassed mother, seated to his right. (I was on the left). Maybe if there had been a little baby brother, my world would have fallen apart, but at least for the time, I had complete faith that the wish was more a joke than anything else" (144).

As busy as Dandy was with his practice and his writing, he was a devoted husband and father who thoroughly enjoyed his home and much preferred it ". . . to going to parties," although when he attended such social affairs "he was always the last one to leave" (145). Actually the Dandys' social life was simple; they rarely entertained other than when it was his turn to host the Wednesday night group of bridge players—Doctors Thomas R. Chambers, Richard Keefer, Ronald Abercrombie, Harvey B. Stone (five including Dandy, so that if one could not be present, there would still be a foursome).

This group regularly played together for ten to fifteen years. While food and drinks were served, these doctors, who took their bridge seriously, did not gather merely to socialize. It was said that Dandy frequently overbid his hand, with the result that his partners could not always support him. On one occasion he blew up and told Ronald Abercrombie that "that was a goddamned stupid play." Later, however, he apologized to Abercrombie. After one of these occasional outbursts, Chambers would say to Dandy, "Walter, I don't know why you haven't been killed" (146).

In June 1938, Dandy took the bridge group to the heavyweight fight in New York between Joe Louis and Max Schmeling, the famous return match, and paid for everything. The fight ended, however, in the first round when Louis knocked out Schmeling. Disappointed with such abruptness, Dandy made some comment about the expensive seats for such a short fight. In recalling this event nearly 30 years later, Harvey Stone observed that the host "was just as extravagantly generous as he was" on occasion rude or discourteous (147).

As Dandy was at home most evenings, the family learned never to talk with him about problems before dinner. It was wiser to wait until he had had an opportunity to enjoy his dinner and glass of beer and to hold forth on some aspect of his day's activities—"I had a beautiful brain abscess today"—with a kind of "contagious enthusiasm" (148).

While he was keenly interested in his children and their development, it is doubtful, as one daughter perceptively observed, that he "knew what he was doing" in raising them "any more than most of the parents of his generation did (in the sense that we now consider the intentionality behind raising children)" (148). He was more concerned with the results they achieved, such as grades or excelling in some sport or other extracurricular activity, than in the learning processes involved in the preparation of a theme or the solving of a mathematical problem. What mattered to Dandy was that each child was "to be special somehow" and that each would be "good at something or other" (149). But whatever they accomplished, he admonished them, "Don't boast" (150).

No doubt Dandy reflected his generation's thinking about the relative importance of boys' education to that of girls'. He probably did not take his daughters' education as seriously as he did that of Walter Jr. While he wanted the girls to have a good education—all of the children attended private schools—he apparently was not interested in it being career oriented. When, in her teens, Mary Ellen began to think about a career, she expressed an interest in becoming a physician; however, her father did not give her much, if any, encouragement (151).

One of the interesting aspects of Dandy's role in the rearing of the children was his determination to avoid spoiling them with material possessions, except for good athletic equipment. Consequently, they had few toys. "He had plenty of money but didn't want us to think," remembered Kitty, "we could have anything we wanted. When I needed a bicycle when I was about twelve, I bought a second-hand clumsy thing with balloon tires; I never had a radio or record player or watch, or any 'unnecessary' luxuries like that, because he was determined that we not be spoiled" (152). He did not hesitate to buy them, however, the best tennis rackets and other sports equipment.

Dandy's likes and dislikes concerning people, work, and recreation were as pronounced by the time he was 50 (1936) as his views about overindulging children. "He liked people who achieved, whether it was a good bartender, prizefighter, cook, doctor, or anything. If the person did his job well, he liked them [sic]. He disliked people who told dirty jokes, who drank too much, who were careless in their work, who didn't try" (153). Achievement, for Dandy, was everything.

Aside from the professional journals and the writings of such pioneers in neurology and neurosurgery as Sir Charles Bell, Hughlings Jackson, and Sir William Macewen, he constantly read newspapers, which on a summer Sunday afternoon were usually scattered around him under the hammock in the backyard or, at other times, on the living room rug. He enjoyed biographies, especially of Lincoln and Napoleon, and histories of the Civil War, such as Douglas Southall Freeman's *Lee's Lieutenants.* He also found pleasure in poring over dictionaries, encyclopedias, and railroad timetables, the last of which, as noted earlier, he kept in abundant supply in an office desk drawer. And regularly he returned to what he considered "a classic," Charles Dickens' *Christmas Carol* which, as he wrote to a friend, he had "enjoyed more than almost anything" (154).

An all too common mistake in comparing Dandy with Harvey Cushing outside the operating room is to note the older man's taste in the acquisition of rare medical books and the consequent development of an excellent private library and to ignore his former pupil's similar interest. Wilder Penfield, the Montreal neurosurgeon, made such a comparison in his autobiography when he said: "Dandy was Halsted-trained, as Cushing was, but he lacked the things that Cushing acquired when he sought out the friendship of Osler [the love of books, their collection, and the history of medicine]. Generalization is dangerous and yet I would say that the best specialists are those who, in later life, keep the windows of the mind and heart open to the world beyond their specialty" (155). Penfield's comment about Dandy's alleged lack of cultural accomplishment and interest in books is considerably wide of the mark. Dandy actually had a fine collection of old and rare medical books which—not as large or as extensive, to be sure, as Cushing's—he kept at his home in built-in bookcases with glass doors. His interest in the history of medicine was not only reflected in his library but in gifts of such books as René Fülöp-Miller's *Triumph Over Pain*, James Thomas Flexner's *Doctors on Horseback*, and Loyal Davis's *J.B. Murphy: Stormy Petrel of Surgery* to friends (156).

Moreover, he was delighted to learn from Fred Reichert about his new course in the history of medicine at Stanford: "It will be such a great thing for young students to get the proper slant on medicine from this angle" (157). Dandy's enthusiasm for medical history, however, did not extend to Henry E. Sigerist (1891–1957) who, with an established reputation as a scholar in the field, came to Hopkins in 1932 as the William H. Welch Professor of the History of Medicine. In fact, Dandy "detested" him (158), perhaps because of Sigerist's sympathetic view of socialized medicine as set forth in his book, *Socialized Medicine in the Soviet Union* (New York, W.W. Norton, 1937); and Hopkins' neurosurgeon had an abiding dislike and distrust of socialism-communism.

Besides his love of reading and of sports—he regularly played golf on Thursday and Saturday afternoons at the Baltimore Country Club—Dandy's zeal for life included other interests. Since his days in Vienna, he enjoyed opera and preferred it to the theater; his hearing difficulty and his somewhat prudish taste precluded his full enjoyment of the latter. In radio programs his taste centered on classical and semiclassical music, as well as such comedians as Jack Benny, Fred Allen, and Eddie Cantor. His enjoyment of movies, especially the antics of Charlie Chaplin and the Marx Brothers, was enhanced in the fall of 1935 when Albert Warner gave him a gold pass to any of the Warner Brothers' theaters. Frequently on Friday nights, Dandy and the family would make use of the pass at a downtown theater (159) where, upon entering, he would leave his cigar on the wall ledge at the back of the auditorium and would pick it up on the way out!

Although he had hoped to give up cigarettes late in 1938, he never was able to do so. Members of the brain team understood that Mrs. Dandy did not wish for him to smoke cigarettes, and so he did not carry them. As he smoked Chesterfields, every resident also smoked them or at least had a pack of them with him when they made rounds so that the "Old Man" would be readily supplied. Contrary to the stories about Sadie's insistence that her husband give up cigarettes, she never urged him, she said years later, to stop. Wives, she noted, are often blamed or used as an excuse for something the husbands do or do not want to do (160).

By the mid-1930s Dandy, with his wife's encouragement, regularly went to Florida for a winter vacation of swimming, fishing, and golf. Whereas warm weather made her uncomfortable, he thrived on it—"He was a sun worshipper" (161)—and never seemd to mind the hot Baltimore summers devoid of air conditioning. His annual sojourn at Jekyll Island before his marriage actually set the pattern of winter vacations. For several years, his friend from Jekyll Island days, Clarence H. Geist, gave him a courtesy card to the beautiful Boca Raton Club at Boca Raton, FL, which Geist had bought for a fraction of its original cost of $10,000,000 (6%). ". . . In all my halcyeon [sic] days I never saw such finery and luxury," wrote Dandy to his mother and father. "The club roster reads like a directory of Wall Street and big business although not the men of such caliber as old Jekyll [Island] used to show" (162). In later years Dandy went to Ponte Vedra, just south of Jacksonville, which had "the nicest course" he had ever played (163).

But Florida vacations, professional accomplishments, and a happy home life could not erase the sorrow he felt with the death of his mother, Rachel, at the age of 75 in July 1936. As an only child of immigrants and with no other relatives here, Dandy, as noted earlier, had been very close to both his mother and father, whom he regularly visited on Sunday afternoons at their home on Arunah Avenue in Baltimore. In the spring of 1940 John Dandy died, having celebrated his 83rd birthday the preceding August. This was an added sorrow to a devoted son.

As a renowned brain surgeon, Dandy came to know many famous people. One of them was H.L. Mencken, the celebrated Baltimore journalist, critic, and linguistic scholar who, late in 1936, was a patient at Hopkins, though not on Dandy's service. On New Year's Eve as he was about to leave the hospital, Mencken wrote as follows to his friend in neurosurgery:

Dear Doctor:
  My very best thanks for that elegant flask of rye. It undoubtedly saved my life. The brethren here have grown tired of me and so propose to ship me off this afternoon. You were kind indeed to drop in on me and cheer me up. I hope we meet again soon after I escape.

Yours,
H.L. Mencken (164)

Among Dandy's other friends of renown were the Klebergs of Texas, owners of the huge King Ranch, not far from Corpus Christi, which he briefly visited on one occasion. The sister of Dick Kleberg, a United States Senator, and Robert who ran the ranch, Sarah Kleberg Shelton (Mrs. Joe Shelton) whose first husband died after a long illness following a brain tumor operation at Hopkins, had been patients of Dandy's. Sarah Shelton (formerly Mrs. Johnson) and her first husband honored him by naming their son "B," B. Dandy Kleberg Johnson. In answer to "a lovely letter" he received from Sarah Shelton in the fall in 1937, Dandy wrote in part: "I love to hear about your happiness and, of course, it always makes me feel so good when I know the game fight you have made [she was in an automobile accident five years before]. Some of these days we may drop in on you again. Do remember me to little "B," who is now quite a big boy; also to your mother and brothers. Every now and then I read something about them and the great ranch, which I was so fortunate in seeing for a few hours" (165).

Meanwhile, although Dandy had never known George Gershwin, the brilliant young American composer, he was dramatically involved in an effort to save his life. The Dandys had been invited to spend a weekend in July with Governor Harry W. Nice, cruising Chesapeake Bay on the Maryland state yacht *du Pont*. Dandy did not particularly like Nice but Sadie, who has always been fond of boats and the water, successfully countered with the observation that it would be quiet and pleasant aboard the governor's yacht. In the meantime Gershwin, who was suffering from a brain tumor, was readmitted to Cedars of Lebanon Hospital, Los Angeles, in a coma on the night of July 9, having been discharged the same morning, stating that he was anxious to resume work. After a short delay, an appeal for Dandy's services was made. The Coast Guard finally reached him by telephone at Cambridge, MD, where the yacht had tied up. He was then flown to the Newark, NJ airport, where he was to take a transcontinental flight to Los Angeles. But at Newark he learned that Gershwin had died from the tumor located in the right temporal lobe (July 11, 1937).

Four weeks later, Gabriel Segall, the attending physician, gave Dandy at his request a detailed diagnosis of Gershwin's condition and the subsequent surgery employed, together with a pathological report. In his response to Segall's report, Dandy was most understanding: "I do not see what more you could have done for Mr. Gershwin. It was just one of those fulminating tumors. There are not many tumors that have uncinate attacks [seizures that begin with olfactory hallucinations, such as a foul odor which Gershwin had experienced] that are removable, and it would be my impression that although the tumor in a large part might have been extirpated and he would have recovered for a little while, it would have recurred very quickly since the whole thing fulminated so suddenly at the onset. I think the outcome is much the best for himself, for a man as brilliant as he with a recurring tumor it would have been terrible: it would have been a slow death" (166).

A year after Gershwin died, Thomas Wolfe, the talented young author of *Look Homeward, Angel* and *You Can't Go Home Again*, became ill in Seattle while on a western trip. Believing that his condition possibly involved a brain tumor or abscess, Doctor George W. Swift arranged with Dandy to send Wolfe by train to Baltimore. Upon arrival Dandy found him to be dangerously ill and doubted if he could do anything to help him. But as he told Wolfe's mother and sister, even "if he had only one chance in a million, he had the right to that chance." After opening his skull, Dandy found that Wolfe had miliary tuberculosis of the brain. Tubercles covered the brain so that there was nothing surgically to do. "As Dandy later diagnosed it, Wolfe at some time in his youth had contracted a tuberculosis of the lung which cured itself, but the encapsulated lesion had been reopened by the [recent] pneumonia, and the tubercle bacilli entering the bloodstream had been carried to the brain (167)." Momentarily, Wolfe's condition improved, and Dandy remembered a similar case 12 years before in which the tubercles of the patient, after 50 days, just dried up and so he survived. Such was not to be Wolfe's fate, as he went into coma, was weakened by pneumonia, and peacefully died (168). "If he had lived in a succeeding generation, this great novelist might not have met death at the age of thirty-eight" (169).

Another famous writer on whom Dandy operated for a spinal cord tumor was Margaret Mitchell (1900–1949), the author of *Gone With the Wind*, for which she received the Pulitzer Prize in 1936. She was reportedly a difficult patient during her hospitalization (170).

In addition to his dramatic involvement with the Gershwin and Wolfe cases, Dandy was asked in August 1940 to try to save the life of Leon Trotsky, the exiled Russian revolutionary leader whom Ramon Mercader, possibly a Stalinist agent, had attacked with an alpenstock at the political exile's suburban home at Mexico City. Dandy was to go with Albert Goodman of Chicago, Trotsky's American attorney, and was to be joined in the Mexican capital by Harry Fischler, a Los Angeles surgeon. On August 21st, the day after the attack, Trotsky died at the age of 61, so that Dandy, who was traveling by train, went only as far as Washington, DC, where the news reached him.

Included in the broad spectrum of lesions that neurosurgeons are called upon to treat are aneurysms of the carotid artery (localized, abnormal dilatations of blood vessels filled with blood and pulsating tumors with a bruit or murmur heard on auscultation) which, given their nature, are often life threatening. In 1935 and 1939 Dandy published, respectively, articles in *Annals of Surgery* on "The Treatment of Carotid Cavernous Arteriovenous Aneurysms" and "The Treatment of Internal Carotid Aneurysms within the Cavernous Sinus and the Cranial Chamber." His interest in aneurysms and their surgical treatment led him to publish some years later a book entitled *Intracranial Arterial Aneurysms*, which is considered a classic on the subject and is still in print.

Noting in the first paper, which was drawn from eight cases of carotid cavernous arteriovenous aneurysms, that "arteriovenous aneurysms of this type are more common than arteriovenous aneurysms in any other part of the body" and that they ". . . occur with greater frequency than all arteriovenous aneurysms combined" (such an aneurysm is an abnormal direct communication between an artery and a vein without the interconnection of the capillaries), Dandy pointed to the uniqueness of the vascular factors affecting the area. "It is . . . the only location in which an artery actually passes through a venous channel and that accounts, as does also the situation of the lesion, for the high frequency of these aneurysms" (171). Three conditions, according to the Hopkins neurosurgeon, clearly define the syndrome: "(1) exophthalmos [abnormal protrusion of the eyeball], (2) pulsation of the protruding eye, (3) a subjective roar which to the observer is a systolic murmur on auscultation" (171). Treatment in general had been undertaken "either from the arterial side or from the venous side"; with the latter approach Dandy had had no experience, although he acknowledged that good results had been reported. He was largely concerned with patients who had not been cured by either partial or total arterial ligations. His procedure was to place a silver clip on the intracranial portion of the internal carotid artery just before it divides in order to isolate the aneurysm. "The exact treatment which one should use," Dandy advised, "depends, of course, upon whether or not the carotid artery can be sacrificed without cerebral disturbances. The physiologic test—compression of this artery with the thumb—should always be made beforehand in order to determine the exact type of ligation to be used" (172). Only if the collateral circulation is adequate should total arterial occlusion be attempted. Dandy closed with the admonition that "intracranial ligation of the internal carotid artery is advocated only when all other arterial ligations have failed to cure" (172). By establishing a successful procedure for ligating intracranially the internal carotid artery, he had made yet another contribution to the advancement of neurological surgery.

In his paper of 1939 Dandy reported on the favorable treatment of three cases of intracranial aneurysms which occurred ". . . in the intracavernous portion of the internal carotid artery or just as the carotid artery enters the cranial chamber. All projected into the cranial chamber alongside the carotid artery" (173). Dandy's approach, which was similar to his method of treating carotid-cavernous arteriovenous aneurysms, was to trap the aneurysm between ligations in the neck, using a silk ligature, and intracranially, employing a silver clip.

This paper was of added interest, as it revealed Dandy's guarded endorsement of and concern with arteriography, a diagnostic procedure which Antonio Egas Moniz (1874–1955), a Portuguese neurosurgeon, had introduced just a few years before. Dandy recognized that arteriography gave ". . . every promise of the greatest help in precisely diagnosing and localizing intracranial aneurysms. Already, quite a number have been so graphically demonstrated by the intra-cranial (internal or common carotid) injections of thorotrast that one cannot be skeptical of its importance." Yet, he was reluctant ". . . to use arteriography, fearing thrombosis of the big arterial trunk, or some cerebral complication from thrombosis of one of the smaller trunks, possibly even the induction of hemorrhages from the aneurysm. This may well be a prejudice of one who withholds all accessory methods in diagnosis, even lumbar punctures and ventriculography, unless there are very necessary indications of their employment. It is always my feeling that the least done to a patient, the better. Complications are bound to arise from time to time as a result of seemingly trivial accessory examinations (lumbar punctures and air injections, intravenous injections, etc., for example) and the patient may lose his life as a result" (174).

Dandy was thus fearful of the potential complications arising from arteriography and consequently avoided using it at Hopkins; however, he occasionally operated on a patient who had undergone the procedure elsewhere, such as at Baltimore City Hospitals (175). Despite this fear, Dandy, it may be said, could include among his achievements "the operative treatment of intracranial aneurysm, a field in which he alone achieved much success for a number of years" (176).

The year 1939 witnessed the outbreak of World War II when, on September 1, Germany launched an attack with over a million and a half men against Poland. Alarmed by the rapidity of the German drive, the so-called *Blitzkrieg*, the Soviet Union invaded Poland from the east on the 17th, and 2 days later met up with the Germans. A little more than a week later Warsaw surrendered, thus ending Polish organized opposition. Hitler's rejection of the Anglo-French demand for German withdrawal from Poland resulted in France and Great Britain declaring war on the Third Reich 2 days after the initial attack. Dandy, like millions of others, was ultimately going to be involved in this second great conflict of the century.

Meanwhile, the year had not begun well for him or the family. In January, he was attacked by mumps and flu at the same time, and the Dandy household had, concurrently, three cases of the mumps, "all contracted," Dandy later told a friend, "through that little rascal baby [Margaret] that we could not restrain" (177). In addition to these illnesses, he had sprained a hip joint while tossing Margaret in the air, which prevented him from playing as much golf as he would have liked during his midwinter vacation in Florida.

Then, early in May, Walter Jr. suffered a serious accident when a Coca-Cola bottle exploded after he had hit it on cement. The glass cut a gash in one eye, going through the iris and into the lens. Fortunately, he recovered, "though with some reduced vision" (178).

Even though Dandy's attorney doubted that negligence could be proved against the bottling company (Robert W. Wood, the attending eye surgeon at Hopkins, did not think that excessive internal pressure caused the bottle to explode), Dandy pressed legal action with the result that the company settled out of court to the extent of paying for Walter Jr.'s 3 weeks of hospital care (179). It was another instance of Dandy's determination to settle accounts when he felt that he was right, although in this case he may not have been.

As parents, the Dandys were understandably concerned with the seriousness of Walter Jr.'s accident. They both had planned attending the following September the Pan-Pacific Surgical Association Congress in Honolulu, at which Dandy was to give papers on the diagnosis and treatment of intracranial aneurysms and Ménière's disease (180). But, fearing an unforeseen change in Walter Jr.'s recovery might occur while they were away, Mrs. Dandy decided not to go. As he had been committed for a year to participating in this meeting, Dandy planned to make the trip, however, and had invited Edwin N. Broyles, a friend and Hopkins otolaryngologist, to join him. Dandy suggested to Fred Reichert that Broyles be put on the program, as "he has a very nice operation for carcinoma of the larynx . . . " (181).

Besides his two papers Dandy readily agreed to speak at a community health meeting in Honolulu on "the advances in the field of neurology" (182). Everything about this trip he enjoyed immensely and looked "forward to coming again" (183). His enthusiasm for Hawaii and its people is best reflected in a letter to one of the children:

Here we are in the mid-Pacific Ocean in a most lovely spot. The vegetation is so luxuriant, the colors & flowers so beautiful. It's probably the loveliest spot on the globe. The native Hawaiians are a simple, unsophisticated people who haven't or at least don't seem to have learned the meanness that shows so quickly in most people. They meet you at the boat with wreaths of flowers to throw over your neck. They call them "lei." I had six before I reached the [Royal Hawaiian] hotel which is the finest in the world (184).

Halfway round the earth while Dandy was on his way to Hawaii by train and steamship, war had broken out. Five years later and under different circumstances he would return to Honolulu.

END NOTES

1. Dandy WE: 'Avertin' anesthesia in neurologic surgery. *JAMA* 96:1860, May 31, 1931.
2. Dandy WE: 'Avertin' anesthesia in neurologic surgery. *JAMA* 96:1861, 1931.
3. W.E.D. to The Winthrop Chemical Co., New York City, letter, July 22, 1930, Dandy MSS.
3a. Dandy WE: 'Avertin' anesthesia in neurologic surgery. *JAMA* 96:1861, 1931.
4. Grace L. Smith, Baltimore, interview with the author, Oct 2, 1966. Dandy thought enough of Grace Smith that on occasion he would give her $1000 for a trip.
5. Irving J. Sherman, M.D., Bridgeport, CT, to the author, letter, Oct 20, 1976. "On one occasion," Sherman recalled, "Dr. Dandy stepped backward and almost fell off the back of the platform. As he teetered on the edge, the entire staff stood there in horror with a feeling as though catastrophe were about to strike the entire universe. Had Dr. Dandy been injured, this would have been considered a catastrophe of the highest magnitude by all of us." Irving J. Sherman, Bridgeport, CT, to the author, letter, Sept 17, 1976.
6. W.E.D. to Dr. H.A.B. Dunning, Hynson, Westcott & Dunning Pharmaceutical Laboratory, Baltimore, letter, April 20, 1927; H.A.B. Dunning, Baltimore, to W.E.D., letter, April 25, 1927; W.E.D. to Francis C. Grant, M.D., Philadelphia, letter, July 24, 1928; W.E.D. to Frederick L. Reichert, M.D., San Francisco, letter, Aug 27, 1928 & Dec 16, 1929, Dandy MSS. Dandy had a high regard for the Hynson, Westcott & Dunning Pharmaceutical Laboratory.

7. W.E.D. to Gov. Harry W. Nice of Maryland, Annapolis, MD, letter, June 4, 1938, Dandy MSS.
8. Dorcas Hager, Baltimore, to W.E.D., letter, July 3, 1928, Dandy MSS.
9. Hugo V. Rizzoli, M.D., Washington, D.C., telephone interview with the author, May 15, 1981. Dandy WE: *Intracranial Arterial Aneurysms.* Cornell University, Ithaca, NY, Comstock Publishing, 1944, pp 67–90.
10. Dandy WE: *Intracranial Arterial Aneurysms.* Cornell University, Ithaca, NY, 1944, p 67.
11. Mrs. Walter E. Dandy, Baltimore, interview by telephone with the author, May 6, 1981.
12. Fox JD: Walter Dandy—super-surgeon. *Henry Ford Hospital Medical Journal,* 25(3):163–164, 1977.
13. Kathleen Louise Dandy Gladstone (Mrs. Richard Gladstone), Washington Hilton Hotel, Washington, D.C., interview with the author, April 22, 1967. Hugo V. Rizzoli, M.D., Washington, D.C., interview by telephone with the author, May 15, 1981.
14. Chambers JW: Frank Rodolph Ford, Oct 21, 1892–Oct 24, 1970. *The Johns Hopkins Med J* 128(2):98, 1971.
15. Ford FR: *Diseases of the Nervous System in Infancy, Childhood and Adolescence,* ed 6. Springfield, IL, Charles C Thomas, 1973.
16. Curt P. Richter, Johns Hopkins University School of Medicine, Baltimore, to the author, letter, Sept 13, 1976.
17. Frank R. Ford, M.D., Baltimore, interview with the author, May 21, 1968.
18. W.E.D. to Ralph Greene, Coral Gables, FL, letter, April 6, 1938, Dandy MSS.
19. Turner FB: *Heritage of Excellence: The Johns Hopkins Medical Institutions, 1914–1947.* Baltimore, The Johns Hopkins University Press, 1974, p 431.
20. Charles E. Troland, M.D.: Doctor Dandy, Unpublished paper delivered at the Annual Meeting of the Neurosurgical Society of America, San Juan, Puerto Rico, 1965, p 7.
21. Charles E. Troland, M.D., Doctor Dandy, Unpublished paper delivered at the Annual Meeting of the Neurosurgical Society of America, San Juan, Puerto Rico, 1965, p 8.
22. Fisher RG: Walter Edward Dandy 1886–1946: *A History of Neurological Surgery,* edited by A. Earl Walker, p 113; Grace L. Smith, Baltimore, interview with the author, Oct 2, 1966; Fox JD: Walter Dandy—super-surgeon. *Henry Ford Hospital Medical Journal* 25(3):158–159, 1977.
23. Charles E. Troland, M.D., Richmond, VA, interview with the author, June 4, 1981.
24. Hugo V. Rizzoli, M.D., Washington, DC, interview with the author, Nov 19, 1980.
25. Charles E. Troland, M.D., Richmond, VA, interview with the author, June 4, 1981.
26. Fox JD: Walter Dandy—super-surgeon. *Henry Ford Hospital Medical Journal* 25(3): 158, 1977. Charles E. Troland, Richmond, VA, interview with the author, June 4, 1981.
27. Fox JD: Walter Dandy–super-surgeon. *Henry Ford Hospital Medical Journal* 25(3):159, 1977.
28. Mary Beatrice Hutton, R.N., Brinklow, MD, interview with the author, June 28, 1966.
29. Charles E. Troland, M.D., Richmond, VA, to the author, letter, March 16, 1981.
30. Mary Beatrice Hutton, R.N., Brinklow, MD, interview with the author, June 28, 1966.
31. "Neurosurgeons today are tending to get away from the sitting position due to the problem of air embolism." Hugo V. Rizzoli, M.D., Washington, DC, interview with the author, Nov 19, 1980.
32. Warfield M. Firor, M.D., Baltimore, interview with the author, Jan 29, 1966.
33. Hugo V. Rizzoli, M.D., Washington, DC, to the author, letter, Dec 19, 1977.
34. Grace L. Smith, R.N., Baltimore, interview with the author, Oct 2, 1966.
35. Hugo V. Rizzoli, M.D., Washington, DC, to the author, letter, Dec 19, 1977.
36. Harvey B. Stone, M.D., Baltimore, interview with the author, May 25, 1967.
37. Richard J. Otenasek, M.D., Baltimore, interview by telephone with the author, July 31, 1980.
38. Dr. Richard J. Otenasek, Baltimore, kindly furnished the author with a copy of this operative note.
39. Charles E. Troland, M.D., Richmond, VA, to the author, letter, June 24, 1981.
40. Otenasek FJ: Ruminations about Walter E. Dandy. Unpublished ms delivered infor-

mally at the Annual Meeting of the Florida Association of Neurosurgeons, Hollywood-by-the-Sea, May 19, 1963, p 17.

41. Troland CE: Doctor Dandy. Unpublished ms, p 6.

42. Troland CE: Doctor Dandy. Unpublished ms, pp 12–13.

43. Earl R. Carlson, Yale University School of Medicine, New Haven, CT, to W.E.D., letter, July 5, 1927; Dr. T.D. Tyson, High Point, NC, to Mrs. Walter E. Dandy, letter, June 29, 1946; W.E.D. to Mrs. Margaret Bell, Baltimore, letter, July 25, 1928, Dandy MSS; Grace L. Smith, R.N., Baltimore, interview with the author, Oct 2, 1966.

44. Charles E. Troland, M.D., Doctor Dandy. Unpublished ms, p 11.

45. Raymond E. Lenhard, M.D., Baltimore, interview with the author, Nov 8, 1975.

46. Mrs. Walter E. Dandy, Falmouth, MA, to the author, letter, July 28, 1975.

47. Charles E. Troland, M.D., Richmond, VA, interview with the author, June 4, 1981.

48. Troland CE: Doctor Dandy. Unpublished ms, pp 11–12.

49. Fox JD: Walter Dandy—super-surgeon. *Henry Ford Hospital Medical Journal* 25(3):164, 1977.

50. Barnes Woodhall, M.D., Duke Hospital, Durham, NC, to Mrs. Walter E. Dandy, letter, April 27, 1946, Dandy MSS.

51. Mrs. Walter E. Dandy, Baltimore, interview with the author, Nov 23, 1976.

52. W.E.D. to R. Eustace Semmes, M.D., Memphis, TN, letter, Nov 4, 1944, Dandy MSS.

53. W.E.D. to Dr. Ricardo Finochietto, Buenos Aires, Argentina, letter, Sept 29, 1937, Dandy MSS.

54. W.E.D. to Kenneth D. Blackfan, M.D., Boston, MA, letter, April 6, 1935, Dandy MSS.

55. W.E.D. to Joseph Colt Bloodgood, M.D., Baltimore, letter, April 10, 1935, Dandy MSS. See also W.E.D. to Paul C. Bucy, Iowa City, IA, letter, May 12, 1926, Dandy MSS. Bucy was then a medical student; he later became a prominent neurosurgeon.

56. W.E.D. to Dr. Henry Allen Moe, New York City, letter, Oct 31, 1934, Dandy MSS.

57. John S. Tytus, M.D., The Mason Clinic, Seattle, WA, to the author, letter, Aug 29, 1975.

58. Frank J. Otenasek, M.D., Baltimore, to the author, letter, Nov 8, 1966.

59. Hugo V. Rizzoli, M.D., Washington, DC, to the author, letter, Dec 19, 1977. Irving J. Sherman, M.D., Bridgeport, CT to the author, letter, Sept 17, 1976.

60. Charles E. Troland, M.D., Richmond, VA, to the author, letter, March 16, 1981.

61. Charles E. Troland, M.D., Richmond, VA, interview with the author, June 4, 1981.

62. Penfield W: *No Man Alone: A Neurosurgeon's Life.* Boston, Little, Brown and Co., 1977, p 43.

63. W.E.D. to Dr. Newdigate M. Owensby, Atlanta, letter, March 6, 1933, Dandy MSS.

64. Otenasek FJ: Ruminations about Walter E. Dandy. Unpublished ms, pp 7–8.

65. Otenasek FJ: Ruminations about Walter E. Dandy. Unpublished ms, p 7. In reference to his tonsillectomy, Ralph Greene, the Jacksonville neurologist, poked gentle fun at Dandy's penchant for the straight razor when he wrote: "Outside of two slight needle pricks, there was no more discomfort than a shave with a safety razor. I cannot testify about the antiquated method of shaving with a straight razor in hot water for you advised me to do this, and consequently, daily, I think of you. I hope you will pardon my connecting you with such a low-brow memory association." Ralph Greene, Coral Gables, FL, to W.E.D., letter, June 5, 1939, Dandy MSS.

66. Mary Ellen Dandy Marmaduke, Baltimore, interview with the author at her mother's home, July 21, 1976. Kathleen Louise Dandy Gladstone (Mrs. Richard Gladstone), Wellesley Hills, MA, to the author, letter, March 31, 1976.

67. W.E.D. to Dr. Caroline I. Buttrick, Scarsdale, NY, letter, Nov 1, 1937, Dandy MSS.

68. Charles E. Troland, M.D., Richmond, VA, interview with the author, June 4, 1981.

69. Fox JD: Walter Dandy—super-surgeon. *Henry Ford Hospital Med J* 25(3):163, 1977.

70. Kathleen Louise Dandy Gladstone (Mrs. Richard Gladstone), Washington, DC, interview with the author, April 22, 1967.

71. W.E.D. to Kathryn French, Miami, FL, letter, May 6, 1938; W.E.D. to Mrs. L.E. Griffith, Worcester, MA, letter, Feb 19, 1938; W.E.D. to Sister Mary Raymond, New York City, letter, March 4, 1939, Dandy MSS.

72. W.E.D. to Dr. Carlos Ottolina, Caracas, Venezuela, letter, Aug 15, 1939, Dandy MSS. Mrs. Walter E. Dandy, Baltimore, interview with the author, June 10, 1976.

73. Charles E. Troland, M.D., Richmond, VA, interview with the author, June 4, 1981.
74. Warfield M. Firor, M.D., Baltimore, interview with the author, Jan 29, 1966.
75. W.E.D. to John S. Swift, St. Louis, letter, Sept 24, 1938, Dandy MSS. Dandy's charges for an examination by 1939 were "always $25.00" or "$50.00." W.E.D. to Charles J. Brooks, Baltimore, letter, Oct 19, 1939; W.E.D. to Dr. Hugh E. Wyman, Columbia, SC, letter, Feb 13, 1939, Dandy MSS. Dr. Peter D. Olch thinks that a charge of $1000.00 for a brain operation in 1930 was not at all unreasonable when one considered the field and the risk. From his knowledge of Johns Hopkins' surgeons in particular and others in general he feels that Dandy was not known as a gouger. Peter D. Olch, M.D., Deputy Chief, History of Medicine Division, National Library of Medicine, Bethesda, MD, telephone interview with the author, June 23, 1975.
76. Hugo V. Rizzoli, M.D., Washington, DC, interview with the author, Jan 18, 1978.
77. Barnes Woodhall, M.D., Durham, NC, interview with the author in Bethesda, MD, Dec 4, 1968.
78. W.E.D. to Dr. Ralph Greene, Jacksonville, FL, letter, July 29, 1926; W.E.D. to Ralph Greene, Jacksonville, FL, letter, Jan 25, 1929, Dandy MSS: Mrs. Walter E. Dandy, Baltimore, interview with the author, Nov 23, 1976; Raymond E. Lenhard, M.D., Blue Hill, PA, interview with the author in Baltimore, Nov 8, 1975. Charles E. Troland recalls that when he was Dandy's resident a man from Chicago (no ethnic origin given), who pleaded poverty, brought his wife to Dandy for surgery. Dandy told him that the charge would be $500.00. When Troland later told his mentor that the man was flying back and forth between Baltimore and Chicago, Dandy became suspicious, learned that the man was really wealthy, and then told him to take his wife out of "my" hospital. The man pleaded with Dandy to relent and apologized for the deception. Finally Dandy softened but told him that the charge would be $10,000.00! Charles E. Troland, M.D., Richmond, VA, interview with the author, June 4, 1981.
79. F.J.S. Grace, New York City, to W.E.D., letter, Dec 8, 1938; W.E.D. to F.J.S. Grace, letter, Dec 9, 1938, Dandy MSS.
80. Ervan F. Kushner, Paterson, NJ, to Mrs. Walter E. Dandy, Baltimore, letter, April 22, 1946, Dandy MSS.
81. Turner FB: Heritage of Excellence: The Johns Hopkins Medical Institutions, 1914–1947. Baltimore, The Johns Hopkins University Press, 1974, p 508.
82. W.E.D. to Dr. Winford H. Smith, Baltimore, letter, May 10, 1933, Dandy MSS.
83. Winford H. Smith, Baltimore, to W.E.D., letter, May 16, 1933, Dandy MSS. Two and a half years before, Smith had gently taken Dandy to task for purchasing instruments in the amount of $66.25 without proper authorization: "There is one thing, as a matter of policy, that I can not permit—and that is to allow every surgical and medical man in the Hospital to go out and pick up what instruments he likes wihout any previous authorization." Dandy promptly apologized, stating that he was sorry "to have run counter to your policy concerning instruments. I did not realize it. As a matter of fact, they were instruments I needed promptly for a new operation, otherwise, there would not have been the haste. I have not paid the bill, and perhaps you can still get the usual hospital reduction." Winford H. Smith, Baltimore, to W.E.D., letter, Nov 3, 1980; W.E.D. to Winford H. Smith, letter, Nov 6, 1930, Dandy MSS.
84. W.E.D. to Winford H. Smith, Baltimore, letter, Oct 1, 1934, Dandy MSS.
85. See Bibliography: "The Complete Writings of Walter E. Dandy."
86. Dandy WE: An operation for the treatment of spasmodic torticollis. Arch Surg 20:1032, 1930.
87. John M.T. Finney, Baltimore, to Major F.V. Schneider, U.S.A., Albany, GA, letter (copy), Nov 30, 1929. Mrs. Walter E. Dandy, Baltimore, to the author, note, n.d. See Finney JMT, Hughson W: Spasmodic torticollis. Ann Surg 81:255–269, 1925.
88. Dandy WE: Treatment of hemicrania (migraine) by removal of the inferior and first thoracic sympathetic ganglia. Bull Johns Hopkins Hosp 48:361, 1931.
89. Hugo V. Rizzoli, M.D., Washington, DC, to the author, letter, Dec 19, 1977.
90. W.E.D. to John H. Baird, M.D., Chillicothe, OH, letter, July 8, 1931, Dandy MSS; Dandy WE: Surgery of the Brain. Hagerstown, MD, W.F. Prior Co., 1945, p 642.
91. Dandy WE: Effects of total removal of left temporal lobe in a right-handed person:

Localization of areas of brain concerned with speech. *Arch Neurol Psychiatry* 27:224, 1932.

92. Dandy WE: Physiological studies following extirpation of the right cerebral hemisphere in man. *Bull Johns Hopkins Hosp* 53:31–51, 1933. Podolsky E: *Medicine Marches On.* New York and London, Harper & Bros., 1934, pp 64–65.

93. Dandy WE: Physiological studies following extirpation of the right cerebral hemisphere in man. *Bull Johns Hopkins Hosp* 53:32, 1933.

94. Dandy WE: Physiological Studies following extirpation of the right cerebral hemisphere in man. *Bull Johns Hopkins Hosp* 53:48–49, 1933.

95. Dr. W.W. Keen, Philadelphia, to W.E.D., letter, March 21, 1928, Dandy MSS.

96. Starr MA: *Brain Surgery.* New York, William Wood, 1893, p xii.

97. W.E.D. to Dr. M. Allen Starr, New York City, letter, Feb 10, 1923, Dandy MSS.

98. Dandy WE: *Surgery of the Brain.* Hagerstown, MD, W.F. Prior, 1945, p 93.

99. Dandy WE: *Surgery of the Brain.* Hagerstown, MD, W.F. Prior, 1945, p 431.

100. Dandy WE: *Surgery of the Brain.* Hagerstown, MD, W.F. Prior, 1945, p 432.

101. W.E.D. to Monica Sullivan, Olean, NY, letter, May 31, 1924, Dandy MSS.

102. Dandy WE: *Surgery of the Brain.* Hagerstown, MD, W.F. Prior, 1945, p 431; W.E.D. to Dr. M. Allen Starr, New York City, letter, Feb 10, 1923, Dandy MSS.

103. Youmans JR (ed): *Neurological Surgery: A Comprehensive Reference Guide to the Diagnosis and Management of Neurosurgical Problems.* Philadelphia and London, and Toronto, W.B. Saunders, 1973, vol III, p 1310.

104. Dandy WE: *Surgery of the Brain.* Hagerstown, MD, W.F. Prior, 1945, p 478.

105. Dandy WE: *Surgery of the Brain.* Hagerstown, MD, W.F. Prior, 1945, p 642.

106. W.E.D. to Frederick L. Reichert, San Francisco, letter, Jan 22, 1931, Dandy MSS.

107. Walker AE: Walter Edward Dandy (1886–1946). In Haymaker W: *The Founders of Neurology.* Springfield, IL, Charles C Thomas, 1953, p 419.

108. Dorcas Hager Padget, in a letter of July 7, 1971, to Walter E. Dandy, Jr., M.D., wrote of his father's generous acknowledgment of her work in *Surgery of the Brain*, as follows: "Have just checked something in my 1945 second edition of your father's famous and fattest book, now, of course, reprinted but the original a collector's item. Had almost forgotten how generous he was in the inscription in his beautiful handwriting (and cute too, since he never called me anything but 'Miss Hager'!): 'To Mrs. Dorcas Hager Padget, who is largely responsible for this book, with my great admiration and esteem—Walter E. Dandy, Dec 18, 1945.'"

109. Dandy WE: Benign tumors in the third ventricle of the brain: Diagnosis and treatment. *Ann Surg* 98:841–845, 1933.

110. Dandy WE: *Benign Tumors in the Third Ventricle of the Brain: Diagnosis and Treatment.* Springfield, IL, Charles C Thomas, 1933.

111. Dandy WE: *Benign Tumors in the Third Ventricle of the Brain: Diagnosis and Treatment.* Springfield, IL, 1933, p 2.

112. Dandy WE: *Benign Tumors in the Third Ventricle of the Brain: Diagnosis and Treatment.* Springfield, IL, 1933, p 3.

113. Dandy WE: *Benign Tumors in the Third Ventricle of the Brain: Diagnosis and Treatment.* Springfield, IL, Charles C Thomas, 1933, p 169.

114. McLean AJ, review of *Benign Tumors in the Third Ventricle of the Brain: Diagnosis and Treatment* by Dandy WE: *Western J Surg Obstet Gynecol* 42(9):552, 1934.

115. W.E.D. to Karl H. Martzloff, M.D., Portland, OR, letter, Jan 24, 1935, Dandy MSS.

116. Frederick L. Reichert, San Francisco, to The Nobel Committee for Physiology and Medicine, The Royal Caroline Medical Institute, Stockholm, letter, Dec 7, 1933, Dandy MSS.

117. Frederick L. Reichert, San Francisco, to W.E.D., letter, Jan 22, 1934, Dandy MSS.

118. Mrs. Walter E. Dandy, Baltimore, interview by telephone with the author, Sept 21, 1981.

119. Dandy was elected an honorary member of the Neurological Society of Estonia in 1937 and of the Sociedad Argentina de Neurologia y Psiquiatria de Rosario in 1945. He was awarded posthumously the Republic of Panama's National Decoration of the Order of Vasco Nunez de Balboa, degree of Commander. J.J. Vallarino, Ambassador, Embassy of Panama, Washington, DC, to Mrs. Walter E. Dandy, letter, June 13, 1946, Dandy MSS.

120. W.E.D. to Frederick L. Reichert, San Francisco, letter, Sept 23, 1932, Dandy MSS.
121. See Bibliography: *The Complete Writings of Walter E. Dandy.*
122. W.E.D. to Paul Hoeber, New York City, letter, June 6, 1934, Dandy MSS.
123. Dandy WE: *Benign, Encapsulated Tumors in the Lateral Ventricles of the Brain: Diagnosis and Treatment.* Baltimore, Williams & Wilkins, 1934, p 184.
124. Dandy WE: *Benign, Encapsulated Tumors in the Lateral Ventricles of the Brain: Diagnosis and Treatment.* Baltimore, Williams & Wilkins, 1934, p 185.
125. For a criticism of Dandy's digital extirpation of an encapsulated brain tumor, see Davis L: *A Surgeon's Odyssey.* Garden City, NY, Doubleday, 1973, p 127.
126. Dandy WE: *Benign Encapsulated Tumors in the Lateral Ventricles of the Brain: Diagnosis and Treatment,* p 184. With young patients Dandy told his friend Ralph Greene that "tapping the head and feeling the inion [external protuberance at the back of the head] are my two standbys in tumors in young children." W.E.D. to Ralph Greene, M.D., Jacksonville, FL, letter, Feb 26, 1935, Dandy MSS.
127. Unsigned review of *Benign Encapsulated Tumors in the Lateral Ventricles of the Brain: Diagnosis and Treatment. JAMA* 104:243, 1935; Charles E. Troland, M.D., Richmond, VA, interview with the author, June 4, 1981.
128. W.E.D. to Ralph Greene, Jacksonville, FL, letter, Feb 1, 1935, Dandy MSS.
129. Dr. C. Wharton Smith, Secretary of the Executive Committee of the Active Staff, Union Memorial Hospital, Baltimore, to W.E.D., letter, May 22, 1934, Dandy MSS.
130. W.E.D. to Dr. C. Wharton Smith, Baltimore, letter, May 25, 1934, Dandy MSS.
131. In 1937 he resigned from the Southern Psychiatric Association because he thought at the start ". . . it would be more neurological but since it is pure psychiatry, it is out of my line." The following year he was made an honorary member of the Association as an expression of appreciation for his splendid paper "The Treatment of Intra-Cranial Aneurysms." W.E.D. to N.M. Owensby, Atlanta, letter, Sept 10, 1938; N.M. Owensby, Atlanta, to W.E.D., letter, Oct 18, 1938, Dandy MSS.
132. Fisher RG: Walter Edward Dandy. In: *A History of Neurological Surgery.* New York, Hafner Publishing Co., 1967, p 113.
133. W.E.D. to Dr. J.C. Villagrana, Mexico City, letter, Sept 11, 1931, Dandy MSS. Dandy did not know Spanish. He knew enough French to read the medical journals but was quite proficient in German. Mrs. Walter E. Dandy, Baltimore, to the author, letter, Nov 17, 1977.
134. W.E.D. to Dr. José Iglesias Torres, Havana, letter, Nov 6, 1933, Dandy MSS.
135. Owen H. Wangensteen, M.D., Minneapolis, to the author, letter, June 30, 1975.
136. W.E.D. to Frederick L. Reichert, M.D., San Francisco, letter, Jan 13, 1936, Dandy MSS.
137. Dr. Robert Wartenberg, Nervenklinik, Freiburg, Germany, to W.E.D., letter, Aug 24, 1933, Dandy MSS.
138. W.E.D. to Robert Wartenberg, Freiburg, Germany, letter, Oct 18, 1933, Dandy MSS.
139. W.E.D. to Robert Wartenberg, Freiburg, Germany, letter, March 24, 1934, Dandy MSS.
140. W.E.D. to Robert Wartenberg, Freiburg, Germany, letter, May 28, 1934, Dandy MSS.
141. W.E.D. to Robert Wartenberg, Freiburg, Germany, letter, July 1, 1935, Dandy MSS.
142. Robert Wartenberg, New York City, to W.E.D., letter, April 18, 1936, Dandy MSS.
143. W.E.D. to Dr. Arthur Schüller, Vienna, letter, Feb 14, 1939, Dandy MSS.
144. Mrs. Margaret D. Gontrum, Eugene, OR, to the author, letter, Feb 17, 1976.
145. Mrs. Kathleen Louise D. Gladstone, Wellesley Hills, MA, to the author, letter, March 31, 1976.
146. Harvey B. Stone, M.D., Baltimore, interview with the author, May 25, 1967. Grace Smith, Dandy's anesthetist for many years, felt that he was obsessed with his work, golf, and cards. Grace L. Smith, Baltimore, interview with the author, Oct 2, 1966.
147. Harvey B. Stone, M.D., Baltimore, interview with the author, May 25, 1967.
148. Mrs. Mary Ellen D. Marmaduke, Baltimore, interview with the author, July 21, 1976; Mrs. Margaret D. Gontrum, Eugene, OR, to the author, letter, Feb 17, 1976.
149. Mrs. Kathleen Louise D. Gladstone, Wellesley Hills, MA, to the author, letter, March 31, 1976; Mrs. Margaret D. Gontrum, Eugene, OR, to the author, letter, Feb 17, 1976.
150. Mrs. Walter E. Dandy, Baltimore, interview with the author, April 7, 1981.

151. Mrs. Mary Ellen D. Marmaduke, Baltimore, interview with the author, July 21, 1976.
152. Mrs. Kathleen Louise D. Gladstone, Wellesley Hills, MA, to the author, letter, March 31, 1976.
153. Mrs. Kathleen Louise D. Gladstone, Wellesley Hills, MA, to the author, letter, March 31, 1976; Dandy's joke-telling was largely confined to shaggy-dog stories such as the one about the man who looked out the window of a plane and reported he saw 200 cows in one spot. Asked by a companion how he knew there were 200 cows, the man replied that he counted their legs and divided by four! Mrs. Kathleen Louise D. Gladstone, Washington, DC, interview with the author, April 22, 1967.
154. W.E.D. to Frederick L. Reichert, San Francisco, letter, Dec. 15, 1943, Dandy MSS.
155. Penfield W: *No Man Alone: A Neurosurgeon's Life*. Boston, Little, Brown and Co., 1977, p 359.
156. Writing in the fall of 1934 to Dr. Henry W. Woltman of the Mayo Clinic, Dandy enthusiastically acknowledged: "I have read your sketch of Sir Charles Bell [1774–1842] with the greatest interest and profit. I was particularly thrilled to know of the rare idea of a new anatomy of the brain and shall avail myself of the opportunity of seeking it in the Surgeon-General's Library. I have been very much interested in the Bells. Recently I acquired from Doctor [Eugene R.] Corson his entire collection of [John and Charles] Bells' work. Of course, this rare volume [Charles Bell, *Idea of a New Anatomy* (privately printed, 1811); reprinted London: Dawnsons of Pall Mall, 1966] was not among them." W.E.D. to Henry W. Woltman, Clinical Section on Neurology, Mayo Clinic, Rochester, MN, letter, Sept 27, 1934, Dandy MSS.
157. W.E.D. to Frederick L. Reichert, San Francisco, letter, Feb 23, 1928, Dandy MSS.
158. Walter E. Dandy, Jr., M.D., Baltimore, to the author, letter, Aug 22, 1980.
159. Mrs. Walter E. Dandy, Baltimore, to the author, letter, June 12, 1975; Albert Warner, New York City, to W.E.D., letter, Oct 15, 1935, Dandy MSS; Mrs. Ellen D. Marmaduke, Baltimore, interview with the author, July 21, 1976; Mrs. Kathleen Louise D. Gladstone, Wellesley Hills, MA, to the author, letter, March 31, 1976.
160. W.E.D. to Frederick L. Reichert, San Francisco, letter, Dec 23, 1938, Dandy MSS; Irving J. Sherman, M.D., Bridgeport, CT, to the author, letter, Oct 20, 1976; Frank J. Otenasek, M.D., "Ruminations about Walter E. Dandy," unpublished ms., p 17; Mrs. Walter E. Dandy, Baltimore, interview with the author, Nov 23, 1976.
161. Mrs. Kathleen Louise D. Gladstone, Wellesley Hills, MA, to the author, letter, March 31, 1975.
162. W.E.D., Boca Raton, FL, to Mr. and Mrs. John Dandy, Baltimore, letter, Jan 31, 1936, Dandy MSS. Dandy told a friend in 1935 that "everyone should go to Florida in the winter after they [sic] are fifty." W.E.D. to C.M. Sheaffer, Lakeland, FL, letter, March 19, 1935, Dandy MSS.
163. W.E.D. to Dr. Chalmers H. Moore, Birmingham, AL, letter, April 8, 1940, Dandy MSS.
164. H.L. Mencken, Baltimore, to W.E.D., letter, Dec 31, 1936, Dandy MSS. In the spring of 1940 Dandy approached Mencken about the possibility of Mencken's interceding with Dr. Isaiah Bowman about the enforced retirement of their friend, Max Broedel, Hopkins' distinguished medical illustrator. Mencken thought " that it would do more harm than good" to approach the University's president in this regard, and he was not sure what Broedel's attitude was. Nonetheless, Mencken added that "certainly it seems insane to throw out a man of his eminence, especially as no adequate substitute is in sight." H.L. Mencken, Baltimore, to W.E.D., letter, May 10, 1940, Dandy MSS.
165. W.E.D. to Mrs. J.B. Shelton, Kingville, TX, letter, Nov 26, 1937, Dandy MSS.
166. W.E.D. to Gabriel Segall, M.D., Los Angeles, letter, Aug 13, 1937; Gabriel Segall, Los Angeles, to W.E.D., letter, Aug 9, 1937, Dandy MSS; *The New York Times*, July 11, 1937, p 1.
167. Turnbull A: *Thomas Wolfe*. New York, Charles Scribner's Sons, 1967, pp 318 & 319.
168. Turnbull A: *Thomas Wolfe*. New York, Charles Scribner's Sons, 1967, pp 318, 319.
169. Harvey AM: *Adventures in Medical Research*. Baltimore, Johns Hopkins University Press, 1974, 1975, 1976, p 66.
170. Mrs. Walter E. Dandy, Baltimore, interview with the author, April 6, 1978.
171. Dandy WE: The treatment of carotid cavernous arteriovenous aneurysms. *Ann Surg* 102:916, 1935.

172. Dandy WE: The treatment of carotid cavernous arteriovenous aneurysms. *Ann Surg* 102:916, 1935.

173. Dandy WE: The treatment of internal carotid aneurysms within the cavernous sinus and the cranial chamber. *Ann Surg* 109:690, 1939.

174. Dandy WE: The treatment of internal carotid aneurysms within the cavernous sinus and the cranial chamber. *Ann Surg* 109:701, 1939.

175. John W. Chambers, M.D., Baltimore, to the author, letter, July 13, 1967; Hugo V. Rizzoli, M.D., Washington, D.C., to the author, letter, Dec. 19, 1977. The late Frank B. Walsh, Hopkins' distinguished neuro-ophthalmologist and close associate of Dandy, saw an interesting parallel with Cushing as "the greatest critic of ventriculography" and Dandy as arteriography's "greatest critic." Frank B. Walsh, M.D., Baltimore, interview with the author, Feb 8, 1968.

176. Frank J. Otenasek, M.D., Tribute Proposed for the Semi-annual Staff Meeting of the Union Memorial Hospital, April 10, 1947, on the Death of Doctor Walter Edward Dandy. Unpublished ms, W.E.D. MSS.

177. W.E.D. to Frederick L. Reichert, San Francisco, letter, Feb 6, 1939, Dandy MSS.

178. W.E.D. to Ralph Greene, Coral Gables, FL, letter, June 1, 1939, Dandy MSS.

179. H. Vernon Eney, Baltimore, to W.E.D., letter, Feb 26, 1941, Dandy MSS; Mrs. Walter E. Dandy, Baltimore, interview with the author, Dec 21, 1977. In this interview Mrs. Dandy indicated that she does not feel that the Coca-Cola Company was necessarily responsible.

180. See Bibliography: "The Complete Writings of Walter E. Dandy."

181. W.E.D. to Frederick L. Reichert, San Francisco, letter, June 9, 1939, Dandy MSS.

182. W.E.D. to F.J. Pinkerton, M.D., Secretary-Treasurer, Pan-Pacific Surgical Association, Honolulu, letter, July 26, 1939, Dandy MSS.

183. W.E.D. to Frederick L. Reichert, San Francisco, letter, Oct 23, 1939, Dandy MSS.

184. W.E.D., Honolulu, to "Dear Daddy" (?), letter, Sept 13, 1939, Dandy MSS.

CHAPTER 10

The Later Years

Early in April 1939, as the war clouds were gathering over Europe, The Harvey Cushing Society held its eighth annual meeting at the Yale University School of Medicine to celebrate Doctor Cushing's 70th birthday (April 8). Six years before, Cushing had moved from Boston to his alma mater in New Haven, where he joined the Yale medical faculty as Sterling Professor of Neurology. He held this position for 4 years until, according to university regulations, he again had to retire. Many of his friends and former pupils gathered in New Haven to honor him on reaching the 70th milestone. As Dandy was not a member of the Cushing Society, he was not among them. But neither was he among those who sent letters and telegrams which, together with speeches honoring the renowned neurosurgeon, were published by The Harvey Cushing Society after his death 7 months later (1). The breach in their relations was obviously never healed, although in a letter six years after Cushing's death to his official biographer, John F. Fulton, Dandy alluded to some small effort by his former mentor "to make amends," as was discussed in Chapter 6.

Meanwhile, at Hopkins, Dean Lewis, who had not been in good health for some time, retired in March 1939 as professor of surgery and surgeon-in-chief. W. M. ("Monty") Firor, who had been substituting for the ailing Lewis, was formally appointed acting head of the department, having agreed to postpone his decision to enter private practice. In turn, he became an active candidate for the permanent position which was first tendered to Evarts A. Graham, professor of surgery at Washington University, St. Louis, and next to Dandy's old friend and best man, Mont R. Reid, professor of surgery at the University of Cincinnati, both of whom for various reasons declined the offer. Alfred Blalock of Vanderbilt University, Alton Oschsner, professor of surgery at Tulane University, and

Firor then became the candidates in the second and final round of the search for a successor to Lewis (2). Dandy thought that Firor had been doing "a good job" as acting head for the twin posts (3), and he had admired and been friends with Blalock for nearly 20 years. President Isaiah Bowman chose Blalock (1899–1964), who accepted in December 1940 the full-time appointment as professor of surgery at a salary of $16,000 per year. Believing that Firor was "better off without it" (4), Dandy was pleased with Blalock and his administrative skills.

Upon arrival at Hopkins, Blalock, who was "the last major appointment" before the United States entered the war, began to reorganize the department with " . . . subdivisions of orthopedic surgery, neurological surgery, urology, and otolaryngology on a full-time basis, but this could not be accomplished until World War II was over"(5). Since his earlier days at Hopkins as a medical student and a house officer, Blalock had the highest regard for its neurosurgeon and "would have done anything Dandy wanted. He named one child [A.] Dandy Blalock." Even though they were good friends, Dandy, however, "would not have gone full-time for anyone" (6). Such a status would have to await a successor.

Dandy reciprocated Blalock's affection, as revealed in the following letter of June 1942 to Herbert E. Picket, the director of the Hyde Bay Camp, Cooperstown, NY, where Walter Jr. had been a camper:

> May I presume to ask a favor of you? The little Blalock boy [Bill] is coming to your Camp for just a month because his father cannot afford the extra time. Doctor Blalock has just operated upon my two little girls and, of course, I cannot pay him for it, and I wondered if you would not write to him sometime about the middle of the month and tell him you are very much interested in the little boy and that you would like to carry him on for the full term without any extra charge, and bill me for the difference. I should not want Doctor Blalock to know this for he would not accept it if he knew it. He is a lovely little boy and you will enjoy having him (7).

In addition to reorganizing the Department of Surgery, Blalock decided to abandon the rotating residency system which Halsted had begun. For Dandy this meant that general surgeons would no longer be rotated onto the brain team; instead, a separate residency for each of the departmental subdivisions was established. Thus he would have complete control, from beginning to end, of the neurosurgical training. Wishing to start afresh with his own residents, Blalock informed Charles Troland, who had already had a year as resident with Dandy under the old system, that there would not be a place for him. When Dandy learned of this upon return from vacation, he quickly interceded, with the result that Troland became the first neurosurgical resident under this new system (8).

Two months after Blalock had accepted appointment as the professor of surgery, Dandy was one of three faculty to be honored by the presentation of their portraits at the 65th Commemoration Day of Johns Hopkins University (February 22, 1941). A committee of 12 in the meantime had arranged for the painting of his portrait, the cost of which was borne by seventy "personal acquaintances and classmates" and some who, though not solicited, "requested permission to contribute" (9).

When he presented the portrait of Dandy to the University on this occasion, Edwards A. ("Ned") Park (1877–1969), a long-time friend and chief of pediatrics, reviewed his friend's career, selecting "eight achievements . . . for the reason that the least important is sufficient to have established the reputation of any man." In his concluding remarks Park set forth what he thought were the secrets of his colleague's success:

> He is a lone worker. He questions all existing knowledge and in that spirit develops fresh, highly individualistic and often most original points of view. His daring stops at no obstacle. His intensely imaginative mind is constantly active; it is of the intuitive type. Suddenly it seizes upon an idea which seems to come from nowhere and with an impetuous energy and complete faith puts it in execution. He is able to perform feats of surgical skill which few, if any, can duplicate.
>
> Mr. President [Clarence Addison Dykstra], in behalf of a group of friends and admirers of Dr. Dandy, I present his portrait to the University. It is the portrait of a great surgeon, a man of colorful personality, with a truly original mind and other attributes of genius who has brought great distinction on this University (10).

A few years before the presentation of this portrait Emil Seletz, a young Los Angeles neurosurgeon had been a visiting voluntary resident on the neurosurgical service (1936–1937), thus not a regular resident. He subsequently did a bust of Dandy that was also presented to the Hospital. Seletz' respect and admiration for him was shown, not only in doing this sculpture but also in his recommendation of Dandy when George Gershwin lay critically ill (11).

About the time of presentation of his portrait, Dandy made for Larry S. MacPhail, the president of the Brooklyn Dodgers, a protective baseball cap with pockets on both sides in which caps of plastic or compressed fiber could be inserted for protection of the vulnerable parts of the skull when the player was at bat. After a St. Louis player was injured earlier by a pitched ball, Dandy began working on the idea of a protective cap which he initially conceived for the Baltimore Orioles of the International League, but upon learning that the Brooklyn Dodgers were trying out a protective helmet designed by MacPhail, he promptly offered it to the Dodgers' president. The Dodgers immediately tried out his cap, which was subsequently modified at the suggestion of Leo Durocher, the manager, MacPhail, and Dandy himself (12).

Shortly, Dandy sensed that MacPhail wished "to take out the patent in his own name." This led to a 2-year patent dispute between the two men, during which Dandy appealed to President Ford C. Frick of the National League and Judge Kenesaw M. Landis, commissioner of major league baseball, both of whom replied that it was a matter between the Dodgers' president and the Baltimore surgeon (12). In the concluding paragraphs of his appeal to Frick, Dandy clearly stated his position:

> I had planned to take out a patent on it in my name and turn it over to the major leagues with no financial return except the cost of the procedure. Mr. MacPhail called me from Miami and told me that he would take out the patent in my name, saving me the expense, and that his lawyers would do the work. This was perfectly satisfactory to me. He now denies this entirely, although that was the sole object of his calling me. I have since learned from a patent attorney that he could not take out the patent for me, and he now says that he never had any intention of doing so. I rather sensed that this was his plan when I saw the reports in the papers, in which he was claiming the major credit for this procedure, and giving me a very minor part in its development
>
> I still am not interested in any financial return, but I think I have been played a dirty trick. All I want is credit for helping baseball, and I surely expected this degree of gratitude in return for my efforts (14).

Through his patent attorney, J. Hanson Boyden of Washington, DC, Dandy filed an application for a patent on the cap in June 1941. Five months later, the Patent Office denied the patent ". . . in view of a large number of prior patents to which attention was called" (15). But Boyden talked with a principal examiner who agreed to review the conclusion reached by an assistant examiner, which was subsequently overturned.

The following spring the Patent Office reported that an interference contest had been set up between MacPhail's application and that filed by Dandy (MacPhail vs. Dandy, Interference No. 80,079) who, as the issue dragged on from month to month, became concerned with the rising legal costs, "especially as there is nothing in it," as he told Boyden, "if I win" (16). Meanwhile Branch Rickey, who had become president of the Brooklyn Dodgers when MacPhail entered the army, wanted ". . . to call the whole thing off and quit spending money on lawyers." In response Dandy told Rickey that he ". . . was not interested except to get the credit." He rather thought the Dodgers' president ". . . would approve of our getting the patent and turning it over to baseball" (17). Five months later the Board of Examiners adjudged Dandy to be the inventor of the cap and thus entitled to the patent which was issued to him on November 9, 1943 (Patent No. 2,333,987).

Boyden suggested at the time the patent was granted that Dandy, in order to be reimbursed for the considerable legal expense which he had assumed in establishing his priority over MacPhail, might wish to sue the Dodgers for infringement. But the inventor did not want to sue them for they (Rickey) had been "very decent"; however, he wondered if it would be worthwile to go after MacPhail (18). He never did sue the former Dodgers' president. Yet, he had the satisfaction of knowing that the Baltimore Orioles planned to use the cap, as one of their players had been seriously injured in 1944; and A.G. Spalding & Brothers, the large athletic equipment manufacturer, wished to manufacture the cap "on a royalty basis" (19).

Interestingly, the baseball batting hat or helmet that is worn today and "that completely surrounds the head" is akin to that which MacPhail designed. As Dandy told Boyden (20), "It had nothing whatever to do with the selective protection of the vulnerable part of the skull. His [MacPhail's] was entirely impractical!" One of Dandy's caps, which Spalding manufactured, is today in the Baseball Hall of Fame at Cooperstown, NY.

In 1941 Dandy published what has been described as a classic in the field (21), *Orbital Tumors: Results following the Transcranial Operative Attack*, in which he presented 24 cases of intraorbital tumors (the orbit is the bony socket containing the eye) that he treated by the transcranial approach, the same route he used for hypophyseal tumors. "The great advantage of this approach lies in the much fuller and safer exposure of the intraorbital contents. The optic nerve, the eyeball, three of the extraocular muscles, the ophthalmic veins and arteries can be well exposed and avoided during the dissection of the orbital tumor" (22). Since frequently ". . . the orbital tumor is but a small fraction of the large but silent intracranial tumor which is usually the primary growth," Dandy's intracranial approach, first tried in 1921, made possible a direct attack on both (23). It involved the removal of the roof of the orbit, next the evacuation of the cistern chiasmatis (the subarachnoid space around the optic chiasm), and then the retraction of the frontal lobe permitting, thereby, sufficient operating room. "Of the series of twenty-four intraorbital tumors that have been operated upon by the intracranial route," noted Dandy in his conclusion, "six, or 20%, were confined to the orbit; eighteen, 80%, were combined intraorbital and intracranial growths; one of the former and two of the latter were metastatic" (24). His operative mortality for this procedure was low, only 4.1 percent.

In a less serious vein, the year 1941 was of significance to Dandy, as it marked the family's introduction to Capon Springs and Farms, WV, a family-operated summer resort some 30 miles west-south-west of Winchester, VA. "He loved everything about that place, especially the informal atmosphere & the country food" (25). He could play golf, swim two or three times a day in the spring-fed outdoor pool, and play bridge in the evening. The informality of dress—the wearing of coats and ties is not permitted in the dining room—he clearly appreciated. Capon Springs had become popular with several of the Johns Hopkins medical staff, including Raymond E. Lenhard, an orthopedic surgeon who introduced Dandy to it (26).

The late Louis L. ("Lou") Austin, the proprietor of Capon Springs, remembered Dandy's objection, on his first night or so there, to the policy of turning off the lights at 11 o'clock at night (except in one's room), while he was playing bridge in the lodge or Main House. Dandy told Austin that he did not like being treated as a child, while Austin explained that the curfew was in the best interests of the guests who had been exercising during the day and needed their rest. Later, Dandy admitted to "Lou" that he did not know how tired he was after all the golfing and swimming he had done and that such a curfew was a good idea (27)—somewhat typical of his willingness, initial feelings to the contrary, to change his mind if he thought an idea were good.

During the several summers that the Dandys vacationed at Capon Springs, Austin and Dandy became good friends. Upon leaving one summer, Dandy gave his friend a signed check without filling in the amount due, saying that no sum of money was too much for the wonderful time that he and the family had enjoyed at Capon Springs which, as he told a friend, was "a delightful spot" (28).

Another instance of his largesse there involved a young waitress whom he liked and thought should have the opportunity of a college education. "He wasn't very subtle or tactful or good at his timing, however, so he blurted out in the middle of lunch one day 'How would you like me to send you to college?' She declined, probably more because of astonishment than anything else" (29). While she might have responded affirmatively if he had quietly taken the young woman aside to make his offer, his spontaneous feeling was in keeping with his direct, forthright manner. To be sure, there were other instances when he quietly helped someone else who was deserving.

In September following the Dandys' first visit to Capon Springs, Dandy, on a trip to the West Coast, visited the Los Angeles studios of Warner Brothers Pictures, Inc., at the invitation of Major Albert Warner, whom he had known for some years. Warner invited him on the set of *King's Row* (1941), where he met and was photographed with the actors, the director, Warner, and Emil Seletz, the neurosurgeon-sculptor who had accompanied him. One of the actors was Ronald Reagan, now the President of the United States (see the autographed photograph that Warner presented to Dandy).

Three months later the United States, as a result of the Japanese strike at Pearl Harbor, was at war. In several ways The Johns Hopkins Medical Institutions mobilized for the conflict. ". . . The accelerated program was in operation from June 1942 until March 1946, and five classes were graduated during this 4-year period, certainly a contribution to professional manpower requirements. Some 88 faculty members had joined the army, 19 the navy, and 5 the U.S. Publich Health Service, excluding house officers who went directly into the services. Many other faculty members served as civilian consultants to the armed services, and 39 research projects related to the war effort were initiated" (29a).

Dandy wasted no time in offering his services as a civilian consultant to the Navy. Shortly, he received official notice of his appointment from then acting secretary of the Navy, James V. Forrestal:

Upon authority of references, you are hereby appointed as Honorary Consultant to the Medical Department of the Navy, in the Bureau of Medicine and Surgery, Navy Department, with pay at the rate of $1.00 per annum, chargeable to the appropriation "Salaries, Bureau of Medicine and Surgery," effective when you execute the required oath of office (29b).

In December 1942, Admiral Ross T. McIntire, the surgeon general of the Navy, scheduled a meeting of honorary consultants so that a review of the personnel requirements from 1943 to 1944 in the training of medical personnel in neurosurgery, their assignment following training, and "the best use" of neurosurgical teams if they "are to be organized" could be made. The minutes of this meeting reflected Dandy's thoughts on these important topics: "The committee advised by Dr. Dandy agrees with his opinion, and the experience of the Navy up to now, that it can further train an adequate number of neurosurgeons and to best advantage by doing so in a Navy hospital where neurosurgery of the type met with in war is being done and under experienced Navy neurosurgeons. It is of the further opinion that neurosurgical teams can be utilized to the best advantage in certain naval hospitals, in this country, so located as to most conveniently receive such injuries from the various fronts. If those facilities and the number of men thus trained prove inadequate, civilian hospitals can be utilized" (30).

A few days after this meeting of consultants, Dandy sent McIntire several copies of his work on brain surgery for distribution among Navy hospitals (31). And as further evidence of his desire to be of service, he went with a fellow neurosurgeon whom he highly regarded, Captain Winchell M. Craig, on leave from the Mayo Clinic, in the spring of 1943 on an inspection of Naval hospitals on the Pacific Coast (32). He and "Wink" Craig became good friends. Craig recalled a few years later how much he enjoyed his trips with "Walter" and that he "counted it a rare privilege to be asked to go along with him. We had much in common and frequently talked about our families—both being fortunate in having lovely wives and devoted families" (33).

In the report (34) of his inspection tour of Naval hospitals on the West Coast and at Great Lakes Naval Training Center in Illinois to the surgeon general, Dandy has nothing but praise for "the high quality and standards in each of the hospitals." He found "no weak links" in general or in neurosurgery. Moreover, he "could not believe that there were so many high class neurosurgeons throughout the great number of these hospitals. . . ."

Later in the report he recommended that surgery for peripheral nerve lesions should be undertaken within 24 to 48 hours after injury; for if it were not done, a large part of the affected nerve must be subsequently resected, making it difficult to bring the ends together and to "get a good result." In his general criticism of the diagnostic and surgical treatment of ruptured disk cases in the Navy hospitals, Dandy felt that the surgeons involved should be trained in the most up-to-date methods and that such cases should be handled in only two hospitals, "perhaps one at Seattle and one in California."

Dandy also mentioned that at the San Diego Naval Hospital the Navy had "one of the best plastic surgeons in the world—Doctor [Harold Laurens Dundas] Kirkham. Plastic surgery should not be handled by the men at the front except for an emergency type of work, and so much of it being done by men who are not qualified, and there is probably no branch of surgery that demands a higher grade of skill. It would be my suggestion that Doctor Kirham and his department have charge of all plastic surgery on the West Coast and that all cases be referred to them. He is in a position to really develop a great school of plastic surgery in this hospital" (34).

In the closing lines of this detailed report Dandy noted that the tour had been "a remarkable and instructive experience" for him and that above all he wished to commend to the surgeon general the work of Doctor Du, a neurologist, and Doctor Kenneth H. Abbot, a neurosurgeon at Oakland Naval Hospital, on subdural hydromas, which he considered "a great discovery"—"I should be very proud indeed to have made this discovery" (34). Admiral McIntire appreciated the report and hoped that Dandy could come over to Washington soon to give him his firsthand impressions (35).

In 1944 Dandy's service to the Navy ended with a trip he made with Winchell Craig in the fall to Honolulu (36). Their visit to U.S. Naval Hospital, Navy No. 10, was much appreciated, according to the commanding officer, who indicated that it was "one of the big events of the year." Captain Hargrave added that "the table talk continues but not nearly so pungent as when our distinguished guests were with us" (37). In reply Dandy was equally complimentary: "You have a great hospital and a lovely one. Never have I seen, nor do I expect to see, a greater surgeon and a finer man than Howard [K.] Gray [on leave from the Mayo Clinic]. He will make any hospital great, and I know full well that he is doing a great job, largely through you" (38).

During the last months of the war and those that immediately followed, Dandy readily advised the personnel officer of the Navy's Medical Department when called upon (39). Although he never donned a uniform, his record of service to the Navy as a dollar-a-year man was just as impressive as if he had (39).

In the spring of 1942, a month or two after he had become an Honorary Consultant to the Surgeon General of the Navy, Dandy was invited to read the draft of a novel with a medical setting which

Jeanette Seletz, the sister of Emil Seletz, the neurosurgeon-sculptor, had written. Not only did Dandy object to the obvious similarity between himself and one of the characters (Jone Brent) in the story but to the author's sharp criticism of the medical profession. He sent a draft of a letter to the Macmillan Company, the publisher, to the author's brother for his comments and in a covering note warned: "I think it would be a great injustice to you if you were ostracized by the publication of this book, and I think you almost surely would be. You and I know that there have been many mistakes in medicine, but I do not think it [sic] should be aired in lay publications. It certainly would create a very bad taste among the members of the profession, and I should think justly so" (40).

Seletz promptly urged his former mentor to defer sending the letter to Macmillan until he came east to discuss it. He emphasized that Dandy's proposed letter to the publisher "would irreparably wreck" his sister's career and that the book could easily be revised. And he added that "we will completely eradicate every possible reference to you and to your institution; we will change the tone of the book to make it inoffensive to the profession" (41).

Dandy replied that he had not realized his proposed letter to Macmillan was as strong as it appeared to Seletz. "I, of course, recognize at once," he continued, "you are trying to compliment me." In turn, he was sending his former voluntary resident a revised letter which, if it were "satisfactory," he would forward to the publisher; thus, a trip to Baltimore was unnecessary. He closed with a caveat that Seletz' "sister should not dwell upon the medical errors to such an extent; it leaves a very bad taste" (42).

Under the title *Hope Deferred* ("Hope deferred maketh the heart sick: but when the desire cometh it is a tree of life." Proverbs XIII: 12), the book was published the following year with a prefatory note: "All characters and institutions named in this book are purely fictitious and any resemblance to real institutions or to characters, living or dead, is purely coincidental" (43). As it turned out, the novel was not a memorable piece of literature.

During these war years Dandy's surgical schedule continued as before, except when his duties with the Navy called him away. Late in 1942 or 1943, the mother of movie actress Dorothy Lamour was admitted to the neurosurgical service, suffering from a ruptured lumbar disc for which surgery had been recommended. She wished to defer the operation, however, until her daughter arrived. Shortly Dorothy Lamour appeared, and her mother then underwent sur-

gery. Frank Otenasek, who was the resident on Dandy's service at
the time, recalled a humorous incident involving the "Old Man"
while Miss Lamour's mother was in the hospital:

> . . . Dr. Dandy never failed to stop in the mother's room in making rounds
> anywhere in the Hospital. He was however a trifle absent-minded. Sometime
> during the postoperative period, we made rounds when Dottie was in her room.
> Her companion at that time was a captain in the regular Navy with all of his
> scrambled eggs and what-not. This was a period of time when many of Dr.
> Dandy's friends around the Hospital would come up to him to shake his hand
> and say goodbye. He was in the habit of saying to them "And what Service are
> you in?" He would then be told that it was the Army, the Navy, or Public Health
> [Service], or whatnot. When Dottie made the introduction and introduced Dr.
> Dandy to Captain So-and-So, he shook hands and promptly asked "And what
> Service are you in?" even in the face of four stripes and scrambled eggs on the
> cap. He never realized the faux pas, but I could see the captain shudder (44).

Another humorous faux pas that Dandy committed in this period
involved the wife of John L. Lewis, president of the United Mine
Workers of America, founder of the C.I.O. (Congress of Industrial
Organizations), and bitter enemy of William Green, the president
of the American Federation of Labor. Shortly after Mrs. Lewis was
admitted to Dandy's service with a lump on the head, a tumor of
the skull, he came to her room. As he greeted her, he looked around
and thoughtfully said, "'Hello, and where is Mr. Green?'" Mrs.
Lewis graciously replied, "'Oh, you mean Mr. Lewis.'" Dandy
apparently never knew what a slip he had made (45).

Although his wife subsequently died Lewis, who had great regard
for the medical profession, expressed appreciation to Dandy for his
professional services, "together with the deep understanding and
warm, human sympathy" that he exhibited (46).

Dandy used his strong concern for patient care to get his way at
the hospital. When, for instance, he wished to look over some films
in the Radiology Department, he was immediately accommodated.
"The same was true of all other services in the hospital. The patient
always had a neuro-ophthalmological consultation the day he arrived in [the] Hospital, and if he had none on admission never failed
to have one on discharge. This was all taken for granted" (47).

One rather humorous instance of Dandy getting his way occurred
one night when the resident had to call him at home about a patient
with a glioma who had gone into a coma prior to the day of her
scheduled craniotomy. At about 2:00 a.m. Dandy came in, completed the craniotomy by 4:00 o'clock, and then "suggested that it
was foolish to attempt to go to bed and get back to the Operating
Room by 7:30 a.m., and that" they "should, therefore, complete

the day's scheduled surgery" (48). The three or four patients with herniated lumbar disks, who were to have surgery later that day, were aroused, given their preoperative medicine, and operated on one by one. By 7:30 or 8:00 a.m. the operative schedule for the day on the neurosurgical service was finished! "As Dandy left the operating room . . ., he had a broad grin on his face and said: 'Huh, we've finished a day's work'" (47). It is doubtful that many others at Hopkins could have upset the hospital routine this way and gotten away with it.

Demanding as Dandy often was, he could at the same time be considerate and generous, not only, as we already know, to members of the brain team but also to both the Hospital and the University as well. In December 1942 he quietly gave $5000.00 to the University for the support of the Department of Surgery. President Bowman, though most appreciative of the gift, expressed ". . . regret that we cannot make public acknowledgement of it, but since you wish the gift to remain anonymous so it shall be" (49).

While it may be argued that by World War II Dandy ". . . seemed to have less interest in scientific problems . . ." as related to the laboratory (50), certainly his interest in new surgical procedures and improved techniques was not in any way diminished. He introduced, in September 1943, a new procedure for the correction of scaphocephaly, 6 years after J.E.J. King performed the first operation for this condition. "Acrocephaly [more commonly known as oxycephaly] and scaphocephaly are related deformities of the skull in infants and children. They are due to unexplained premature closure of the cranial sutures and result in crowding the brain within a space that is too small for its present size and its subsequent growth. As a result the eyeball may (or may not) protrude and the child is listless and mentally backward and has headaches. Papilledema is frequently present, and there is convolutional atrophy of the skull and compression of the ventricular system. All the signs and symptoms are the result of a general intracranial pressure" (51).

Whereas King's procedure called for "cutting into loosely lying fragments most of the vault of the skull on both sides, thus allowing the cranial chamber to expand before the fragments reunite" (the dura was not opened) (51). Dandy's operation made possible the enlargement of the narrow head by lifting "a large bone flap on each side and holding it in position by a transplant of bone (from the bone flap)" (52). The surgery, which also involved incising the dura so that brain could expand, was done for each side of the skull so as to provide symmetry in separate procedures 2 or 3 weeks apart. Dandy believed that while the operation could more easily transform the long, narrow head of scaphocephaly into a normally shaped head than attempting the same for the pointed, short head of acrocephalus, "relief of cerebral symptoms should be secured equally well for either condition"(53).

The first patient on whom Dandy employed this procedure was only 5 months old. After the first operation the child was immediately alert "and showed a remarkable change from the preoperative listlessness and rather stupid appearance"(53). Ten months after the first operation the baby was active and normal, and its skull was completely firm.

In addition to this procedure, Dandy, by the 1940s, had resumed his earlier interest in the diagnosis and treatment of ruptured intervertebral disks and wished recognition for having first called attention to this condition and its surgical resolution in his article "Loose Cartilage from Intervertebral Disk Simulating Tumor of the Spinal Cord," which was discussed in Chapter 8. His concern for such recognition is shown in the following letter of August 30, 1939, to Eustace Semmes, his friend and classmate at both Missouri and Johns Hopkins, as well as a fellow neurosurgeon:

Dear Eustace:
    Your publications appear so rarely that I hesitate to call your attention to a little error. I am referring to your article on ruptured intervertebral discs in the *Yale Journal of Biology and Medicine.* If you will read my article on ruptured intervertebral disc in the *Archives of Surgery*, 1929, you will find that this was the beginning of the attack upon this lesion. [W. J.] Mixter came very much later and added nothing except the recognition of the lesion with a partial block (54).

Dandy's interest in disk surgery was reflected in operations on over 2000 disks that he and the brain team performed and in some half dozen articles that he published on the subject during the 1940s. (See The Complete Writings of Walter E. Dandy.) There were, he noted, three steps in the development of low back pain and sciatica: "(1) A sudden, severe lift, or twist, tears the capsule at the lateral articulations, and loosens the joints. (2) These loose joints automatically throw an additional strain on intervertebral cartilages, which is the third component in the articulations between the vertebrae. (3) The result of this sustained trauma is an injured disk which protrudes and impinges upon the emerging spinal nerve lying immediately in contact with the intervertebral disk" (55). Believing that this condition ". . . is one of the most satisfactory lesions to treat surgically" (56), Dandy considered the term *ruptured disk* "a misnomer," even though on occasion he used it. Rather, he preferred to speak of "protruding disk" and "concealed disk," the latter of which he found in about a quarter of the cases "protrudes so slightly that it can hardly be found at operation unless one explored the subdural region with great care, but at the same time the findings are just as definite and unequivocal as the large protruding disks" (57).

He also argued that the diagnosis and the localization of affected disks did not require intraspinal injections of lipiodol or air as they did more harm than good and were quite painful. Clinical diagnosis and the mobility test for localization ". . . at operation by pushing a spinous process in the horizontal direction" were quite sufficient. A spinal cord tumor, which occurred in less than 1 percent of the cases, however, was the one possibility for diagnostic error (58).

It should be noted that whereas Dandy believed that all back pain was disk oriented, some orthopedists, especially the conservatives, did not necessarily agree with him. His friend and Hopkins colleague, Raymond E. Lenhard, an orthopedist, suggested to him that a follow-up study be done on people who had undergone disk operations on the neurosurgical service. Although Dandy thought it was a good idea, he suggested that inasmuch as he did not have the time to undertake such a study, Lenhard should do so. From some 800 cases Lenhard, who was interested in the end results, received some 500 replies; and 150 people showed up for an interview. Lenhard ". . . found that about 60% were symptom free. About 20% were improved and about 20% were not improved" (59). In other words, approximately 80 percent of Dandy's disk patients were either free from pain or indicated improvement. Such results were indeed commendable and compare favorably with those of disk surgery today (60).

Midway during the war years Dandy received the John Scott Award, given by the city of Philadelphia, for his development of ventriculography in 1918. Very few physicians had been so honored. At the Hall of the American Philosophical Society on December 16, 1943, Vannevar Bush, who was head of the Office of Scientific Research and Development, Samuel Caldwell of M.I.T., who had developed a differential analyzer, Chevalier Jackson, Honorary Professor of Broncho-Esophagology at Temple University, who had devised instruments and methods useful in bronchoscopy, and the Johns Hopkins neurosurgeon were each given the John Scott medal and a premium of $100.00, a "lovely honor" indeed. Dandy was most appreciative of the recognition and the efforts of Doctor Thomas A. Shallow of Philadelphia, a member of the John Scott Award Committee, on his behalf (61).

The year following, Dandy published *Intracranial Arterial Aneurysms*, his next to last major publication, that was predicated on a study of 108 patients with 138 aneurysms which he ". . . verified by either necropsy or operation or both" (62). In this monograph, unquestionably an important contribution to the literature of neurological surgery, the author, following an introduction covering such topics as surgery's recent aids to diagnosis and the types of ruptured and unruptured aneurysms, dealt with the localization of aneurysms, the anatomy of the circle of Willis (Chapter 3 of which he invited Dorcas Hager Padget, his longtime illustrator, to write), preoperative procedures, and surgical treatment. A little over 6 years before, Dandy operated upon what turned out to be the first "cured" aneurysm, with a diagnosis of the condition in hand before surgery. In the interim he developed six methods for treating aneuryms by: "(1) Clipping the neck of the aneurysmal sac. (2) Trapping the aneurysm between an intracranial clip and a ligature in the neck. (3) Trapping the aneurysm between two intracranial clips. (4) Excision of the aneurysm and closure of the entering vessel. (5) Opening the aneurysm and quickly inserting a piece of muscle large enough to fill the sac; the muscle is then thoroughly coagulated with the electrocautery. (6) Turning back the aneurysm and coagulating the neck of the sac and the aneurysm itself" (62). The surgeon must remember, the author counseled, that "one of the great risks attending any treatment of intracranial carotid aneurysms is injury to the posterior communicating artery" (62). Should the internal carotid and posterior communicating arteries be sacrificed, the entire circulation of the brain must then be borne from the opposite side by the anterior communicating and anterior cerebral arteries. Such a link may not be sufficient. Dandy had found that it was "adequate in two cases and inadequate in four" (62). In order to diagnose the condition and to determine the most appropriate course of action, the aneurysm must actually be exposed as any attempt to treat it by simple ligation of the cervical internal carotid artery was at best "a shot in the dark" and "usually ineffective" (62).

The year 1944 not only marked the publication of *Intracranial Artery Aneurysms* but, more important for the world at the moment, the Allied invasion of Europe and the reelection to a 4th term of President Franklin D. Roosevelt, whom Dandy intensely disliked, as was mentioned earlier. By contrast, a public official for whom he had the highest regard was J. Edgar Hoover, the director of the Federal Bureau of Investigation. He had known Hoover for some 10 years, having operated on two special agents of the FBI. Hoover reciprocated Dandy's regard, and on one occasion invited the Dandy family to tour the Bureau. Dandy was ecstatic in expressing his appreciation to the director: "Both young and old agree that it is one of the most interesting afternoons of a life time, and we are all convinced there is nothing in the governmental set-up that can begin to compare. When the time comes that a non-politician can become President of the United States no one will be a more ardent supporter of you than I" (63).

A few years later, in the spring of 1944, Hoover sent his friend and admirer at Hopkins a copy of his address before the 53rd Continental Congress of the Daughters of the American Revolution at the Waldorf-Astoria in New York. Thanking him promptly for the "splendid address," Dandy added with what might be described as a touch of naiveté: "I always approve of everything you say: the only thing, you do not say enough. More power to you. I only wish the country had a dozen men like yourself and that they were in a position to run the government; our troubles would then be over" (64). One must remember that many people at that time shared this view of J. Edgar Hoover, who by his conduct and overextended administration, ultimately fulfilled Lord Acton's famous dictum, "Power tends to corrupt and absolute power corrupts absolutely."

Another contemporary whom Dandy considered "the greatest living American" was Charles F. Kettering (1876–1958), the automotive engineer and manufacturer who had perfected the electric self-starter and had invented lighting and ignition systems. Dandy thought that if Kettering were appointed chairman of the board of trustees of The Johns Hopkins University, ". . . it would be the best assurance of maintaining the University's greatness." To his old friend, Roy McClure of Henry Ford Hospital, Detroit, he suggested that "sometime when Mr. Kettering is in Baltimore and you would be with him, we could have a dinner at which Doctor Bowman could be present, also Wink [Winchell M.] Craig, Doctor Blalock, and perhaps Admiral McIntire of the Navy. I know how much influence you have with Doctor Bowman, and perhaps it would open his eyes to such a possibility. This is just entre nous. I have never met Mr. Kettering, but I would almost go across the continent for such an opportunity. He has long been my idol of greatness" (65).

During the war years, despite the entreaties of Fred Reichert, his close friend and first resident, Dandy did not slow down his pace of living. In thanking him for sending a copy of Doctor Llewellys Barker's autobiography, Reichert reflected that Barker "and his wife are beautiful examples of taking one's age with dignity. When I see you again I'll give you a Sunday school lesson on that subject, i.e. slowing up and aging gradually" (66). While mildly diabetic and somewhat overweight, Dandy was not hypertensive. As he had a slight disk problem, he was careful in his movement (67) and so got ". . . along quite well. . . ." He continued to maintain a full schedule of operating—sometimes as many as five disk operations in one day—writing, and lecturing but with time set aside for golf, a midwinter vacation, and a summer sojourn with the family at Capon Springs. He was not interested in such domestic pursuits as the care of the lawn or the vegetable garden, though he relished the fresh spring onions and radishes that the garden produced. A delightfully humorous exception occurred one day when the family had gone and left him "in peace." Years later (68) Margaret, the youngest daughter, aptly described what they found him doing when they returned: "When we came back and pulled up at the base of the driveway, there he was, sitting above us on the front lawn, with a trowel in one hand and a pile of garlic-type weeds on the other. I'll never forget the broad, proud, and at the same time sly grin which announced, in effect, 'You didn't think I did such things but I surprised you, didn't I?'"

Although Sadie and the children regularly attended Sunday services at The Brown Memorial (Presbyterian) Church, Dandy seldom did so even though he liked the minister, The Reverend Doctor T. Guthrie Speers. He did not enjoy going to church, partly because he had difficulty hearing; and although he was Christian-oriented, organized religion held no interest for him. Golf or reading the Sunday paper were greater attractions. On the few occasions when he did attend, he would absent-mindedly sit there jingling the change in his pocket, much to the family's embarrassment; his deafness in one ear may have encouraged this practice (69).

With the German surrender early in May and the Japanese capitulation in mid-August 1945, World War II came to an end. Walter Jr. was well along in his premedical program at Princeton University and would enter that fall The Johns Hopkins School of Medicine; and Mary Ellen, the oldest daughter, having just graduated from the Roland Park Country Day School, as would subsequently the other girls, had been admitted to Wellesley College.

During that summer Dandy published an article in *Archives of Surgery* on the "Diagnosis and Treatment of Strictures of the Aqueduct of Sylvius (Causing Hydrocephalus)" that showed his continuing interest in hydrocephalus which dated back 30 years before to the important research that Kenneth Blackfan and he had done. And the following April, *Archives* would publish, as it turned out, his last article on hydrocephalus, "The Treatment of An Unusual Subdural Hydroma (External Hydrocephalus)." (See The Complete Writings of Walter E. Dandy.)

Meanwhile, Winford Smith, the director of the Hospital, had informed him of his annual reappointment as visiting surgeon to The Johns Hopkins Hospital and neurosurgeon of its Diagnostic Clinic (70). And, of course, his twin appointment as adjunct professor of surgery continued. He was much impressed with Blalock's leadership of the Department and his recent blue-baby operation, which he and Helen B. Taussig, a pediatric heart specialist, had developed.

Not only was Dandy involved in sponsoring a fund for a portrait of Blalock in 1945, he wished to propose him for the Nobel Prize. Writing to Abraham Flexner of the Carnegie Foundation for the Advancement of Teaching for advice, Dandy noted that Blalock had "... done a piece of work [the Blalock-Taussig operation] that is most extraordinary and it is so fundamental in that it opens up new lines of therapy. It seems to me that he would stand an excellent chance in competition with others for this prize. You probably know him from Vanderbilt where he was associated with Dr. [Barney R.] Brooks for many years before coming here. He is a great professor of surgery" (71). Flexner advised that if Blalock's work were important enough, it would be picked up by those responsible for the Nobel Prize in Medicine or Physiology (72). Consequently Dandy did not pursue the matter further. Like his older friend in neurosurgery, Blalock never did receive the prize.

Meanwhile, Dandy was concerned that Blalock, who had been invited to become professor of surgery at the Columbia University

Medical Center and Presbyterian Hospital, might be leaving Hopkins. Blalock, however, remained there until his retirement many years later.

Early in 1946, Dandy, who loved traveling and wished that he could have done more, went "... to Panama going down through Central America and saw the Mayan ruins at Merida." Upon his return he wrote to Roy McClure that if he wanted "a vacation in a lovely spot, you should go to Guatemala" (73).

In this same letter he also discussed another, less exotic subject. Like many other Americans of the day Dandy had had to get along during the war years with his old car. Now that the war was over, he asked if, with McClure's "great influence," he "could get a Lincoln car in the near future" and added: "My car is getting quite feeble and I do not know how long it is going to last. I had in mind a blue sedan. I have also thought of a Zephyr, but I like a heavy car. I do not know whether this is a proper request to make or not, but if it is not just disregard it" (73). He did subsequently buy a new car.

Sometime late in 1945 or early 1946, Dandy prepared a paper, "The Location of the Conscious Center of the Brain—The Corpus Striatum." It was to be his last and was published posthumously (74). The paper was most interesting, as he had not dealt with this subject before. In discussing the significance of "consciousness" Dandy observed:

There has been much discussion about the meaning of consciousness. If in its original sense consciousness implies the recognition and utilization of afferent impressions, the only way of recognizing consciousness is by the efferent manifestations of speech and motion. The definition is doubtless reversible, for if, with intact pathways of speech and movement, there is no outward expression of speech and movement, the assumption of recognition of incoming impressions could not be assumed and these functions are in all probability abolished also. In these cases practically all activities of the body (there are a few minor movements) are lost except the autonomic—and that certainly means the loss of consciousness. The center for consciousness is, therefore, the "integrator" of all the voluntary activities of the brain. With the loss of this center the body becomes a vegetative organism. Doubtless it is this center of consciousness that is concerned with sleep. With its complete destruction there have been, of course, no periods of recurring sleep (75).

In the 10 cases Dandy presented in this paper "consciousness was immediately, almost totally and probably permanently lost after..." resecting a frontal lobe (7 cases), removing tumors from the third ventricle (2 cases), and ligating both anterior cerebral arteries at the internal carotids (1 case) (76). "These cases," he concluded, "merely indicate that the center for consciousness is located somewhere in the basal ganglia [corpus striatum or the corpus striatum and thalamus considered together as the important central subcortical centers on each side of the brain] or thalamus [the middle and larger portion of the diencephalon which is the main relay center for sensory impulses going to the cerebral cortex] , but do not indicate the precise location" (77). He deduced, however, in resecting the frontal lobe in seven cases that "...the injured part of the basal ganglia or of its blood supply must lie in the path of the resection and this could only be in the anterior part of the corpus striatum" hence, the conscious center of the brain.

But others have had different views. Hugo V. Rizzoli of Washington, DC, a former resident of Dandy's, thinks that he erred in locating the conscious center of the brain in the corpus striatum and believes that the question has not been resolved (78). Another former resident, Charles E. Troland of Richmond, Virginia, does not think that a definitive answer can be given to this question. "It is my feeling," he states, "that the corpus striatum is certainly the area controlling consciousness. Other areas of the brain probably exert their effect on consciousness thru the corpus striatum. This can be done by pressure or by other measures. However, I do not believe that a final statement can be made at this time." And the late Wilder Penfield (80), the Montreal neurologist and neurosurgeon, wondered: "Do brain-mechanisms [sensory, motor, psychical] account for the mind? Can the mind be explained by what is now known about the brain?"

Thirty-seven years after the publication of Dandy's last article the question is still unresolved. More than likely he would have agreed with Penfield, though, that "...the day will dawn when the mystery of the mind will no longer be a mystery" (81).

Some months before, Dandy had accepted an invitation from Wilder Penfield to speak on April 10, 1946, at a meeting of the Montreal Neurological Society, but on the first of April had to decline after he was hospitalized following a heart attack. He had operated right up to the time of the attack. Perhaps while in the hospital he had some premonition that he would not live much longer, as he repeated himself about having to take it easier than he had (82). He told one visitor, however, "that the diagnosis of a coronary thrombosis was all wrong as he was free from pain and he 'obviously had a gall bladder colic' " (83). Yet, while in the hospital he asked his secretary, Bertha B. Schauck, to help him prepare his will, which he signed on April 9 with his friends Al Blalock and "Monty" Firor serving as subscribing witnesses.

Meanwhile, the arrangements for a celebration of Dandy's 60th birthday (April 6), for which Frank Otenasek was in charge, had to be canceled as the result of his illness. But the plans for a birthday number of the prestigious publication *Surgery*, which professional friends from Australia had suggested, went ahead. Blalock, who was associate editor and obviously much involved with the arrange-ments, wrote the introduction to the "Dr. Walter E. Dandy Birthday Number" of *Surgery*, which included, besides a heart-felt appreci-ation by Fred Reichert, some dozen articles by other friends and admirers here and abroad (84). As there were several causes for delay in the publication, Dandy unfortunately died before it ap-peared. He would have been pleased to have been thus honored.

Following diagnosis and treatment at the hospital he went home, but his convalescence was cut short by a second heart attack. Margaret and "Kitty" ". . . were alone in the house when he had his final attack on April 18." Recalled Margaret: "I remember very well his face, again reddening [as it had a few days before when he attempted to help her start a vegetable garden], and again in a great deal of pain as he asked me to call the doctor. I couldn't do it. It was Kitty who came to the rescue" (85). Although Doctor Warde Allan had been at home sick with infectious mononucleosis, he came quickly to the Dandy home, where he ordered an ambulance for his patient-colleague. On the following day, April 19, 13 days after his 60th birthday, Walter Dandy died of a myocardial infarct (86). In a way, his death at The Johns Hopkins Hospital, where he had spent his entire career and to which he had contributed so much to its far-reaching reputation, was befitting.

On the following Monday, April 22, The Reverend Doctor T. Guthrie Speers, the minister of The Brown Memorial (Presbyterian) Church in Baltimore, conducted the funeral service, which a large number of Dandy's colleagues and friends attended. In the printed order of service that a friend whom the Dandys had come to know at Capon Springs quietly provided, Speers spoke movingly of the departed neurosurgeon: "We rejoice to remember the heritage into which he was born and all that he added to the good name he bore by his own strength and usefulness and integrity" (87). Burial followed in Druid Ridge Cemetery in nearby Pikesville.

In the days and weeks that followed, letters of sympathy and tribute from colleagues, friends, and former patients were received. Warfield T. Longcope, professor of medicine at The Johns Hopkins School of Medicine, wrote to Sadie that the neurologist Foster Kennedy once told him that Dandy "...had the genius of a Lister combined with the brilliant technique of Victor Horsley. He commanded respect and admiration from everyone who came in contact with him, and for those of us who saw him often, these were combined in addition with great affection" (88). From Manchester, England, Sir Geoffrey Jefferson wrote that "...Dr. Dandy was one of the great surgeons of all time..." and added the perceptive observation: "I hope that I was right in thinking him a shy man and, I suspected, a very sensitive one in spite of his being so often on the attack" (89). And a former patient of Dandy's spoke warmly of what he had done for her and her family:

> Mrs. Dandy, to me, and my family Dr. Dandy will always live in our memories. His passing had the same effect on me as if he were my parent, or dear member of our family.
> We are of Jewish faith, and one of our customs is to light a candle each year on the day of passing of our dear ones. And I can assure you we will always remember Dr. Dandy on that day, as well as every day of my life, thanks to Dr. Dandy. I don't like to bother you with my case history at this time, but before I came to Dr. Dandy [the] Mayo Clinic gave me no chance to live if they [sic] operated or not and were so mean & sarcastic. Dr. Dandy comforted us and talked to me and my family as though we were members of his family or dear friends (90).

A year and a half after Dandy's death Antonio Gonzalez-Revilla of Panama, Republic of Panama, a former resident on Dandy's service, informed Sadie that the Walter E. Dandy Institute of Neurology and Neurosurgery at the Santo Tomas Hospital in the city of Panama had been established. "The Dandy Institute is small: It consists of 20 beds, not including private ones. It has its own operating room, X-ray Dept., electroencefalography [sic], experimental laboratory, Neuropathology and outpatient Dept. When the number of cases increases," continued Revilla, "the Institute will be enlarged" (91). After more than 30 years, the Dandy Institute remains "quite active," and "ninety percent of the neurological surgeons of Panama had their training there" (92).

In the meantime, the Dandy family had with courage resumed their tasks and responsibilities. There was, of course, the necessity of probating the will, Dandy having made his wife and son the executors. The total gross estate, as revealed in the will, amounted approximately to $1,460,000, the largest portion of which was in stocks and bonds. Dandy's generosity was reflected in not only providing the sum of $50,000 for each of the four children upon reaching their 25th birthday but a bequest of $20,000 to his devoted secretary, Bertha Schauck, and $5,000 to Helen Dorsey, the Dandys' beloved maid (92). As he had forgotten to make provision in the will for Polly, the family laundress, he asked Sadie before he went to the hospital for the last time to remember her (94). The bulk of the estate he left to his widow, who in turn had to pay some $450,000 in federal and state taxes (95). Thus the net value of the estate, after payment of these taxes, was about $750,000, a substantial sum indeed but nowhere near the figures that others have reported (96).

By a life of hard work, thrift, and prudent investment Walter Dandy had left, what was considered in the 1940s, an impressive estate.

Following his death, Blalock put Frank Otenasek, who was only an instructor, in charge of neurosurgery until a permanent appointment could be made. After Barnes Woodhall of Duke University, one of Dandy's former residents, turned down the appointment, the chief of surgery turned to Doctor A. Earl Walker of the University of Chicago. A year and a half after the death of Dandy, Walker became the first, full-time (salaried) professor of neurological surgery and thus inaugurated a new chapter in the history of that specialty at The Johns Hopkins Medical Institutions.

END NOTES

1. *Harvey Cushing's Seventieth Birthday Party April 8, 1939: Speeches, Letters, and Tributes.* Published for The Harvey Cushing Society. Charles C Thomas, Springfield, IL, 1939, p vii.
2. Turner TB: *Heritage of Excellence: The Johns Hopkins Medical Institutions, 1914–1947.* Baltimore, The Johns Hopkins University Press, 1974, pp 75–76.
3. W.E.D. to Frederick L. Reichert, San Francisco, letter, Oct 25, 1939, Dandy MSS.
4. W.E.D. to Frederick L. Reichert, San Francisco, letter, Dec 26, 1940, Dandy MSS.
5. Turner TB: *Heritage of Excellence: The Johns Hopkins Medical Institutions, 1914–1947.* Baltimore, The Johns Hopkins University Press, 1974, pp 499, 462–463.
6. W.M. Firor, M.D., Baltimore, to the author, letter, March 15, 1976.
7. W.E.D. to Herbert E. Pickett, Cooperstown, NY, letter, June 24, 1942, Dandy MSS.
8. Fox JD: Walter Dandy—super-surgeon. *Henry Ford Hospital Med J* 25(3):162, 1977; Charles E. Troland, M.D., Richmond, VA, interview with the author, June 4, 1981.
9. F.R. Ford, M.D., Baltimore, to W.E.D., letter, Jan 30, 1941, Dandy MSS.
10. Park EA: Remarks at Presentation of Dr. Walter E. Dandy's Portrait to Johns Hopkins University. Feb 22, 1941. Unpublished ms, pp 3–4.

11. Emil Seletz, M.D., Los Angeles, to W.E.D., letter, Aug 16, 1937, Dandy MSS.
12. Mrs. Walter E. Dandy, Baltimore, interview with the author, March 24, 1975; W.E..D. to Ford C. Frick, president, National League, letter, May 22, 1941, Dandy MSS.
13. W.E.D. to J. Hanson Boyden, Washington, DC, letter, May 10, 1941; W.E.D. to Ford C. Frick, president, National League, letter, May 22, 1941; Ford C. Frick to W.E.D., letter, May 27, 1941; W.E.D. to Kenesaw M. Landis, commissioner of baseball, letter, June 4, 1941; Kenesaw M. Landis to W.E.D., letter, June 7, 1941, Dandy MSS.
14. W.E.D. to Ford C. Frick, letter, May 22, 1941, Dandy MSS.
15. W. Hanson Boyden, Washington, DC, to W.E.D., letter, Dec 5, 1941, Dandy MSS.
16. J. Hanson Boyden, Washington, DC, to W.E.D., letter, April 7, 1942; W.E.D. to J. Hanson Boyden, Washington, DC, letter, Aug 5, 1942, Dandy MSS.
17. W.E.D. to J. Hanson Boyden, Washington, DC, letter, Feb 26, 1943, Dandy MSS.
18. J. Hanson Boyden, Washington, DC to W.E.D., letter, Nov 12, 1943; W.E.D. to J. Hanson Boyden, letter, Nov 29, 1943, Dandy MSS.
19. W.E.D. to J. Hanson Boyden, Washington, DC, letter, Jan 2, 1945; G.W. Browne, merchandise manager, A.G. Spalding & Bros., Chicopee, MA, to Stone, Boyden & Mack, patent attorneys, Washington, DC, letter, May 28, 1945, Dandy MSS.
20. W.E.D. to J. Hanson Boyden, Washington, DC, letter, Dec 14, 1942, Dandy MSS.
21. Otenasek FJ: Tribute proposed for the semi-annual staff meeting of the Union Memorial Hospital, April 10, 1947, on the death of Doctor Walter Edward Dandy. Dandy MSS.
22. Dandy WE: *Orbital Tumors: Results following the Transcranial Operative Attack.* New York, Oskar Piest, 1941, p 1. The book is no longer in print.
23. Dandy WE: *Orbital Tumors: Results following the Transcranial Operative Attack.* New York, Oskar Piest, 1941, p 2.
24. Dandy WE: *Orbital Tumors: Results following the Transcranial Operative Attack.* New York, Oscar Piest, 1941, p 1.
25. Mrs. Walter E. Dandy, Baltimore, to the author, letter, Jan 17, 1976.
26. Raymond E. Lenhard, M.D., Blue Ridge Summit, PA, interview with the author in Baltimore, Nov 8, 1975.
27. Louis L. Austin, Capon Springs, WV, interview with the author, Sept 29, 1966.
28. Louis L. Austin, Capon Springs, WV, interview with the author, Sept 29, 1966; W.E.D. to Frederick L. Reichert, San Francisco, letter, Sept 9, 1944, Dandy MSS. Mary Ellen, the eldest Dandy daughter, remembered caddying for her father on the Capon Springs golf course but on one occasion threatened to stop if he did not behave himself better; he had thrown his clubs and had sworn following a poor shot. Mrs. Mary Ellen D. Marmaduke, interview with the author at her mother's home, Baltimore, July 21, 1976.
29. Mrs. Kathleen Louise D. Gladstone, Wellesley Hills, MA, to the author, letter, March 31, 1976.
29a.Turner TB: *Heritage of Excellence: The Johns Hopkins Medical Institutions, 1914–1947.* Baltimore, The Johns Hopkins University Press, 1974, pp 475–476.
29b.Rear Adm. Ross T. McIntire, M.C., Surgeon General, U.S. Navy, Washington, DC, to W.E.D., letter, Jan 18, 1942; James V. Forrestal, Washington, DC, to W.E.D., letter, Feb 5, 1942, Dandy MSS.
30. Adm. Ross T. McIntire, Washington, DC, to W.E.D., memorandum, Dec 10, 1942; minutes of meeting of Honorary Consultants, Medical Dept., U.S. Navy, Washington, DC, Dec 11, 1942, Dandy MSS.
31. W.E.D. to Ross T. McIntire, Washington, DC, letter, Dec 14, 1942, Dandy MSS.
32. W.E.D. to Ross T. McIntire, Washington, DC, letter, June 2, 1943, Dandy MSS. In this letter Dandy referred to Craig as "a great surgeon," adding, "You are lucky to have him."
33. Winchell M. Craig, Rochester, MN, to Mrs. Walter E. Dandy, Baltimore, April 26, 1946. Dandy MSS
34. W.E.D. to Ross T. McIntire, Washington, DC, letter, June 5, 1943, Dandy MSS.
35. Adm. Ross T. McIntire, Washington, DC, to W.E.D., letter, June 11, 1943, Dandy MSS.
36. Dandy had received official notice of the termination of his appointment, effective March 13, 1944. His inspection tour of the Naval Hospital at Honolulu that fall suggests, however, that the appointment had been extended. F.G. Crisp, Div. of SECP, Navy Dept., Washington, DC, to W.E.D., dept. form (termination of appointment), March 12, 1944, Dandy MSS.

37. Capt. W.W. Hargrave, U.S. Naval Hospital, Navy No. 10, Fleet P.O., San Francisco, to W.E.D., letter, Nov 30, 1944, Dandy MSS.
38. W.E.D. to Capt. W.W. Hargrave, U.S. Naval Hospital, Navy No. 10, Fleet P.O., San Francisco, letter, Dec 18, 1944, Dandy MSS.
39. Rear Adm. W.J.C. Agnew, U.S.N., Asst. to the Bureau of Medicine and Surgery, Washington, DC, to Mrs. Walter E. Dandy, Baltimore, letter, April 20, 1946, Dandy MSS.
40. W.E.D. to Emil Seletz, M.D., Los Angeles, letter, June 22, 1942, Dandy MSS.
41. Emil Seletz, Los Angeles, to W.E.D., letter, June 25, 1942, Dandy MSS.
42. W.E.D. to Emil Seletz, Los Angeles, letter, July 1, 1942, Dandy MSS.
43. Jeanette Seletz, *Hope Deferred.* New York, The Macmillan Co., 1943, 536 pp. Upon receiving a copy of the book, Dandy wrote the author that he would read it "with the greatest pleasure. I hope it goes over well." W.E.D. to Jeanette Seletz, Hollywood, CA, letter, Sept 3, 1943, Dandy MSS.
44. Otenasek FJ: Ruminations about Walter E. Dandy. Unpublished ms, May 19, 1963. pp 13–14.
45. Otenasek FJ: Ruminations about Walter E. Dandy. Unpublished ms, p 15.
46. John L. Lewis, Washington, DC, to W.E.D., letter, Sept 30, 1942, Dandy MSS. Later, Dandy operated on Lewis's daughter. In response to a snippy editorial about Lewis which Roy D. McClure of Henry Ford Hospital, Detroit, an old friend, sent him a few years later, Dandy gave a brief but interesting assessment of the powerful labor leader: "His wife was one of the loveliest persons I have ever known and I think she educated Mr. Lewis. I doubt that he ever went to a grade school; I have heard this at any rate. He certainly is a polished speaker and slick. I know his reputation as a head of labor but there is no doubt that he has done a lot for the miners, and there is probably no group of labor that needs it more. He was certainly most appreciative of my efforts in his behalf and he is the only man who ever insisted upon paying me more than I charged him." W.E.D. to Roy D. McClure, Detroit, letter, Dec 19, 1945, Dandy MSS.
47. Otenasek FJ: Ruminations about Walter E. Dandy. Unpublished ms, p 16.
48. Irving J. Sherman, M.D., Bridgeport, CT, to the author, letter, Sept 17, 1976.
49. Isaiah Bowman, president, The Johns Hopkins University, Baltimore, to W.E.D., letter, Dec 30, 1942, Dandy MSS.
50. Dr. Curt P. Richter, Dept. of Psychiatry and Behaviorial Sciences, Johns Hopkins University School of Medicine, Baltimore, to the author, letter, Sept 13, 1976. In this letter Richter remembered Dandy's reaction to his telling him about "finding of marked differences in functioning of some of the ganglia of the sympathetic chain: 'Awh, Richter[,] the sympathetic ganglia are all the same like so many peas in a pod.' That settled that."
51. Dandy WE: An operation for scaphocephaly. *Arch Surg* 47:247, 1943.
52. Dandy WE: An operation for scaphocephaly. *Arch Surg* 47:248, 1943.
53. Dandy WE: An operation for scaphocephaly. *Arch Surg* 47:249, 1943.
54. W.E.D. to Dr. R.E. Semmes, Memphis, TN, letter, Aug 30, 1939, Dandy MSS.
55. Dandy WE: Newer aspects of ruptured intervertebral disks. *Ann Surg* 119:481, 1944.
56. Dandy WE: Recent advances in the diagnosis and treatment of ruptured intervertebral disks. *Ann Surg.* 115:516, 1942.
57. W.E.D. to Dr. James H. Young, Mt. Hawthorne, Western Australia, letter, June 27, 1945, Dandy MSS; Dandy WE: Recent advances in the diagnosis and treatment of ruptured intervertebral disks. *Ann Surg* 115:515, 1942.
58. Dandy WE: Recent advances in the diagnosis and treatment of ruptured intervertebral disks. *Ann Surg* 115:517–518, 1942; Dandy WE: Newer aspects of ruptured intervertebral disks. *Ann Surg* 119:483, 1944.
59. Dr. Raymond E. Lenhard, Blue Ridge Summit, PA, interview with the author in Baltimore, Md., Nov 8, 1975; Raymond E. Lenhard, Blue Ridge Summit, Pa., to the author, letter, Nov 23, 1975.
60. Hugo V. Rizzoli, M.D., Washington, DC, interview by telephone with the author, Jan 4, 1982.
61. Dr. Thomas A. Shallow, Philadelphia, to W.E.D., letter, June 4, 1943; Walter R. Russell, secretary, city of Philadelphia Board of Directors of City Trusts, Philadelphia, to W.E.D., letter, Oct 22, 1943; W.E.D. to Thomas A. Shallow, Philadelphia, letter, Jan 7, 1944, Dandy MSS.

62. Dandy WE: *Intracranial Arterial Aneurysms.* Ithaca, NY, Cornell University Press/ Comstock Publishing, 1944, p 136. Through the urging of Dr. Hugo V. Rizzoli the monograph was republished by the Hafner Publishing Co. in 1969 and is still in print.

63. W.E.D. to J. Edgar Hoover, director, Federal Bureau of Investigation, Washington, DC, letter, March 28, 1941, Dandy MSS.

64. W.E.D. to J. Edgar Hoover, Washington, DC, letter, April 21, 1944, Dandy MSS.

65. W.E.D. to Roy D. McClure, Detroit, letter, Dec 7, 1944, Dandy MSS.

66. Frederick L. Reichert, San Francisco, to W.E.D., letter, April 28, 1942, Dandy MSS.

67. Warde Allan, M.D., Baltimore, interview with the author, Feb 11, 1967. Dandy WE: The diagnosis and treatment of ruptured intervertebral discs. *The Medical Comment (Cambria County Pennsylvania Medical Society)* 1944, 6.

68. Margaret D. Gontrum, Eugene, OR, to the author, letter, Feb 17, 1976.

69. Mrs. Walter E. Dandy, Baltimore, interview with the author, June 3, 1975; Harvey B. Stone, M.D., Baltimore, interview with the author, May 25, 1967; Kathleen Louise D. Gladstone, Wellesley Hills, MA, interview with the author in Washington, DC, April 22, 1967.

70. Winford H. Smith, M.D., Baltimore, to W.E.D., letter, June 6 and 18, 1945, Dandy MSS.

71. W.E.D. to Abraham Flexner, New York City, letter, Nov 28, 1945, Dandy MSS.

72. W.E.D. to Abraham Flexner, New York City, letter, March 18, 1945, Dandy MSS.

73. W.E.D. to Roy D. McClure, Detroit, letter, Feb 20, 1946, Dandy MSS.

74. Dandy WE: The location of the conscious center of the brain—the corpus striatum. *Bull Johns Hopkins Hosp* 79:34–58, 1946.

75. Dandy WE: The location of the conscious center of the brain—the corpus striatum. *Bull Johns Hopkins Hosp* 79:53, 1946.

76. Dandy WE: The location of the conscious center of the brain—the corpus striatum. *Bull Johns Hopkins Hosp* 79:56, 1946.

77. Dandy WE: The location of the conscious center of the brain—the corpus striatum. *Bull Johns Hopkins Hosp* 79:57, 1946.

78. Hugo V. Rizzoli, M.D., Washington, DC, interview with the author, Nov 19, 1980.

79. Charles E. Troland, M.D., Richmond, VA, to the author, letter, March 16, 1981.

80. Penfield W: *The Mystery of the Mind: A Critical Study of Consciousness and the Human Brain.* Princeton, NJ, Princeton University Press, 1975, p xiii.

81. Penfield W: *The Mystery of the Mind: A Critical Study of Consciousness and the Human Brain.* Princeton, NJ, Princeton University Press, 1975, p xiii.

82. Charles E. Troland, Richmond, VA, interview with the author, June 4, 1981. Troland visited Dandy in the hospital after his first heart attack.

83. Dr. Antonio Gonzalez-Revilla, Panama, Republic of Panama, to the author, letter, Feb 15, 1978.

84. Dr. Walter E. Dandy Birthday Number. *Surgery* 19(5): May 1946; Dr. Walter E. Dandy Birthday Number (Concluded). *Surgery* 19(6):June, 1946.

85. Margaret D. Gontrum, Eugene, OR, to the author, letter, Feb 17, 1976.

86. Dr. Allan told the author that Dandy's electrocardiogram had been satisfactory. He felt, however, that given the demands and strains of Dandy's work, it is not surprising that he died at age sixty. Warde Allan, M.D., Baltimore, interview with the author, Feb 11, 1967.

87. "Order of Service for the funeral of Dr. Walter E. Dandy Conducted by The Reverend T. Guthrie Speers, D.D., The Brown Memorial Church, Baltimore, Maryland, April 22, 1946." Printed by C. William Schneidereith, Sr., Schneidereith & Sons, Baltimore, Dandy MSS.

88. Warfield T. Longcope, M.D., Baltimore, to Mrs. Walter E. Dandy, letter, April 22, 1946, Dandy MSS.

89. Geoffrey Jefferson, M.D., Manchester, England, to Mrs. Walter E. Dandy, letter, May 23, 1946, Dandy MSS.

90. Mrs. M.H. Greenburg, Minneapolis, MN, to Mrs. Walter E. Dandy, letter, May 4, 1946, Dandy MSS.

91. Antonio Gonzalez-Revilla, M.D., Panama, Republic of Panama, to Mrs. Walter E. Dandy, letter, Dec 18, 1948, Dandy MSS.

92. Antonio Gonzalez-Revilla, M.D., Panama, Republic of Panama, to the author, letter, Feb 15, 1978.

93. Last Will and Testament of Walter E. Dandy, No. 57, Case No. 647, File No. 44923, Office of Register of Wills, Baltimore, MD.

94. Mrs. Walter E. Dandy, Baltimore, MD, interview with the author, April 6, 1978.

95. Estate of Walter E. Dandy, File No. 44923, First Administration Account (approved), April 8, 1948, Office of Register of Wills, Baltimore, MD.

96. Fox JD: Walter Dandy—super-surgeon. *Henry Ford Hospital Med J* 25(3):162, 1977; Louis L. Austin, Capon Springs, WV, interview with the author, Sept 29, 1966.

CHAPTER 11

Looking Back

Thirty years before (1916), a friend had written to Dandy who had recently become Halsted's resident: "You are such a fortunate man. No matter where you go you are bound to succeed" (1). When one looks back on his career of 36 years, several things are apparent: his straight-line approach to the achievement of superiority in his specialty that reflected both his intellectual acuity and power of intense concentration; his constant curiosity about the nervous system which he often revealed at surgery by the questions he asked himself aloud—How? What? Why? Coupled with that curiosity was the courage to break new ground. "Not content with existing procedures when these seemed to be inadequate, his keen observation and deduction often led to a solution which meant the saving of a life in an apparently hopeless situation" (2). As many visitors to his operating room would attest, Dandy possessed an exquisite surgical technique, embodying no wasted effort. Added to these elements of his career were his unremitting emphasis on the importance of patient care to the members of the brain team and the nursing staff; his impressive record of publication of books and articles, written in a clear, readable prose; his loyalty to and consideration of colleagues, friends, and The Johns Hopkins Medical Institutions; and his devotion to his parents, wife, and four children.

One thing Dandy never achieved, as noted in an earlier chapter, but which, as he told his family, he hoped a wealthy patient might provide, was the establishment of a neurological institute at Hopkins, something comparable to the Wilmer (ophthalmological) and Brady (urological) Institutes there. His son and a former resident believe that he *really* did not want such an institute as he on occasion declared, since he was able to do as he pleased under the existing arrangements (3). It is doubtful that he would have been happy in dealing with the administrative details which such an organization requires.

While Dandy had many virtues, he was certainty not without shortcomings. In speaking or writing he would sometimes use for emphasis "always" when more than likely he meant "usually" (4). This left him open to the charge of being "too dogmatic" (5). Short-tempered and at times impatient, Dandy occasionally demonstrated an indifference to the social amenities that amounted to brusqueness, if not rudeness.

He had little use for many of his fellow neurosurgeons, not out of professional jealousy but rather out of what he considered to be their blindness and obstinacy. Gilbert Horrax, one of Cushing's men, with whom Dandy enjoyed a warm friendship, once chided Temple Fay of Philadelphia after the latter had complained about the Hopkins neurosurgeon, saying, "Come, come, Fay, face up to it. The big complaint we have against Dandy is that he is 20 years ahead of all of the rest of us" (6). At the time of Dandy's death, Francis C. Grant, a longtime friend and distinguished Philadelphia neurosurgeon, declared: "Had it not been for Walter & his innovation in neuro-surgery I doubt if this surgical specialty could have long survived" (7).

A man "without guile," Walter Dandy, through his many contributions towards relieving the ill and the afflicted, ". . . was an unlikely and largely reluctant hero, but a hero for all that, to the young physicians and the many patients that came within his orbit" (8). Truly a man of significance in medicine and history.

END NOTES

1. Marion Plossites (?), Baltimore, to W.E.D., letter, Sept 23, 1916, Dandy MSS.
2. Reichert FL: An appreciation. *Surgery* 19:580, 1946.
3. Mrs. Walter E. Dandy, Baltimore, interview with the author, June 10, 1976; Charles E. Troland, M.D., Richmond, VA, to the author, letter, March 16, 1981.
4. Hugo V. Rizzoli, M.D., Washington, DC, telephone interview with the author, Jan 4, 1982.
5. *The Lancet*, obituary, May 11, 1946, p 718.
6. Irving J. Sherman, M.D., Bridgeport, CT, to the author, letter, Sept 17, 1976.
7. Francis C. Grant, M.D., Philadelphia, to Mrs. Walter E. Dandy, letter, n.d. (1946).
8. Louis L. Austin, Capon Springs, WV, interview with the author, Sept 29, 1966; Turner TB: *Heritage of Excellence: The Johns Hopkins Medical Institutions, 1914–1947.* Baltimore, Johns Hopkins University Press, 1974, p 411.

Figure 27. Sadie Dandy at the center of the table, far side; Dandy in the foreground to the right. On a trip to Panama for Panpacific Surgical Meeting, Havana, 1929.

Figure 28. The wedding reception of Elizabeth and Ferdinand Verbeek at the Belvedere Hotel, Baltimore, in the 1930s. Verbeek, a Dutch neurosurgeon, was a visitor on Dandy's service. On the *left* of the bride is Dandy who gave her away. Charles H. Frazier, a Philadelphia neurosurgeon, is holding the two children on the front row. Barnes Woodhall is fourth from the left in the second row.

Figure 29. Walter Dandy with a patient from Middletown, Ohio, December 1936.

Figure 30. Dandy at the University of Missouri while he was serving on the board of trustees of the Medical School Foundation or as a member of the advisory council to the Board of Curators.

Figure 31. Joe Medwick of the Brooklyn Dodgers inserting plastic cup in the baseball cap designed by Dandy (International News Photo).

Figure 32. Dr. Dandy on the set of the Warner picture, "Kings Row." Dandy had treated Albert Warner's niece and was given a tour of the studio. Ronald Reagan is at *lower right.*

Figure 33. Dandy, *upper right*, at the Pithotomy Club Show of 1938 at Johns Hopkins. Note H. L. Mencken, *center right*, looking up.

Figure 34. Captain Winchell ("Wink") M. Craig, U.S.N., on leave from the Mayo Clinic and Dandy on tour of inspection of neurosurgical facilities at the U.S. Naval Hospital, Navy No. 10, Honolulu, 1944.

Figure 35. Dandy, *center*, present at the launching of the S. S. *Sedalia Victory* at the Bethlehem-Fairfield Shipyard, Baltimore.

Figure 36. Dandy, *left*, in the studio of Emil Seletz, *center*, a neurosurgeon and sculptor, who did a bust of his teacher and friend, which he gave to Hopkins.

Figure 37. Emil Seletz, a young Los Angeles neurosurgeon, made this bronze bust of Dandy, which he presented to Johns Hopkins Hospital.

Figure 38. Portrait of Dandy, wearing the hood of his honorary degree from the University of Missouri, that was presented to Johns Hopkins University, and was painted by Julian Lamar.

Figure 39. Dr. Dandy at the airline ticket counter when he was to go to Mexico to care for Trotsky. The trip did not materialize as Trotsky died shortly following the assassination attack.

Figure 40. Walter and Sadie Dandy in their garden just before a dinner that they held in honor of Frederick L. Reichert, his first resident. Reichert took the picture.

Figure 41. The home of Sadie and Walter Dandy, 3904 Juniper Road, Baltimore, in recent years.

Figure 42. Dandy with Walter, Jr., and Mary Ellen.

Figure 43. Dandy with Walter, Jr.

Figure 44.   Dandy with Walter, Jr., about 1929.

Figure 45. Dandy with Walter, Jr., having dinner with his childhood friend, Pauline Battersby Foraker, her husband, H. O. Foraker, and her mother.

Figure 46. Left to right, Sadie Dandy, Dandy, Dorcas Hager Padget, his illustrator, Mrs. Barnes Woodhall, Barnes Woodhall, a former resident of Dandy's who became professor of neurological surgery at Duke University.

Figure 47. Walter Dandy with youngest daughter, Margaret Martin, 10 days after her birth in 1935. He was then 49 years old.

Figure 48. John Dandy with granddaughter, Margaret.

Figure 49. Sadie and Walter Dandy in the living room of their home on Juniper Road.

Figure 50. Dandy was an avid golfer.

Figure 51. Dandy at pool side, Capon Springs and Farms, West Virginia. Sadie Dandy is in the pool. Dorcas Hager, Dandy's illustrator, took the picture.

Figure 52.   Dandy in Florida during the 1940s.

Figure 53. *Left* to *right*: Sadie Dandy, Kathleen Louise (Kitty), Mary Ellen, and Dandy at the front entrance of their home on Juniper Road, Baltimore.

Figure 54.　Dr. Dandy in Florida.

ORDER OF SERVICE

for the funeral of

DR. WALTER E. DANDY

Conducted By

THE REVEREND T. GUTHRIE SPEERS, D. D.

The Brown Memorial Church, Baltimore, Maryland

APRIL 22, 1946

LET US PRAY:

O God, Who in Christ hast shown to us the life that cannot be holden of death, give us the joy that the world cannot give as in the presence of what the world calls death, we praise Thee for a victorious life. Let the light of the eternal day shine now in our hearts. Let the peace of the everlasting gospel be our comfort and our strength. Let the communion of the saints be our living fellowship. Make strong the faith which Thou hast given us through Jesus Christ, our Lord. *Amen.*

THE LORD'S PRAYER

It was noised abroad that Mr. Valiant-for-Truth was taken with a summons . . . Then said he, "I am going to my Father's; and though with great difficulty I am got hither, yet now do I not repent me of the trouble I have been at to arrive where I am. My sword I give to him that shall succeed me in my pilgrimage, and my courage and skill to him that can get it. My marks and scars I carry with me to be a witness for me that I have fought His battles Who now shall be my rewarder." . . . So he passed over, and all the trumpets sounded for him on the other side.

Pilgrim's Progress—John Bunyan.

Pure religion and undefiled before our God and Father is this, to visit the fatherless and widows in their affliction, and to keep one's self unspotted from the world. (James 1:27).

Figure 56. The response of newspapers to the death of Walter E. Dandy.

Bibliography

The Complete Writings of Walter E. Dandy

I. ARTICLES

1910–1914

1. A human embryo with seven pairs of somites measuring about 2 mm. in length. *Am J Anat* 10:85–108, 1910.
2. The blood supply of the pituitary body, with E. Goetsch. *Am J Anat* 11:137–150, 1910–11.
3. The nerve supply to the pituitary body. *Am J Anat* 15:333–343, 1913.
4. An experimental and clinical study of internal hydrocephalus, with K. D. Blackfan. *JAMA* 61:2216–2217, 1913.
5. Peritoneale und pleurale Resorption in ihren Beziehungen zu der Lagerungebehandlung, with L. G. Rowntree. *Beitr Klin Chir* 87:539–567, 1913.
6. Peritoneal and pleural absorption with reference to postural treatment, with L. G. Rowntree, *Ann Surg* 59:587–596, 1914.
7. Internal hydrocephalus, an experimental, clinical and pathological study, with K. D. Blackfan. *Am J Dis Child* 8:406–482, 1914.
8. Hydrocephalus internus, eine experimentalle, klinische und pathologische untersuchung, with K. D. Blackfan. *Beitr Klin Chir* 93:392–486, 1914.
9. Zur Kenntnis Der Gutartigen Appendix Tumoren, Speziell Des Myxoms. *Beitr Klin Chir* 95:1–7, 1914.

1915–1919

10. Extirpation of the pineal body. *J Exp Med* 22:237–248, 1915.
11. A report of seventy cases of brain tumor, with G. J. Heuer. *Johns Hopkins Hosp Bull* 27:224–237, 1916.
12. Roentgenography in the localization of brain tumor; based upon a series of one hundred consecutive cases, with G. J. Heuer. *Johns Hopkins Hosp Bull* 29:311–322, 1916.
13. Internal hydrocephalus, second paper, with K. D. Blackfan. *Am J Dis Child* 14:424–443, 1917.
14. Ventriculography following the injection of air into the cerebral ventricles. *Ann Surg* 68:5–11, 1918.
15. Ventriculography following the injection of air into the cerebral ventricles. *Am J Roentgenol*, n.s., 6:20–26, 1919.
16. Extirpation of the choroid plexus of the lateral ventricles in communicating hydrocephalus. *Ann Surg* 68:560–579, 1918.
17. Fluoroscopy of the cerebral ventricles. *Johns Hopkins Hosp Bull* 30:29–33, 1919.

18. Experimental hydrocephalus. *Ann Surg* 70:129–142, 1919.
19. Pneumoperitoneum: a method of detecting intestinal perforation—an aid in abdominal diagnosis. *Ann Surg* 70:378–384, 1919.
20. Roentgenography of the brain after the injection of air into the spinal canal. *Ann Surg* 70:397–403, 1919.
21. Exhibition of a case of internal hydrocephalus, The Johns Hopkins Medical Society, Jan 21, 1918. *Johns Hopkins Hosp Bull* 29:153–154, 1918.
22. A new hypophysis operation. Devised by G. J. Heuer. Presented by W.E.D. in Heuer's absence. The Johns Hopkins Medical Society, Feb 4, 1918. *Johns Hopkins Hosp Bull* 29:154–155, 1918.

1920–1924

23. Two cases of epilepsy apparently cured by a new form of operative treatment, The Johns Hopkins Medical Society, Feb. 16, 1920. *Johns Hopkins Hosp Bull* 31:137–138, 1920.
24. Localization or elimination of cerebral tumors by ventriculography. *Surg Gynecol Obstet* 31:329–342, 1920.
25. The diagnosis and treatment of hydrocephalus resulting from strictures of the aqueduct of Sylvius. *Surg Gynecol Obstet* 31:340–358, 1920.
26. Hydrocephalus in chondrodystrophy. *Johns Hopkins Hosp Bull* 32:5–8, 1921.
27. The diagnosis and treatment of hydrocephalus due to occlusions of the foramina of Magendie and Luschka. *Surg Gynecol Obstet* 32:112–124, 1921.
28. The cause of so-called idiopathic hydrocephalus. *Johns Hopkins Hosp Bull* 32:67–75, 1921.
29. An operation for the removal of pineal tumors. *Surg Gynecol Obstet* 33:113–119, 1921.
30. The treatment of brain tumors. *JAMA* 77:1853–1859, 1921.
31. Prechiasmal intracranial tumors of the optic nerves. *Am J Ophthalmol* 5:169–188, 1922.
32. Remarks upon certain procedures useful in brain surgery. *Johns Hopkins Hosp Bull* 33:188–190, 1922.
     I. Treatment of non-encapsulated brain tumors by extensive resection of contiguous brain tissues.
     II. Diagnosis, localization and removal of tumors of the third ventricle.
     III. Cerebral ventriculoscopy.
     IV. An operation for the removal of large pituitary tumors.
     V. An operative procedure for hydrocephalus.
     VI. Diagnosis and localization of spinal cord tumors.
33. An operation for the total extirpation of tumors in the cerebello-pontine angle: a preliminary report. *Johns Hopkins Hosp Bull* 33:344–345, 1922.
34. The diagnosis and treatment of brain tumors. *Atlantic Med J* 26:726–728, 1923.
35. A method for the localization of brain tumors in comatose patients: the determination of communication between the cerebral ventricles and the estimation of their position and size without the injection of air (ventricular estimation). *Surg Gynecol Obstet* 36:641–656, 1923.
36. Localization of brain tumors by cerebral pneumography. *Am J Roentgenol Radium Ther* 10:610–612, 1923.
37. The space-compensating function of the cerebrospinal fluid—its connection with cerebral lesions in epilepsy. *Johns Hopkins Hosp Bull* 24:245–251, 1923.
38. Localization of brain tumors by injection of air into the ventricles of the brain. *J Missouri State Med Assoc* 21:329–331, 1924.
39. The treatment of staphylococcus and streptococcus meningitis by continuous drainage of the cisterna magna. *Surg Gynecol Obstet* 39:760–774, 1924.

1925–1929

40. The diagnosis and localization of spinal cord tumors. *Ann Surg* 81:223–254, 1925.
41. Studies in experimental epilepsy, with Robert Elman. *Bull Johns Hopkins Hosp* 36:40–49, 1925.
42. Section of the sensory root of the trigeminal nerve at the pons: preliminary report of the operative procedure. *Bull Johns Hopkins Hosp* 36:105–106, 1925.

43. Studies on experimental hypophysectomy, I. Effect on the maintenance of life, with F. L. Reichert. *Bull Johns Hopkins Hosp* 37:1–13, 1925.
44. An operation for the total removal of cerebello-pontile (acoustic) tumors. *Surg Gynecol Obstet* 41:129–148, 1925.
45. Intracranial tumors and abscesses causing communicating hydrocephalus. *Ann Surg* 82:199–207, 1925.
46. Contributions to brain surgery. A. Removal of certain deep-seated brain tumors. B. Intracranial approach with concealed incisions. *Ann Surg* 82:513–525, 1925.
47. Pneumocephalus (intracranial pneumatocele or aerocele). *Arch Surg* 12:949–982, 1926.
48. Ventriculography. *Int Surg Digest* 2:195–198, 1926.
49. Abscesses and inflammatory tumors in the spinal epidural space (so-called pachymeningitis externa). *Arch Surg* 13:477–494, 1926.
50. A sign and symptom of spinal cord tumors. *Arch Neurol Psychiatry* 16:435–441, 1926.
51. Treatment of chronic abscesses of the brain by tapping. *JAMA* 87:1477–1478, 1926.
52. Diagnose und Behandlung der Hirntumoren. *Dtsch Med Wochenschr* 52:638–639, 1926.
53. Experimental investigations on convulsions. *JAMA* 88:90–91, 1927.
54. Impressions of the pathology of epilepsy from operations. *Am J Psychiatry* 6:519–522, 1927.
55. Diagnosis and treatment of brain tumors. *NY State J Med* 27:285–287, 1927.
56. Glossopharyngeal neuralgia (tic douloureux): its diagnosis and treatment. *Arch Surg* 15:198–214, 1927.
57. Pneumocephalus of bacterial origin. *Arch Surg* 15:913–917, 1927.
58. Removal of right cerebral hemisphere for certain tumors with hemiplegia: preliminary report. *JAMA* 90:823–825, 1928.
59. Ménière's disease: Its diagnosis and a method of treatment. *Arch Surg* 16:1127–1152, 1928.
60. Arteriovenous aneurysms of the brain. *Arch Surg* 17:190–243, 1928.
61. Venous abnormalities and angiomas of the brain. *Arch Surg* 17:715–793, 1928.
62. An operation for the cure of tic douloureux: partial section of the sensory root at the pons. *Arch Surg* 18:687–734, 1929.
63. Where is cerebrospinal fluid absorbed? *JAMA* 92:2012–2014, 1929.
64. Operative relief from pain in lesions of the mouth, tongue and throat. *Arch Surg* 19:143–148, 1929.
65. An operative treatment for certain cases of meningocele (or encephalocele) into the orbit. *Arch Ophthalmol* 2:123–132, 1929.
66. Mechanisms and symptoms of tumors of the third ventricle and pineal body. *Intracranial Pressure in Health and Disease*, vol 8 of a Series of Research Publications, Association for Research in Nervous and Mental Diseases. Baltimore, Williams & Wilkins, 1929, pp 375–385.
67. Loose cartilage from intervertebral disk simulating tumor of the spinal cord. *Arch Surg* 19:660–672, 1929.

1930–1934

68. Injuries to the head. *J Med Soc NJ* 27:91–97, 1930. Also in the *Int J Med Surg* 43:237–242, 1930.
69. An operation for the treatment of spasmodic torticollis. *Arch Surg* 20:1021–1032, 1930.
70. Changes in our conceptions of localization of certain functions in the brain. *Am J Physiol.* 93:643, 1930.
71. The course of the nerve fibers transmitting sensation of taste, with Dean Lewis. *Arch Surg* 21:249–288, 1930.
72. Skull, brain and its membranes. In Graham EA (ed): *Surgical Diagnosis: By American Authors.* Philadelphia, WB Saunders, 1930, vol III, pp 846–898.
73. Congenital cerebral cysts of the cavum septi pellucidi (fifth ventricle) and cavum vergae (sixth ventricle): diagnosis and treatment. *Arch Neurol Psychiatry* 25:44–66, 1931.
74. "Avertin" anesthesia in neurologic surgery, *JAMA* 96:1860–1862, 1931.

75. Treatment of hemicrania (migraine) by removal of the inferior cervical and first thoracic sympathetic ganglion. *Bull Johns Hopkins Hosp* 48:357–361, 1931.
76. Epilepsy. Read at the Annual Meeting of Medical and Surgical Section, American Railway Association, New York City, June 8, 1931, and published in the *Proceedings* of the Association in the Fall 1931, pp 3–12.
77. Diagnosis and treatment of lesions of the cranial nerves. *Bull Assoc Surg Missouri Pacific Railway.* January, 1932.
78. Certain functions of the roots and ganglia of the cranial sensory nerves. *Arch Neurol Psychiatry* 27:22–26, 1932.
79. The importance of more adequate sterilization processes in hospitals. *Bull Am Coll Surg* 16:11–12, 1932.
80. Effect of total removal of left temporal lobe in a right-handed person: localization of areas of brain concerned with speech. *Arch Neurol Psychiatry* 27:221–224, 1932.
81. The treatment of trigeminal neuralgia by the cerebellar route. *Ann Surg* 96:787–795, 1932.
82. The diagnosis and treatment of Ménière's disease. *Trans Am Ther Soc* for 1932, pp 128–130.
83. Ménière's disease: diagnosis and treatment: report of thirty cases. *Am J Surg*, n.s., 20:693–698, 1933.
84. Physiological studies following extirpation of the right cerebral hemisphere in man. *Bull Johns Hopkins Hosp* 53:31–51, 1933.
85. Treatment of Ménière's disease by section of only the vestibular portion of the acoustic nerve. *Bull Johns Hopkins Hosp* 53:52–55, 1933.
86. Diagnosis and treatment of injuries of the head. *JAMA* 101:772–775, 1933.
87. Benign encapsulated tumors in the lateral ventricles of the brain: diagnosis and treatment. *Ann Surg* 98:841–845, 1933.
88. Cerebral (ventricular) hydrodynamic test for thrombosis of the lateral sinus. *Arch Otolaryngol* 19:297–302, 1934.
89. The diagnosis and treatment of lesions of the cranial nerves. *Del State Med J* 6:153–160, 1934.
90. Concerning the cause of trigeminal neuralgia. *Am J Surg*, n.s., 24:447–455, 1934.
91. The effect of hemisection of the cochlear branch of the human auditory nerve. Preliminary report. *Bull Johns Hopkins Hosp* 54:208–210, 1934.
92. Ménière's disease: symptoms, objective findings and treatment in forty-two cases. *Arch Otolaryngol* 20:1–30, 1934.
93. Removal of cerebellopontile (acoustic) tumors through a unilateral approach. *Arch Surg* 29:337–344, 1934.
94. The treatment of so-called pseudo-Ménière's disease. *Bull Johns Hopkins Hosp* 55:232–239, 1934.
95. Effects on hearing after subtotal section of the cochlear branch of the auditory nerve. *Bull Johns Hopkins Hosp* 55:240–243, 1934.

1935–1939

96. The treatment of intracranial hemorrhage resulting from cisternal puncture. *Bull Johns Hopkins Hosp* 56:294–301, 1935.
97. The treatment of carotid cavernous arteriovenous aneurysms. *Ann Surg* 102:916–920, 1935.
98. The treatment of bilateral Ménière's disease and pseudo-Ménière's disease. *Trans Am Neurol Assoc* 61:128–133, 1935; also in *Acta Neuropathol* in honorem Ludovici Puusepp, Tartu, Estonia, *Folia Neuropathol Estoniana* 60:10–14, 1935.
99. Polyuria and polydipsia (diabetes insipidus) and glycosuria resulting from animal experiments on the hypophysis and its environs, with F. L. Reichert. *Bull Johns Hopkins Hosp* 58:418–427, 1936.
100. The treatment of injuries of the head. *Pennsylvania Med J* 39:755–759, 1936.
101. Operative experience in cases of pineal tumor. *Arch Surg* 33:19–46, 1936.
102. [The treatment of carotid cavernous aneurysms, pulsating exophthalmos.] *Soviet Surg* 2:736–739, 1936 (in Russian).
103. Carotid-cavernous aneurysms (pulsating exophthalmos). *Zentralbl Neurochir* 2 Jahr-

gang, N.R. 2:77–113, 1937; N.R. 3:165–206. Also *Int J Neurol Contrib*, Prof. Wilhelm Tönnis, Wurzburg, Germany.

104. Pathological changes in Ménière's disease. *JAMA* 108:931–937, 1937.

105. Ménière's disease: its diagnosis and treatment. *South Med J* 30:621–623, 1937.

106. Etiological and clinical types of so-called nerve deafness. *Laryngoscope* 47:594–597, 1937.

107. Diagnosis and treatment of brain tumors. *Alabama Med Assoc J* 6:162–166, 1936; also *Ohio State Med J* 33:17–18, 1937.

108. Brain tumors. *Texas State J Med* 32:833, 1937.

109. Injuries of the head, *Proceedings of the Seventeenth Annual Meeting of the Medical and Surgical Section of the Association of American Railroads*, June 7–8, 1937, pp 96–105.

110. Intracranial pressure without brain tumor. *Ann Surg* 106:492–513, 1937.

111. Diagnosis and treatment of brain abscess. *Proceedings of the Inter-State Post Graduate Medical Assembly of North America*, 1937, pp 235–238.

112. Studies on experimental hypophysectomy in dogs: III. Somatic, mental and glandular effects, with F. L. Reichert. *Bull Johns Hopkins Hosp* 62:122–155, 1938.

113. Intracranial aneurysm of the internal carotid artery cured by operation. *Ann Surg* 107:654–659, 1938.

114. Diagnosis and treatment of lesions of the cranial nerves. *Rocky Mt Med J* 35:282–288, 1938.

115. The operative treatment of communicating hydrocephalus. *Ann Surg* 108:194–202, 1938.

116. Trigeminal neuralgia and pains in the face. *J Indiana State Med Assoc* 31:669–672, 1938.

117. The surgery of Ménière's disease. In Kopetzky SJ (ed): *Surgery of the Ear, Nelson's Loose-Leaf Surgery of the Ear*. New York and Edinburgh, Thomas Nelsons and Sons, 1938 and 1946, ch 16, pp 387–398.

118. Subdural hematoma: diagnosis and treatment, with P. A. Kunkel. *Arch Surg* 38:24–54, 1939.

119. The treatment of internal carotid aneurysms within the cavernous sinus and the cranial chamber: report of three cases. *Ann Surg* 109:689–709, 1939.

120. Papilloedema without intracranial pressure (optic neuritis). *Ann Surg* 110:161–168, 1939.

121. The central connections of the vestibular pathways: an experimental study, with P. A. Kunkel. *Am J Med Sci* 198:149–155, 1939.

122. Lesions of the cranial nerves: diagnosis and treatment. *J Int Coll Surg* 2:5–14, 1939.

123. Intracranial aneurysms, *Proceedings of the Third Congress of the Pan-Pacific Surgical Association*, Honolulu, Hawaii, September 15–21, 1939, pp 335–336.

124. Ménière's disease, *Proceedings of the Third Congress of the Pan-Pacific Surgical Association*, Honolulu, Hawaii, September 15–21, 1939, pp 357–364.

1940–1946

125. Section of the human hypophyseal stalk: its relation to diabetes insipidus and hypophyseal functions. *JAMA* 114:312–314, 1940.

126. On the relationship of dentistry to certain neurological diseases (Paper given at the Dental Centenary Celebration, Baltimore, March 18, 1940). *Proceedings of the Dental Centenary Celebration*, March, 1940, Sponsors: Maryland State Dental Association and American Dental Association, pp 140–144.

127. Removal of longitudinal sinus involved in tumors. *Arch Surg* 41:244–256, 1940.

128. The surgical treatment of Ménière's disease (Presented before the Clinical Congress of the American College of Surgeons, Chicago, October 21–25, 1940). *Surg Gynecol Obstet* 72:421–425, 1941.

129. Results following the transcranial operative attack on orbital tumors. *Arch Ophthalmol* 25:191–213, 1941.

130. On the pathology of carotid-cavernous aneurysms (pulsating exophthalmos), with R. H. Follis, Jr. *Am J Ophthalmol* 24:365–385, 1941.

131. The surgical treatment of intracranial aneurysms of the internal carotid artery. *Ann Surg* 114:336–339, 1941.

132. Concealed ruptured intervertebral disks: a plea for the elimination of contrast media in diagnosis. *JAMA* 117:821–823, 1941.
133. Recent advances in the diagnosis and treatment of ruptured intervertebral disks. *Ann Surg* 115:514–520, 1942.
134. Serious complications of ruptured intervertebral disks. *JAMA* 119:474–477, 1942.
135. Aneurysm of the anterior cerebral artery. *JAMA* 119:1253–1254, 1942.
136. Improved localization and treatment of ruptured intervertebral disks. *JAMA* 120:605–607, 1942.
137. Intracranial arterial aneurysms in the carotid canal. *Arch Surg* 45:335–350, 1942.
138. Results following ligation of the internal carotid artery. *Arch Surg* 45:521–533, 1942.
139. A method of restoring nerves requiring resection. *JAMA* 122:35–36, 1943.
140. An operation for scaphocephaly. *Arch Surg* 47:247–249, 1943.
141. Recent advances in the treatment of ruptured (lumbar) intervertebral disks. *Ann Surg* 118:639–646, 1943.
142. The treatment of essential hypertension by sympathectomy: a report on twelve patients three to seven years following operation, with James Bordley, III and Morton Galdston. *Bull Johns Hopkins Hosp* 72:127–165, 1943.
143. Newer aspects of ruptured intervertebral disks. *Ann Surg* 119:481–484, 1944.
144. A procedure to correct facial paralysis, with Edward M. Hanrahan. *JAMA* 124:1051–1053, 1944.
145. Pathogenesis of intermittent exophthalmos, with Frank B. Walsh. *Arch Ophthalmol* 32:1–10, 1944.
146. Treatment of rhinorrhea and otorrhea. *Arch Surg* 49:75–85, 1944.
147. Treatment of recurring attacks of low backache without sciatica. *JAMA* 125:1175–1178, 1944.
148. Electroencephalograms taken at the Henry Phipps Psychiatric Clinic on One Hundred Patients on the Neurological Service, The Johns Hopkins Hospital, Baltimore, 1938–1940, 92 pp.
149. Treatment of aneurysms of the brain. *Proceedings of the Twentieth Annual Meeting of the Medical and Surgical Section of the Association of American Railroads*, June 10–11, 1940, pp 51–63.
150. Results of removal of acoustic tumors by the unilateral approach. *Arch Surg* 42:1026–1033, 1941.
151. Diagnosis and treatment of lesions of the cranial nerves. *J Med* 22:239–245, 1941.
152. The diagnosis and treatment of ruptured intervertebral disks. *The Medical Comment*, Johnstown, Pennsylvania, 26:4–7, 17, July, 1944.
153. Recent advances in the diagnosis and treatment of ruptured intervertebral disks. *Neurocirugia*, Santiago, Chile, 2 (Anos 1941–1943), 1944, 4 pp.
154. The treatment of spondylolisthesis. *JAMA* 127:137–139, 1945.
155. Ménière's disease in a deaf-mute. *Arch Surg* 50:74–76, 1945.
156. Diagnosis and treatment of strictures of the aqueduct of Sylvius (causing hydrocephalus). *Arch Surg* 51:1–14, 1945.
157. Arteriovenous aneurysms of the scalp and face. *Arch Surg* 52:1–32, 1946.
158. Results following bands and ligatures on the human internal carotid artery. *Ann Surg* 123:384–396, 1946.
159. The treatment of an unusual subdural hydroma (external hydrocephalus). *Arch Surg* 52:421–428, 1946.
160. The location of the conscious center in the brain—the corpus striatum. *Bull Johns Hopkins Hosp* 79:34–58, 1946.

II. BOOKS

1. Surgery of the brain. In: Lewis D (ed): *Practice of Surgery.* Hagerstown, MD, WF Prior, 1932, vol 12, ch 1.
2. *Benign Tumors in the Third Ventricle of the Brain: Diagnosis and Treatment.* Springfield, IL, Charles C Thomas, 1933, 171 pp.
3. *Benign, Encapsulated Tumors in the Lateral Ventricles of the Brain: Diagnosis and Treatment.* Baltimore, Williams & Wilkins, 1934, 189 pp.

4. *Orbital Tumors: Results Following the Transcranial Operative Attack.* New York, Oskar Piest, 1941, xv, 168 pp.
5. *Intracranial Arterial Aneurysms.* Ithaca, NY, Comstock Publishing Company, Cornell University, 1944, viii, 147 pp.
6. *Surgery of the Brain* (A monograph from Volume 12 of *Lewis' Practice of Surgery*). Hagerstown, MD, WF Prior, 1945, 671 pp.
7. *Selected Writings of Walter E. Dandy.* Compiled by Charles E. Troland and Frank J. Otenasek. Springfield, IL, Charles C Thomas, 1957, vii, 789 pp.
8. *The Brain.* Hagerstown, MD, WF Prior, 1966, 671 pp.

Other Sources on Walter E. Dandy

1. Barcala FJ: *Walter Edward Dandy, su obra en neurocirugia.* Buenos Aires, Imprenta Ferrari Hnos., 1946, 76 pp.
2. Blalock A: Walter Edward Dandy (1886–1946). *Surgery* 19:577, 1946.
3. Campbell E: Walter E. Dandy—surgeon 1886–1946. *J Neurosurg* 8:249, 1951.
4. Crowe SJ: *Halsted of Johns Hopkins: The Man and His Men.* Ch 5, Walter Edward Dandy. Springfield, IL, Charles C Thomas, 1957, pp 85–111.
5. Fairman D: Evolution of neurosurgery through Walter E. Dandy's work. *Surgery* 19:581–604, 1946.
6. Fox JD: Walter Dandy—super-surgeon. *Henry Ford Hosp Med J* 25:149–170, 1977.
7. Fox WL: The Cushing-Dandy controversy. *Surg Neurol* 3:61–66, 1975.
8. Glass RL: Walter Dandy, Sedalia's number one paperboy. *Mo Med*, December, 1965, pp 973–977.
9. Harvey AM: Neurosurgical genius—Walter Edward Dandy. *Johns Hopkins Med J* 135:358–368, 1974. Also in *Adventures in Medical Research: A Century of Discovery at Johns Hopkins.* Ch 7, Neurosurgical Genius: Walter Edward Dandy. Baltimore: Johns Hopkins University Press, 1974, 1975, 1976, pp 60–68.
10. Reichert FL: An appreciation. *Surgery* 19:580, 1946.
11. Semmes RE: Walter Dandy, M.D.: his relationship to the Society of Neurological Surgeons. *Neurosurgery* 4:1–2, 1979.
12. Woodhall B: Neurosurgery in the past—the Dandy era. *Clin Neurosurg* 18:1–15, 1971.
13. Woodhall B: Walter Dandy, M.D.: personal reminiscences. *Neurosurgery* 4:3–6, 1979.

Appendix

Dandy's Residents

Charles Troland
Frank J. Otenasek
Hugo V. Rizzoli
John W. Chambers

Antonio Gonzalez-Revilla
J. Irving Sherman
Arthur B. King
William Burklund

Drs. Sherman, King and Burklund were unable to complete the entire residency because of military duty in World War II and because of Dr. Dandy's death.

Contemporaries of Dandy at Johns Hopkins

R. Eustace Semmes
Ernest Sachs
Howard C. Naffziger
Harvey Cushing
George Heuer
William Sharpe
E. Jefferson Browder

Richard G. Coblentz
Wilder Penfield
Carl W. Rand
Frank R. Ford (*neurology*)
Frank B. Walsh (*ophthalmology*)
Dean Lewis (*surgery*)

Residents in General Surgery Who Were Members of the Brain Team

Frederick L. Reichert°
Warfield M. Firor
J. Deryl Hart
George G. Finney
William F. Rienhoff, Jr.
Rawley M. Pennick
Harry J. Warthen
I. Ridgeway Trimble
Eldridge H. Campbell, Jr.°
Crenshaw D. Briggs
Fred W. Geib°
M. Barnes Woodhall°
Paul A. Kunkel

Edward S. Stafford
David H. Sprong, Jr.
August F. Jonas, Jr.
James M. Mason, III
William G. Watson
Kenneth L. Pickrell
Herbert E. Sloan, Jr. (*intern only*)
William P. Longmire, Jr. (*intern only*)
William E. Gross (*intern only*)
Alan Woods, Jr. (*intern only*)
William H. Muller, Jr. (*intern only*)

° These men became neurosurgeons.

Interns and Students at Johns Hopkins Exposed to Dandy's Service

Henry G. Schwartz
Collin S. MacCarty
Henry L. Heyl (*pediatrics*)
Winchell McK. Craig
James C. White (*pathology*)
John E. Scarff
Henry T. Ballantine
Samuel P. W. Black
Armando Coppola
Charles E. Dowman, III
Gordon S. Dugger
William G. Evans
Edmund M. Fountain
James R. Gay
C. Douglas Hawkes
George J. Hayes
Thomas I. Hoen
A. Beaumont Johnson, II
William C. Kite, Jr.

Joseph A. Mufson
Harold D. Paxton
Averill Stowell
John M. Thompson
Alfred Uihlein, Jr.
James G. Arnold, Jr.
Carl P. Schlicke
Gayle W. Crutchfield
Tracy J. Putnam (*pathology*)
David L. Reeves
Franc D. Ingraham (*surgical research*)
Clinton N. Woolsey (*neurophysiology*)
Vernon B. Mountcastle (*neurophysiology*)
E. Douglas Horning
Thomas S. Bennett
Isidore M. Tarlov

Visitors and Voluntary Assistants to Dandy

A. H. Olivecrona
Wilder Penfield
Geoffrey Jefferson
Loyal Davis
Gordon Holmes
Hugh Cairns
Otfrid Foerster
Francis Grant
Paul Bucy
Temple Fay
James Poppen
Gilbert Horrax
C. C. Coleman
Jost Michelson
A. Kolodny
Ricardo Finochietto (*Argentina*)
A. de Sousa Pereira (*Portugal*)
Paul Martin (*Belgium*)
Dr. Koebcke (*Germany*)
Dr. Vissoli (*Italy*)
R. Arana-Iniguez (*Uruguay*)
Antonio de Vasconcellos Marques (*Portugal*)
Pierre Wertheimer (*Lyon*)
Eduard A. V. Busch (*Denmark*)
Alfonso Asenjo (*Chile*)
Thierry de Martel (*Paris*)

Sixtor Obrador (*Spain*)
F. A. Verbeek (*Holland*)
Daniel Petit-Dutaillis (*Paris*)
Rex A. Money (*Australia*)
Mizuho Nakata (*Japan*)
Leopold Schonbauer (*Austria*)
A. Austregesilo (*Brazil*)
Adams A. McConnell (*Ireland*)
G. Hugo Dickman (*Argentina*)
David Fairman (*Argentina*)
Fermin Barcala (*Argentina*)
R. Douglas Wright (*Australia*)
O. Sjoquist (*Sweden*)
C. H. Lenshrect (*Holland*)
H. Haimovici (*Marseille*)
M. Davila (*Peru*)
M. Bernali (*Peru*)
A. F. Zavalla (*Philippines*)
A. Fajardo (*Colombia*)
D. Oda (*Japan*)
I. Woljenick (*Holland*)
H. Askenasy (*Rumania*)
S. Ferraresi (*Italy*)
M. Ohma (*Japan*)
H. Uchiyama (*Japan*)
J. C. Christensen (*Argentina*)

Neurosurgical Procedures
Walter E. Dandy   *1912–1946*

Gliomas		1435
Cerebral	903	
Cerebellar	393	
Brain stem	93	
Ependymal	21	
Other and unspecified	25	
Pituitary adenomas		337
Meningiomas		291
Acoustic tumors (*neurinomas*)		234
Pineal tumors		48
Orbital tumors		33
Metastatic brain tumors		79
Other brain tumors (*unspecified*)		497
Skull and scalp tumors		69
Tuberculomas		34
Brain abscess		168
Intracranial hematoma		149
Giant aneurysms		13
Aneurysms clipped		27
Carotid ligations (*aneurysm*)		88
Herniated intervertebral disc		2000+
Spinal cord tumors		325
Intraspinal abscess		4
Trigeminal neuralgia		500+
Ménière's syndrome		800+
Hydrocephalus		285+

This incomplete list was compiled from Dr. Dandy's records, operative notes and publications, and is therefore only an approximation of his actual surgical experience.

EXAMPLES of Dr. Dandy's Operative Notes*

<table>
<tr><td></td><td>Halsted 7</td><td>Neurosurgical</td></tr>
<tr><td>V _____ S _____</td><td></td><td>292522</td></tr>
</table>

OPERATION: April 18, 1944
Dr. Dandy
Pentothal sodium 2.5% (50 cc) — Oxygen — Miss Smith

REMOVAL OF PROTRUDING DISK L5, RIGHT

This is a very remarkable and interesting case. The patient was operated on last May, eleven months ago, at which time we removed the third and fourth disks, although at that time we thought they were four and five. Both were concealed. Since the operation she has had no relief from her sciatica, but her backache has been cured. The explanation is not clear. We removed three and four instead of four and five. The fifth lamina was intact and the interspace, which was small, had not been opened, for the ligamentum flavum was also intact. There was no movement at five, none at four, and none at three. All were solid, but the x-ray of five showed a mere line. We then removed part of the lamina from five and found a large mass of fibrous tissue under the nerve mixed with cartilage, spread out over quite an area and tightly bound to the nerve. It went well over the midline, and it took a good deal of division with the periosteal elevator to remove it. The disk was then entered and only the small and finally, the medium curette could be applied. There was very little cartilage in it. Practically all that was removed except a small part of the interior, was from the extruded mass. This is the first time I can recall having missed the count of the vertebrae.

(Dr. Dandy)

ms
Disk no. 1100.

* Courtesy of Dr. Richard J. Otenasek.

W_____ S_____   271871

OPERATION: September 21, 1942
                Dr. Dandy
                Avertin 4 cc (50 mgm)—Ether 10—Miss Smith

PARTIAL REMOVAL LARGE HYPOPHYSEAL ADENOMA
RESECTION OF FRONTAL LOBE

This was a very difficult tumor to handle. There was such severe intracranial pressure that after exposing the tumor briefly it was clear that nothing could be done without resecting the frontal lobe. This was done without difficulty and there was only a fair amount of bleeding. The right nerve was pushed outward and greatly flattened by the tumor which projected in front of and behind the nerve. There was no vision in this eye and it was clear that there could be no return, and it was impossible to tackle the tumor in front of the optic tracts. It was a very hard tumor with an irregular surface. The curette required a great deal of pressure to bring out portions of the tumor. The tumor went so deeply in the sella that we thought it might well fill the sphenoid cavity. As much of it was removed as possible and the left optic nerve freed from tumor, but tumor certainly went backward toward the brain stem and doubtless upward into the brain, but this could not be determined definitely.

The wound was dry when closure was begun. The dura was closed. The bone flap was replaced and wired. The galea and skin were closed with interrupted sutures of silk.

The weight of the tumor removed was 2 grams. The frontal lobe weighed 76.3 grams.

                                                        (Dr. Dandy)

cp

O_____ S_____   314402

OPERATION: Feb. 21, 1944
                Dr. Dandy
                Avertin 5.8 cc (75)—Ether 9—Miss Smith

REMOVAL DURAL TUMOR, OLIVARY EMINENCE

This was a very interesting case for diagnosis, and it was shown on ward rounds. A clean-cut diagnosis of dural tumor of the olivary eminence was made, because the sella was normal. No endocrine disturbance, and no loss of sense of smell.

Usual hypophysial approach was made on the left side. The field for form on this side was normal, but there was hemianopsia for color, and on the opposite side, hemianopsia for color and form. Visual acuity less on the left. No intracranial pressure. There was ample room.

A little red, hard tumor projected slightly in front of the optic nerves, which were rather long. The interior was curetted, the capsule drawn away, and then the whole tumor came out in one piece. It weighed 4.9 grams. There was practically no bleeding. There was a little rough area, where the dural attachment was placed. This was thoroughly cauterized. It was almost exclusively to the left of the midline, but there was a slight extension beyond it to the right.

The dura was closed, the bone flap replaced and wired, and the galea and skin were closed with interrupted sutures of silk.

(Dr. Dandy)

ms

Halsted 7

L_____ S_____   262893

OPERATION: June 30, 1942
             Dr. Dandy
             Avertin 4 cc (65 mgm)—Ether 6—Miss Smith

             TOTAL SECTION FIFTH NERVE RIGHT FOR TIC
             DOULOUREUX

The usual unilateral cerebellar approach was made. The mastoid cells were not seen. The cerebellum was very tight, even after the cisterna magnum and the lateral cisterna were evacuated. It was necessary to resect the cerebellar cap after which the nerve was sectioned totally. There was a very large nerve. It was not possible to see whether or not there was an underlying artery. There was no bleeding or further difficulty. The wound was closed with silk in layers. The cerebellar cap weighed 9 gms.

(Dr. Dandy)

rl

Halsted 7

F_____ S_____

OPERATION: March 10, 1933
               Dr. Dandy
               Avertin 5.9 cc—90 mgm per kilo—Ether oz 6—Miss
               Smith

PARTIAL SECTION EIGHTH NERVE LEFT FOR MÉNIÈRE'S DISEASE

Since patient's hearing was somewhat affected in the opposite ear we felt it a good opportunity to attempt to preserve the auditory division of the nerve in the left ear and, therefore, to divide only the vestibular division. The nerve was easily exposed. It was cocainized with a pledget of cotton emersed in ten per cent procaine. A small tenotomy knife was passed thru the nerve just a little posterior to its middle and the anterior portion divided. Feeling that we had better be on the safe side a little additional part of the auditory branch was divided immediately thereafter. I should think that probably five-eighths of the entire cross section of the nerve was sectioned. There was no bleeding at any time. The facial nerve was not seen and no attempt was made to expose it. The wound was closed in the usual manner with interrupted sutures of silk.

A herniotomy was done immediately afterwards by Dr. Briggs. Patient had no dizziness for forty-eight hours, apparently due to the affects of cocaine as the behavior was exactly like that in the other case, in whom we had cocainized the nerve. *This is the first instance in which the vestibular branch of the nerve alone has been sectioned.*

                                                    (Dr. Dandy)
rs

                    Halsted 7   Neurosurgery

H _____ S _____   570474

OPERATION: December 15, 1945
               Dr. Walter E. Dandy
               Avertin (60) 4.6 cc—Ether 5½—Miss Smith

THIRD VENTRICULOSTOMY, RIGHT APPROACH

There was fluid in the subarachnoid space and when this was evacuated, we could see the floor of the ventricle. It was not a large floor but it was not difficult to puncture it and widen the opening. There was enough tissue, however, about the opening to make one a little apprehensive that it might not stay open. There was no bleeding or difficulties.

                                                    Dr. Dandy
at

HLH 2

A _____ S _____   267870

OPERATION: August 31, 1942
              Dr. Dandy
              Novocaine 1-200
              Avertin 2.7 (75 mgm)—Ether 3—Miss Smith

TREPHINE AND AIR INJECTION
REMOVAL CEREBELLAR GLIOMA

Although we felt very certain that this was a cerebellar tumor because of the high inion, some staggering and a little ataxia, we were not entirely certain there might not be a pineal tumor as there was a little calcification of the pineal. 350 cc of air was injected to replace an equal amount of fluid. It showed a patent aqueduct and a large fourth ventricle in the anterior fourth.

A bilateral cerebellar approach was made. The cerebellum was full and tight, but the pressure was partly relieved by tapping the lateral ventricle. There was no tumor on the surface and a tap for a cyst was negative. We encountered tumor at a depth of about a centimeter. At the lower part of the vermis just at the spinal canal we could see a little tumor when the tonsils were separated. These were far in the spinal canal. The vermis was then split and a very hard circumscribed tumor encountered. This was shelled around with the finger gently. It was very firmly attached to the brain stem. In attempting to shell it out with the finger with considerable force the tumor was broken off and a large slab of it left on the fourth ventricle. We then lifted up the lower pole of the remaining part of the tumor and found that it could be separated from the fourth ventricle although it was firmly fixed, particularly on the sides. With the finger this was gently stripped and finally the mass came out with a fair amount of bleeding which was controlled by a pack.

Respirations were at once affected by this and the breathing stopped, but the pulse remained good and the color was good, so there must have been over a long period of time very shallow respirations. Some artificial respiration was given. The patient was given oxygen and remained about the same condition for about six hours when she died.

The weight of the tumor was 74.2 grams. It was quite well circumscribed and would probably have been cured had she been able to stand the operation. It was an exceedingly large tumor and exactly in the midline. A little of the outer surface of the right lobe was macerated and was removed. It weighed 6.4 grams.

(Dr. Dandy)

cp

Halsted 7

C _____ S _____

OPERATION: February 25, 1943
             Dr. Dandy
             Avertin 5.4 (60 mgm)—Ether 8—Miss Smith

TOTAL SECTION FIFTH NERVE LEFT FOR TIC DOULOUREUX

The usual unilateral approach was made. The mastoid cells were not seen. The bone was quite thick. There was ample room. The petrosal vein spread out for some distance over the dura and had to be divided after cauterization. An artery ran along the posterior border of the nerve and after the nerve was sectioned it was seen that it indented the undersurface. The nerve was farther posteriorly than usual so that the upper part of the nerve was divided first and segments continued to the posterior part. There were no difficulties of bleeding. The wound was closed with silk in layers.

(Dr. Dandy)

cp

About the Author

William Lloyd Fox, Ph.D.
7905 Takoma Avenue
Silver Spring, MD 20910

Professor Emeritus of History
Montgomery College

Doctoral Research Advisor (*currently*)
The American University

President, Washington Society of the History of Medicine, 1964–65

Publications Include:
Book: *J. Franklin Jameson: A Tribute* with Ruth Anna Fisher (1965)

Book: *Montgomery College: Maryland's First Community College 1946–1970* (1970)

Book: *Maryland: A History 1632–1974* (1974) with Richard Walsh; 2nd printing (1983)

List of Doctoral Dissertations in History in Progress or Completed at Colleges and Universities in the United States since 1958 (American Historical Association, 1961)

Articles:
"What is lacking": Dr. Harvey W. Wiley's view of American Medical Education (1874). *Bulletin of the History of Medicine* (May–June 1962)

The Harvard days of Dr. Harvey W. Wiley. *Harvard Alumni Bulletin* (Sept. 1956)

The Cushing-Dandy controversy. *Surgical Neurology* (Feb. 1975)

Walter Edward Dandy and Charles Albert Elsberg. *Dictionary of American Biography*, Supplement Four

Other Articles and Book Reviews Have Appeared In:
The American Historical Review, Maryland Historical Magazine, The Journal of American History, The Journal of Southern History, Agricultural History, American Quarterly, Science Quarterly (A.A.A.S.), *National Genealogical Quarterly*, and *The Washington Post*

Principal Speaker at the 90th anniversary of the founding of The Johns Hopkins Medical History Club (1980). Topic: Walter E. Dandy: "Reluctant Hero"

Recipient of the Certificate of Distinguished Citizenship from the Governor of Maryland (1976)

Index

Page numbers in italics denote figures; those followed by "t" or "f" denote tables or footnotes, respectively.

281